IMAGES
of America

GROSSE POINTE WAR MEMORIAL

On the Cover: Society girl Beth Loomis was one of the lucky passengers on a Wright brothers biplane. Russell Alger was an early investor in the Wright brothers' airplanes. In 1911, he arranged for a Wright Flyer to come to Grosse Pointe and give demonstration rides in order to generate interest in the business.

IMAGES
of America

GROSSE POINTE WAR MEMORIAL

Ann Marie Aliotta and Suzy Berschback

ARCADIA
PUBLISHING

ISBN 978-0-7385-7746-3

Published by Arcadia Publishing
Charleston SC, Chicago IL, Portsmouth NH, San Francisco CA

Printed in the United States of America

Library of Congress Control Number: 2009933633

For all general information contact Arcadia Publishing at:
Telephone 843-853-2070
Fax 843-853-0044
E-mail sales@arcadiapublishing.com
For customer service and orders:
Toll-Free 1-888-313-2665

Visit us on the Internet at www.arcadiapublishing.com

Suzy Berschback would like to dedicate this book to all the veterans who have served our country and allowed us to enjoy the freedoms we take for granted every day. She would especially like to thank her father, Robert "Binks" Skipwith King Jr., who grew up in Grosse Pointe and served in the 25th Infantry Division, assigned to Otsu, Japan. He worked in the labor office, where he assigned Japanese workers jobs to help with the reconstruction of Japan in 1946 and 1947, after the war ended.

Ann Marie Aliotta would like to dedicate this book to her parents, Virginia and Ross John Fazio, who encouraged the belief that she could accomplish anything.

Contents

Acknowledgments

This book has been in the making for about 20 years, since Suzy first started working at the Grosse Pointe War Memorial in public relations. Immediately she was smitten with the Alger family's home and home life and needed to learn all about the family. She started collecting history and writing to family members to learn more. Many people have contributed to the photograph archives and materials. Over the years, many stories have been written about the house, family, and community center. These include articles from the *Grosse Pointe News*, particularly John Lake's column The Grosse Pointe War Memorial as John Lake Remembered It.

We would like to thank the following contributors for sharing their time, resources, and encouragement in the making of this book: Mark R. Weber, Teri L. Carroll, Renee Langer, Lud Schomig, Dick Kay, John Bluth, Jay F. Hunter, Maureen Devine, Chip Berschback, Jerry Aliotta, Chuck Bigelow, Bill Krag, Madeleine Socia, Nancy Dodge Heenan, Hudson Mead, Russell A. Alger IV, the Alger family, the Grosse Pointe War Memorial staff, and the Grosse Pointe Historical Society staff and archives. All photographs are courtesy of the Grosse Pointe Historical Society Alger/War Memorial Collection and the Country Club of Detroit archives.

Other sources consulted while writing this book were: *Tonnancour: Life in Grosse Pointe and along the Shores of Lake St. Clair, Vols. 1 and 2,* by Arthur M. Woodford; *Grosse Pointe 1880–1930* by Madeleine Socia and Suzy Berschback; *The Buildings of Detroit* by W. Hawkins Ferry; *Heritage: A Journal of Grosse Pointe Life* magazine; *The Grosse Pointe News*; and the Grosse Pointe Historical Society Web site, www.gphistorical.org.

INTRODUCTION

This should be a place for the enrichment of community life and the promotion of human well-being—a place of permanence, beauty, dignity and usefulness.

—Alger Shelden, Founding President
Grosse Pointe War Memorial Association
1948

A small hand rests upon the cool bronze plaque bearing the name of a man he never met. His inquisitive eyes look to his mother. "Your great grandfather," she says. "He fought in World War II." He looks up at the wall of names that reaches to the ceiling, each etched in bronze, silent reminders of the great cost of our freedom, but he cannot comprehend the magnitude of their sacrifice. He only knows this place for summer camps and his big brother's dances, as the spot where his parents were married and he said his last goodbye to his grandmother. But this place, the scene of so many vital events in the lives of a whole community, was once the home to a single family. The sprawling mansion called the Grosse Pointe War Memorial is what the Alger children—Fay, Josephine, and Russell Alger III—simply called home. Their father, Russell Alger Jr., a founder of the Packard Motor Company, moved his family in 1910 to the Moorings, an Italian Renaissance home designed by Charles A. Platt that graced the shores of Lake St. Clair.

The Algers held great parties and entertained many famous people of the era, including the Wright brothers, the Dodges, the Fords, and many more. The Moorings was designed for entertaining, with its manicured gardens, billiard room, and lake view terrace. The structure itself was designed to enthrall the senses—the ceilings decorated with intricate carvings, great fireplaces, and well-polished floors. Russell even had wood panel imported from England for his billiard room. Everything about the house was elegant. Its inhabitants were just as vibrant and colorful, Russell with his love of flying and Josephine with her many exuberant adventures on the grounds of the family mansion.

In 1930, Russell A. Alger Jr. passed away, and it was decided that the Moorings would live on as a branch of the Detroit Institute of Arts. In 1949, the Moorings was dedicated as the Grosse Pointe War Memorial—a living memorial in honor of the 3,500 Grosse Pointers who served in World War II and the 126 that gave their lives for our freedom. The Grosse Pointe War Memorial was founded for this great purpose as a 501(c)3 charitable, nonprofit organization. The memorial hosts an estimated 2,000 programs and events while serving nearly 200,000 individuals on an annual basis. It receives no tax dollar support and relies on voluntary contributions for its existence.

Today at this state and national historic site, children and adults alike come to find the names of their relatives on the bronze plaque that lines the walls of the front foyer of the Alger House representing all of our nation's wars since World War II; couples are united in holy matrimony overlooking Marion's gardens; ideas are shared in the library that hosted the great entrepreneurs of the 20th century; and the sounds of life continue to permeate the walls of the Moorings.

Mark R. Weber, Ph.D.
President
Grosse Pointe War Memorial Association

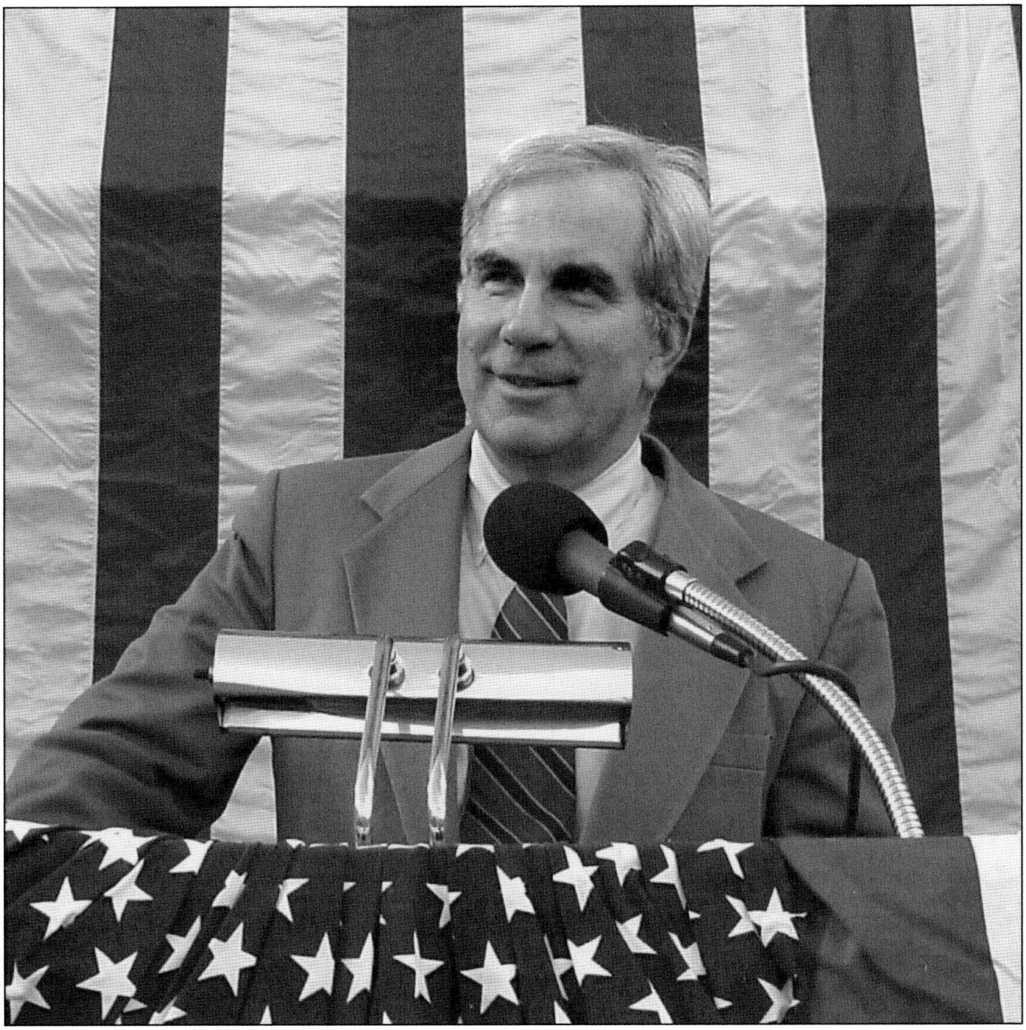

One

Growing Up Alger

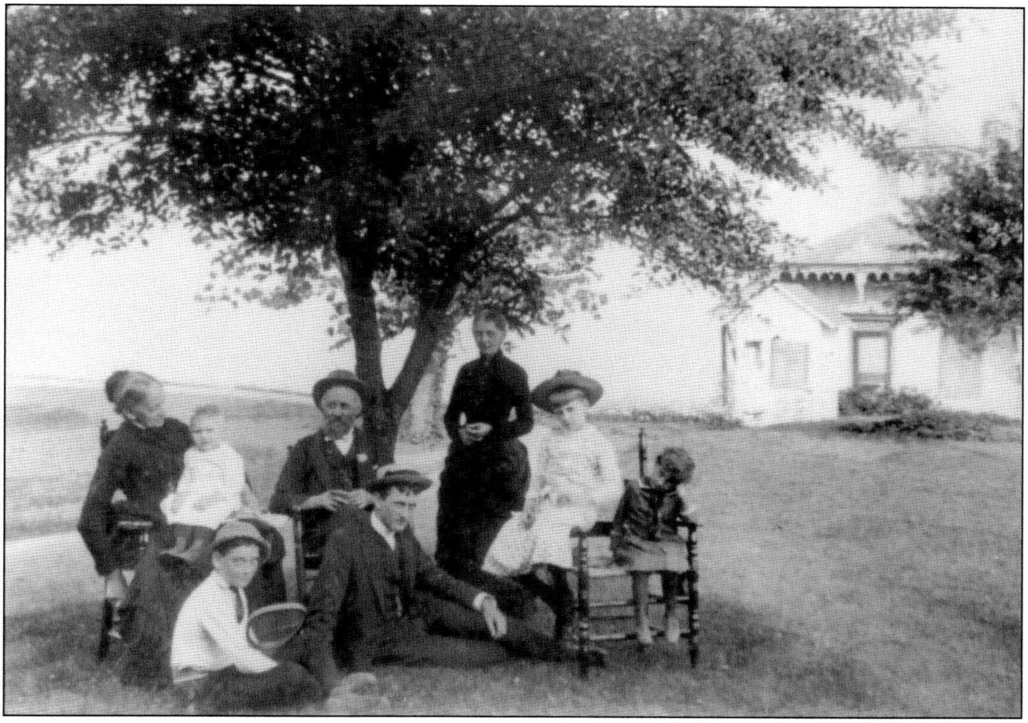

In 1862, Detroit wholesaler Theodore Hinchman built a gingerbread cottage along the shore of Lake St. Clair where the Grosse Pointe War Memorial is today. The area was a popular summer colony for many leading businessmen. Their families would live there from June through September, while the men would commute, often by boat, to jobs in Detroit. Hinchman was not only a successful merchant, but served as state senator and fire commissioner. He and his wife, Louise Chapin, had five children: John M., Ford De Camp, Charles Chapin, Lilly, and Mary.

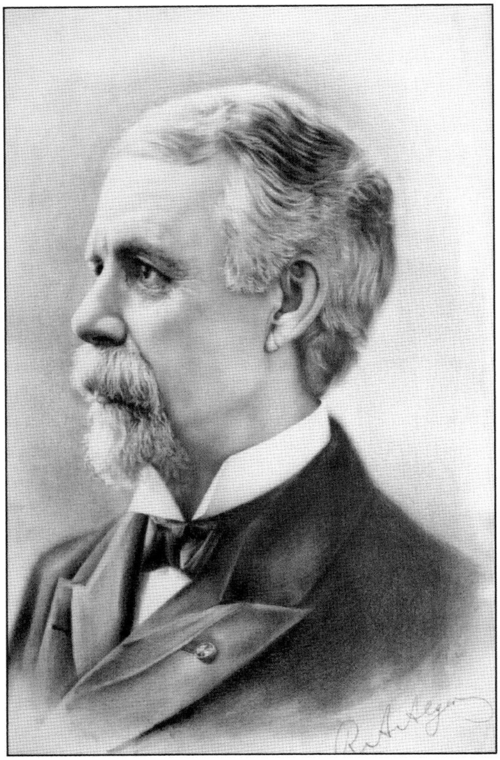

The patriarch of the Alger family, Russell Alexander Alger, led a legendary life. Orphaned at the age of 12, he went on to law school, served valiantly as a major general in the Civil War, and came home to Michigan to found thriving businesses in lumber, mining, and railroads. He ended his career as a prominent politician, serving as the governor of Michigan, secretary of war under President McKinley, and a U.S. senator.

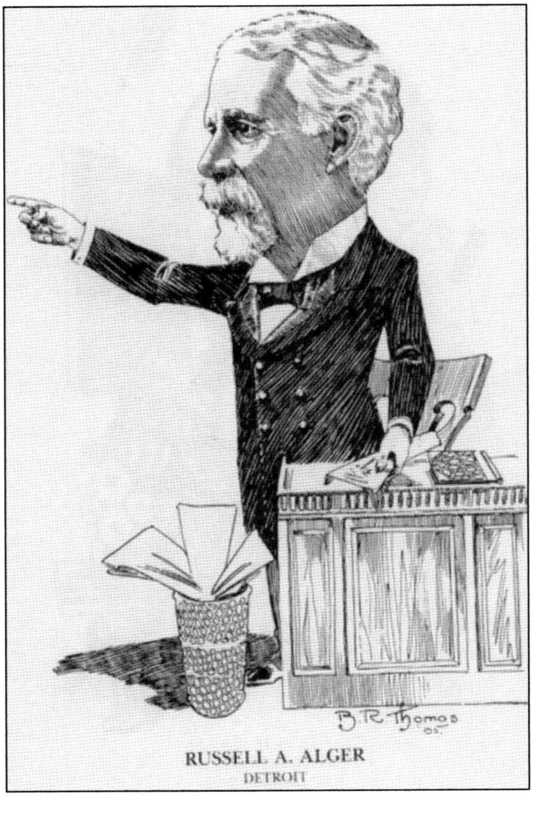

Pictured here in his role as a U.S. senator, Russell Sr. was truly one of the country's leading citizens. His Civil War career alone has a mythic quality. As colonel of the Fifth Michigan Cavalry, he and his regiment served with General Custer's famous Michigan Cavalry Brigade. He later served as private assistant to President Lincoln.

The son of a prominent businessman and politician, Russell Jr. distinguished himself on many fronts. He ran the Alger, Smith and Company, the family lumber business, cofounded the Packard Motor Car Company, and invested in the Wright brothers' first commercial airplane.

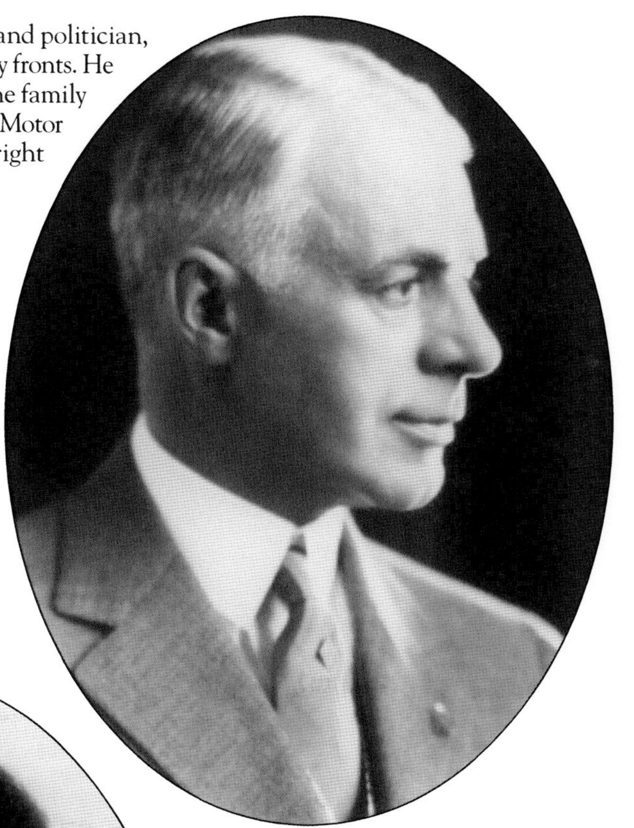

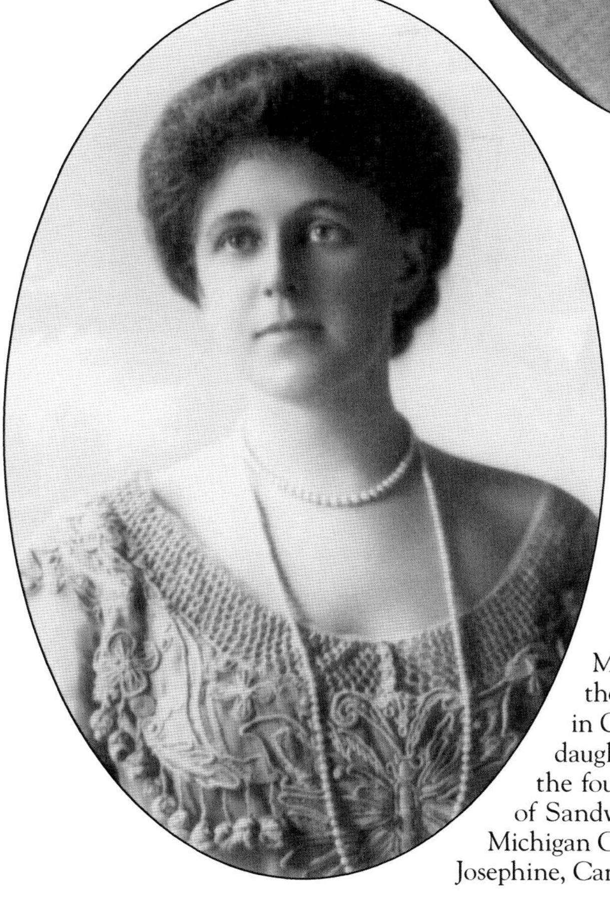

Marion Jarves Alger was the first lady of the Moorings and a great philanthropist in Grosse Pointe and Detroit. She was the daughter of Josephine and Deming Jarves, the founder of the Sandwich Glass Factory of Sandwich, Massachusetts, later known as Michigan Carbon Works. She had three children: Josephine, Caroline Fay, and Russell Alger III.

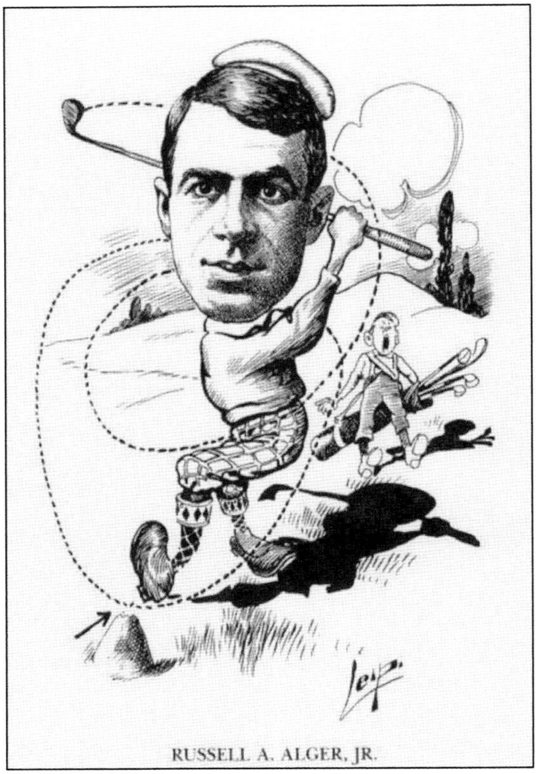

Russell was an avid sportsman who loved the outdoors. Golf was one of his favorite pastimes. He also loved being near the water and built his dream home on the lake. This caricature was included in the 1905 Newspaper Cartoonists' Association of Michigan's gallery of pen sketches entitled "Our Michigan Friends As We See 'Em."

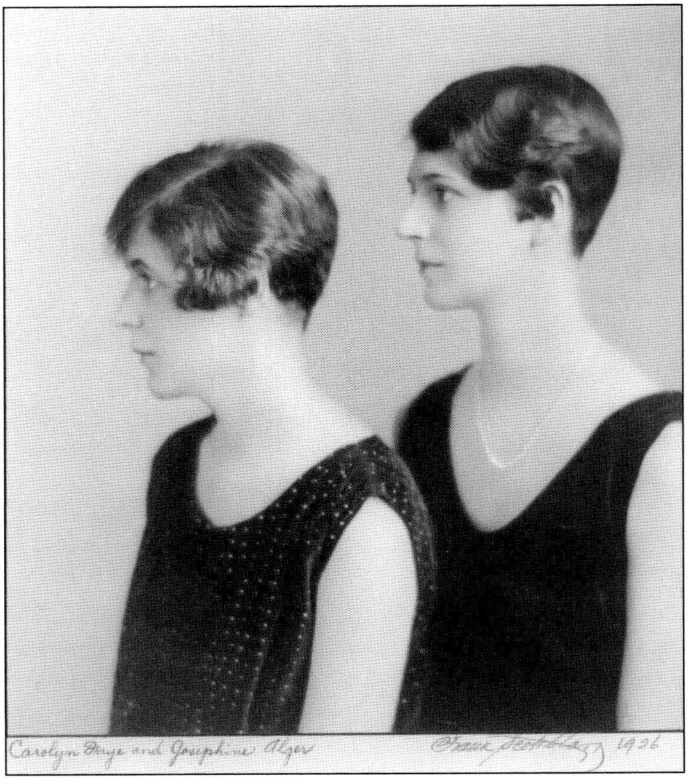

Caroline Fay (left) and Josephine Alger, the darling daughters of Russell Jr. and Marion, are pictured in 1926 sporting the fashionable bobs of the day. The girls were raised at the Moorings.

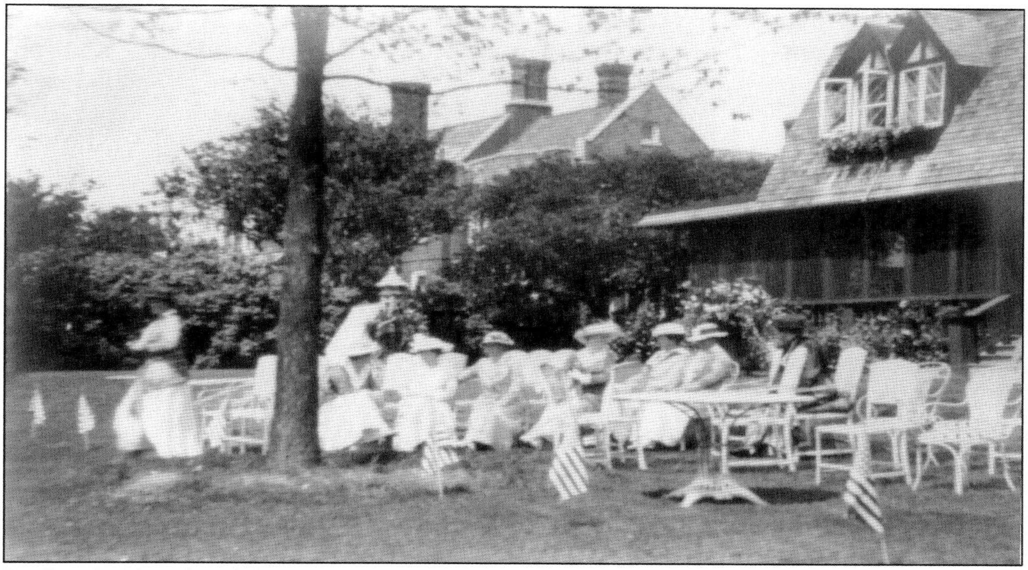

Frederick Alger lived down the street from his older brother Russell in a rambling, English farmhouse-style mansion built in 1908 by Stratton and Baldwin. Friends and family would gather on the lawn overlooking the lake for summer celebrations. The home, which was razed in the 1960s, stood where the street Island Lane is today.

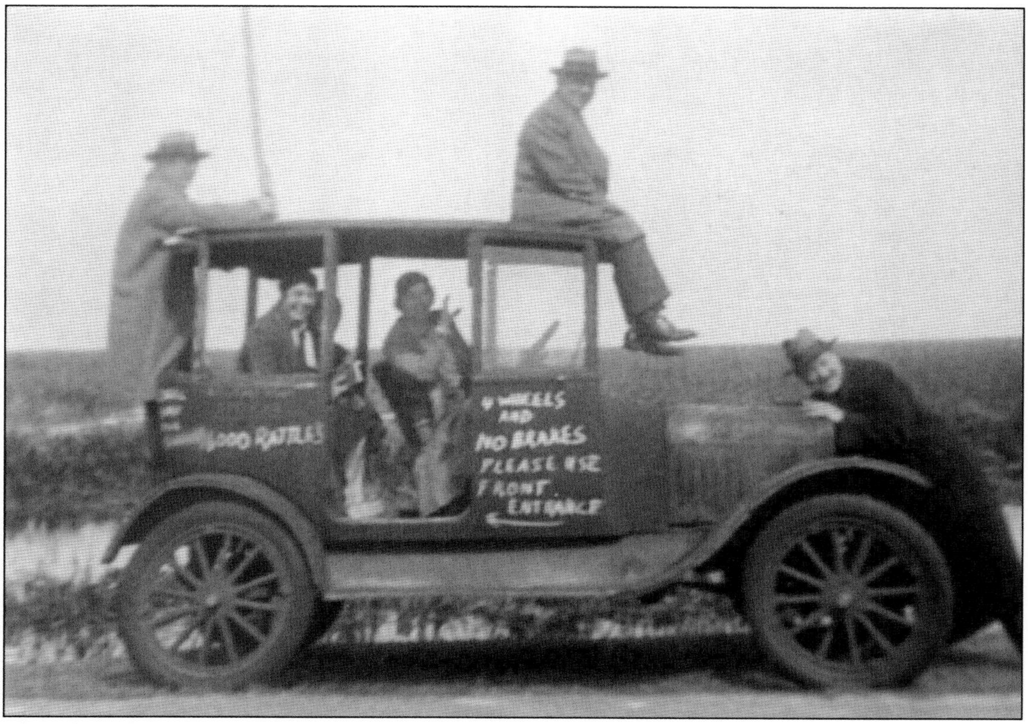

The Alger clan of friends and family mugs for the camera before embarking on a road trip. Written on the photograph is "4 wheels and no brakes/ Please use front entrance/ 1,000 Rattles."

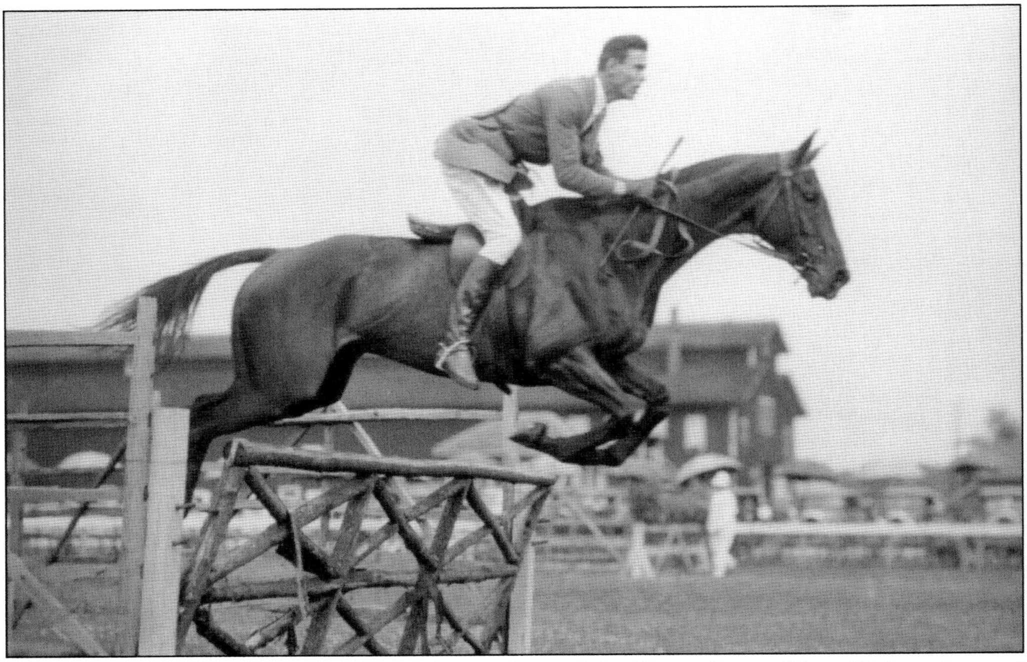

Frederick, an avid horseman, was an early president of the Grosse Pointe Hunt Club and owned stables and land in Metamora, Michigan's horse country. He withdrew from Harvard in 1898 to fight in the Spanish-American War. Some 20 years later, he was commissioned to fight in World War I and earned a promotion to lieutenant colonel.

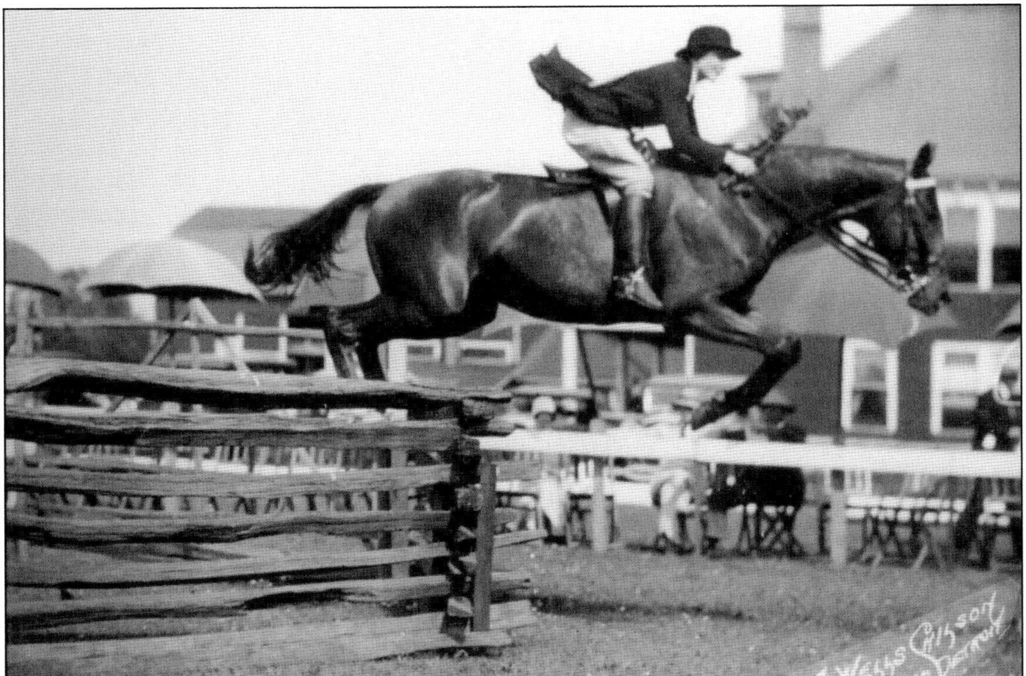

Frederick's wife, Mary Eldridge Swift Alger, was also a skilled rider. Refined and well-educated, she was born in Connecticut, attended the prestigious Dobbs Ferry School, and studied in New York City and Paris.

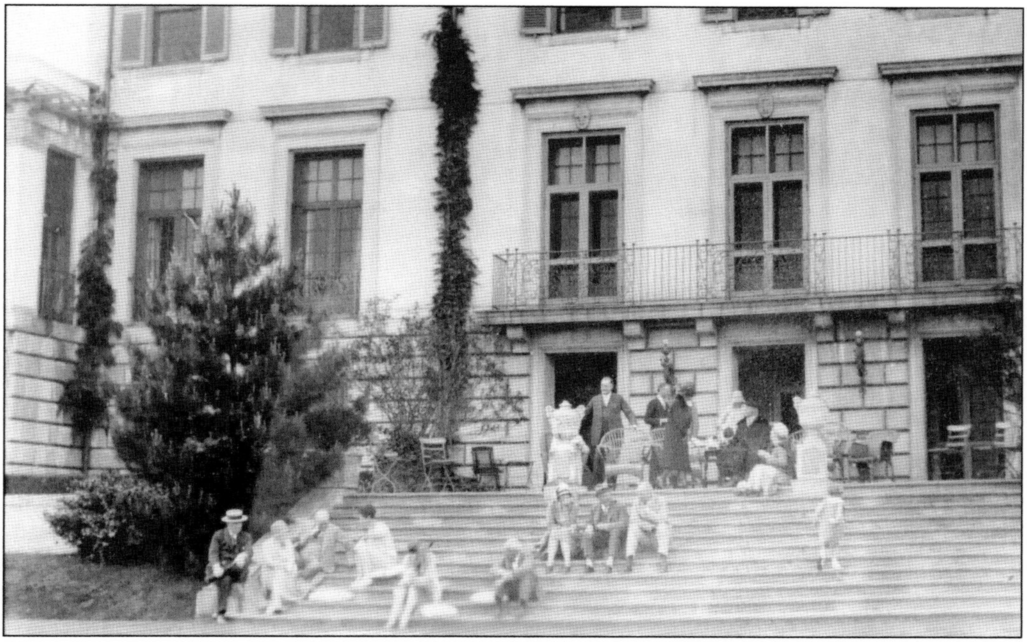

The terrace overlooking the lake was the scene of many gatherings. On Sundays, Russell and Marion often entertained family and friends. Tea was served by the Alger's butler, dressed in formal tails, and his "second man," in a hunter green uniform with a green and yellow striped waistcoat.

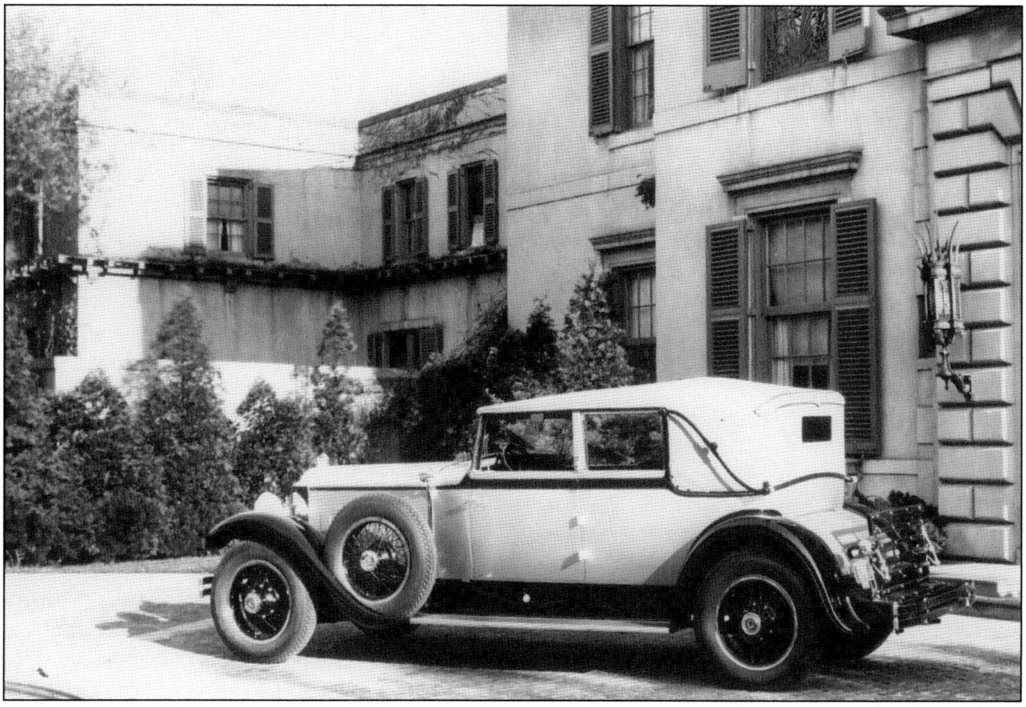

An elegant Packard is parked in front of the Alger's house. Russell Jr. was one of the original investors in the Packard Motor Car Company and served as vice president. At one time, the company was the most successful luxury automobile manufacturer in the country. The company folded in 1958.

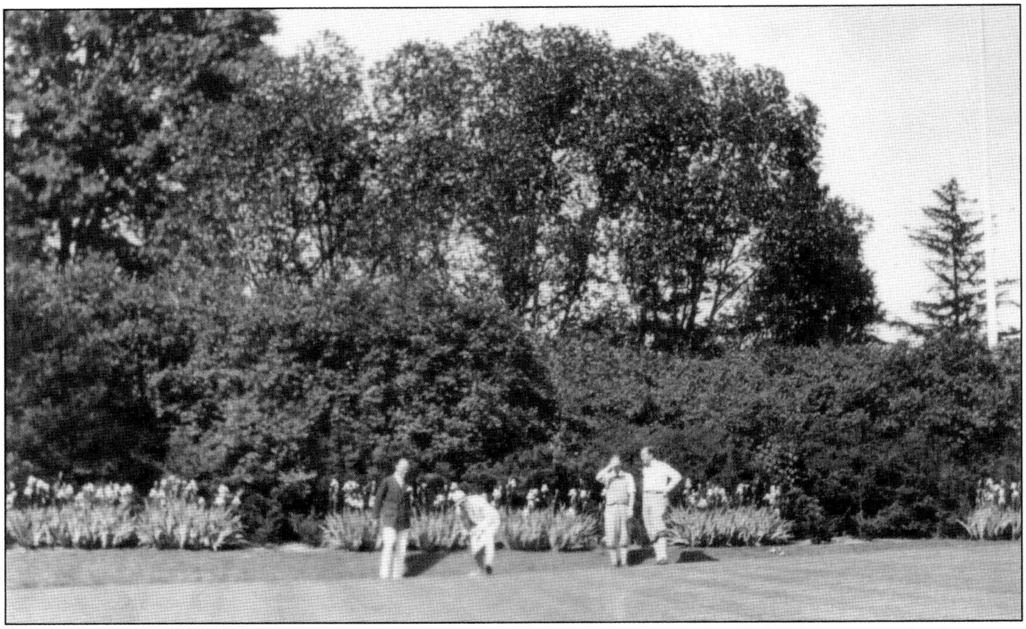

Outdoor get-togethers were a frequent occurrence at the Moorings, and the Algers made the most of the beautiful grounds surrounding their house. Here a few friends bowl on the manicured lawn with irises and trees in the background. Off to the side, the lawn continued down to the lake, with steps that are now buried by fill dirt and a cement sea wall.

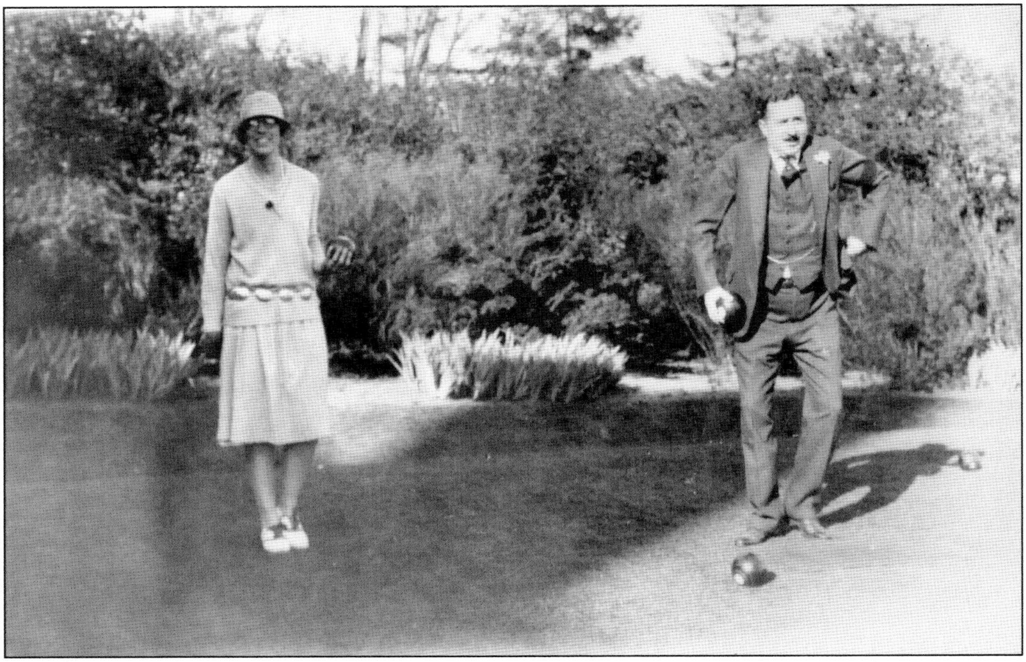

Marion Campbell and Percival Dodge enjoy lawn bowling at the Moorings around 1925. Marion was the daughter of Samuel Campbell, a prominent Detroit lawyer who founded the Grosse Pointe Club. He enjoyed memberships in several exclusive clubs, including the Yondotega Club, the Country Club of Detroit, and the Huron Mountain Club, where he was one of only 50 members who owned a cabin.

Young Marion Miller must have been delighted to spend the afternoon playing on the beautiful lawn of her grandmother Marion's home with her father, Sidney Miller. Behind the group is Lake St. Clair, where they could watch boats sail by and feed the seagulls and mallards if they tired of lawn bowling.

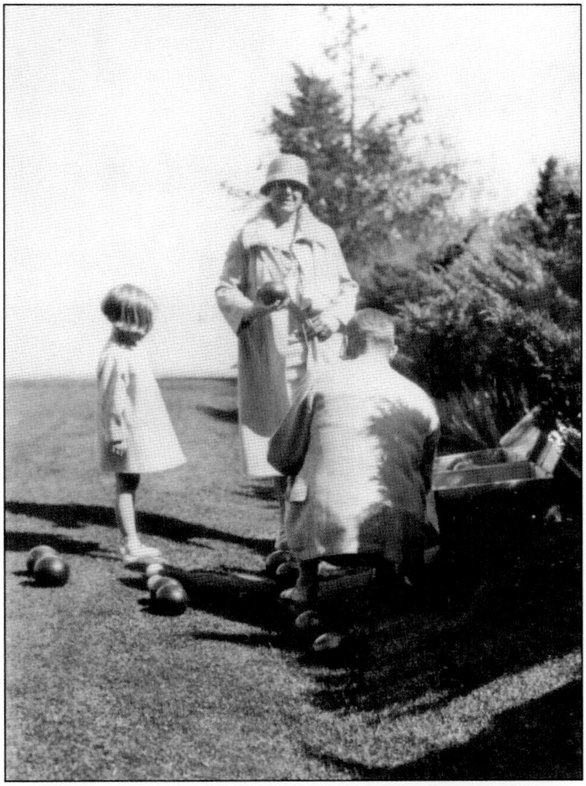

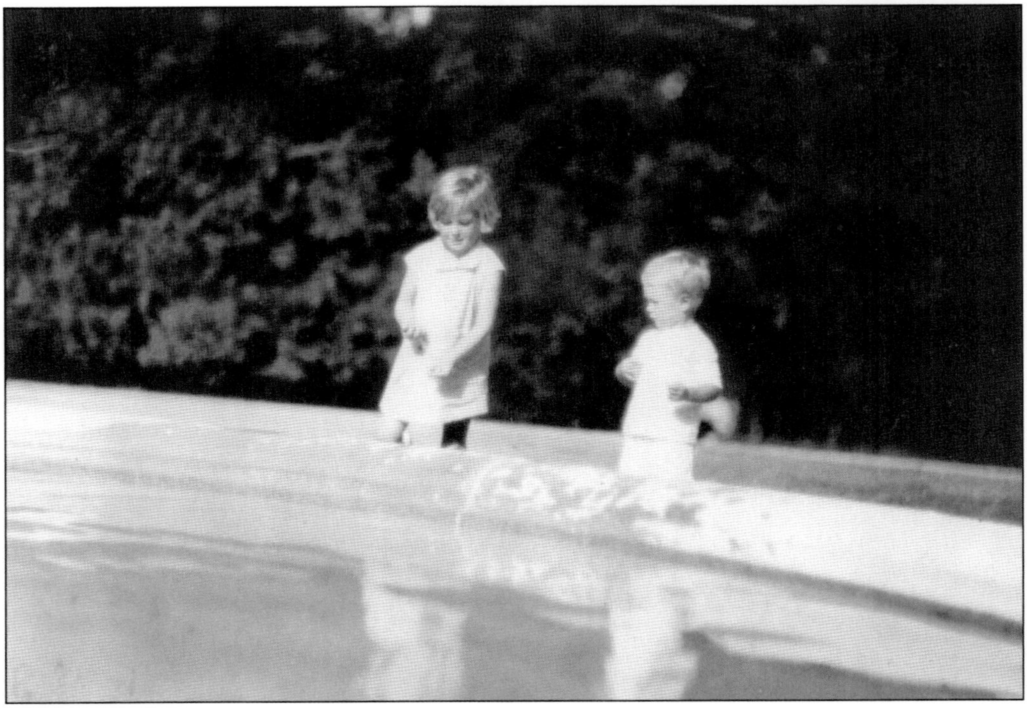

Cousins Marion Miller (daughter of Sidney and Fay Alger Miller) and Russell Alger IV (son of Phoebe Anne Bailey and Russell Alger III) splash in the pool in front of the Moorings.

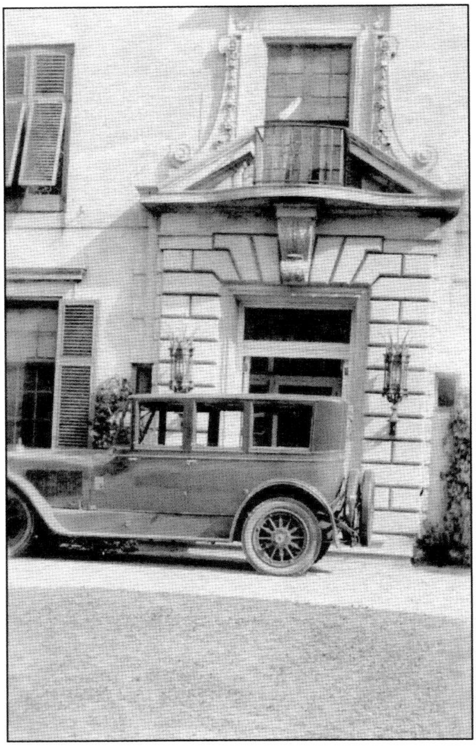

A Packard Twin Six automobile is pictured here. Wealthy Detroiter Henry Bourne Joy was so impressed with the company that he persuaded nine of his colleagues to become investors. In 1902, Russell Alger Jr. put in $50,000, as did Joy. Other backers were Truman and John Newberry, C. A. DuCharme, D. M. Ferry, Joseph Boyer, Phillip H. McMillan, Alger's brother Fred, and Joy's brother Richard.

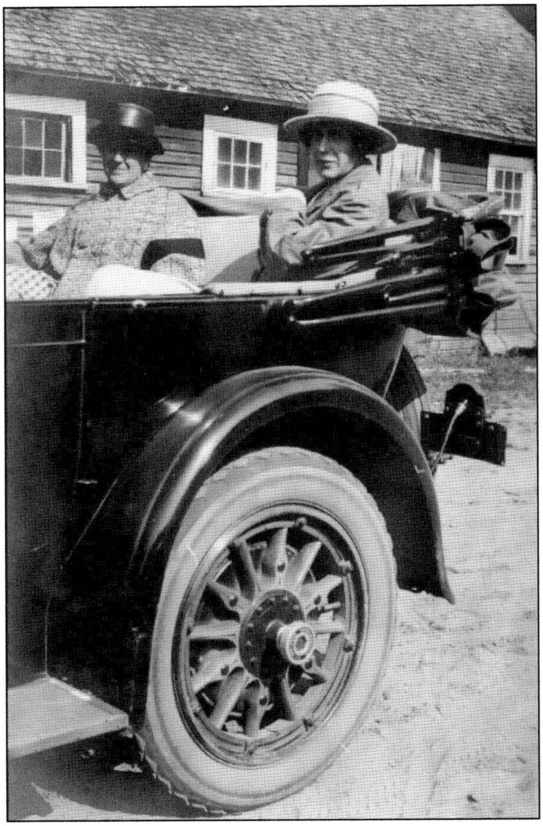

Marion Alger and her daughter Fay are pictured here. The black band around Marion's arm suggests the photograph was taken during World War II. The photograph may have been taken at the Huron Mountain Club, the exclusive private hunting and fishing preserve located in the rugged Upper Peninsula. Wealthy businessmen from Detroit and Chicago founded the club in the late 1890s, and Henry Ford was a member.

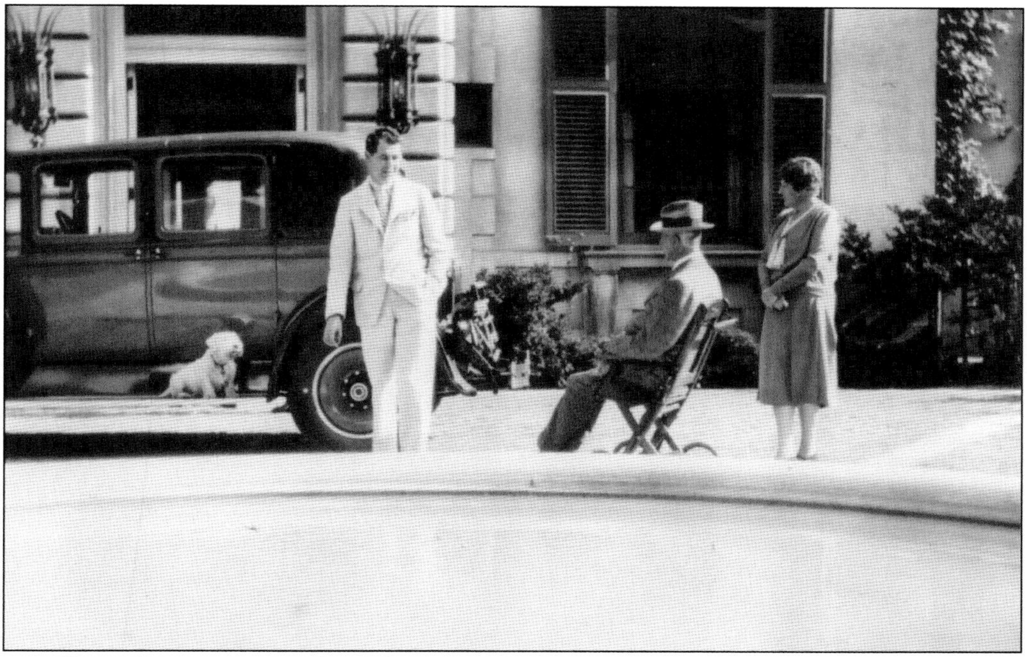

Russell A. Alger III is pictured with his father and mother in front of the Moorings. Russell Alger II sits in a wheelchair. He was paralyzed at the age of 48 after being thrown from a horse chasing hounds at the Grosse Pointe Country Club in 1921. Marion Alger was devoted to her husband and cared for him lovingly through his untimely illness and death.

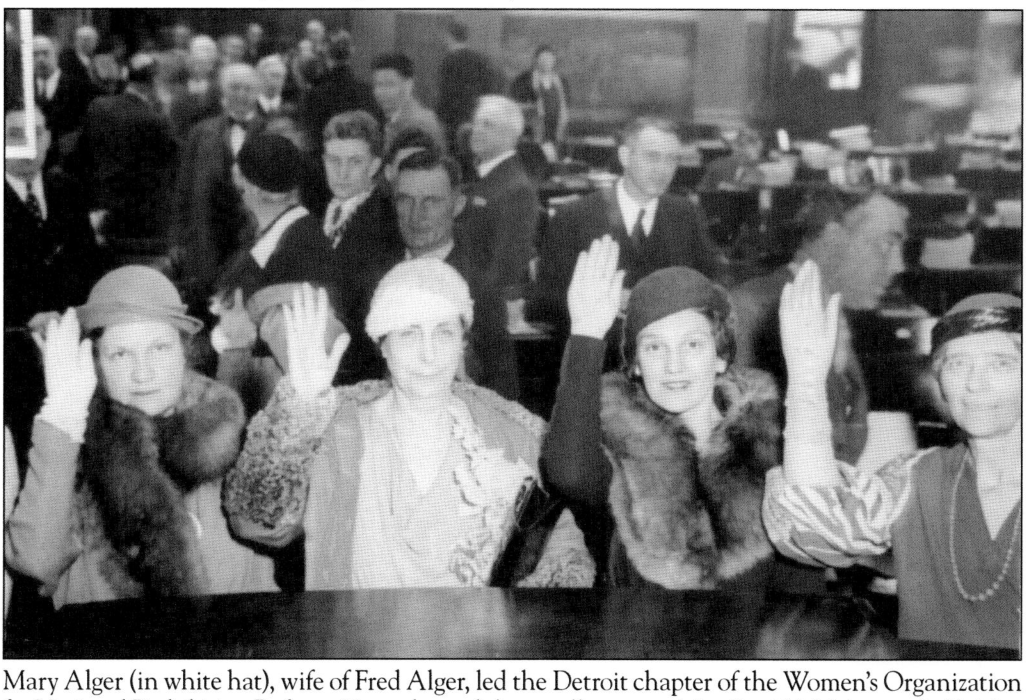

Mary Alger (in white hat), wife of Fred Alger, led the Detroit chapter of the Women's Organization for National Prohibition Reform. Here, she and three colleagues—Mrs. David McMorran (left), Mrs. Thomas McAllister (third from the left), and Catherine D. Doren—testify in favor of repealing the 19th Amendment. Mary Alger was later named to the Michigan Liquor Control Commission.

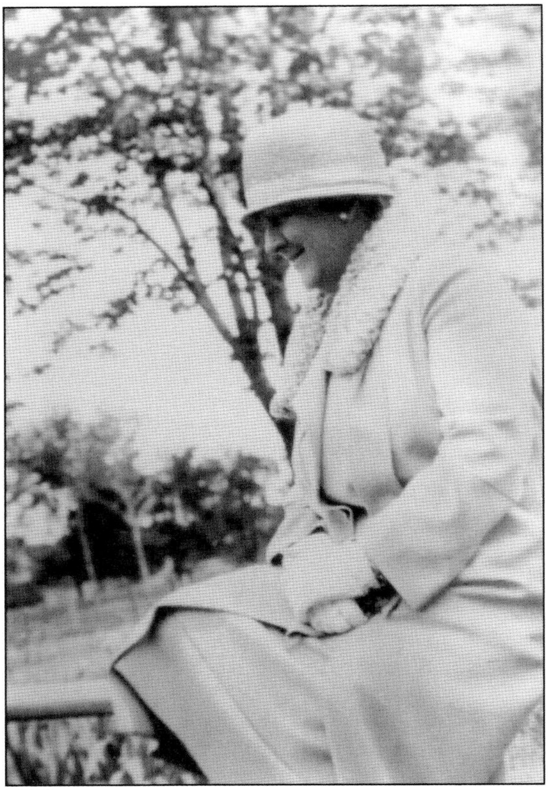

Marion sits outside her home, no doubt smiling as she watches her guests. Marion was committed to her family and loved nothing better than to have them spend time with her and Russell. Her concern for others went beyond her family—in the late 1920s, she and a few friends founded the Neighborhood Thrift Shop to help needy residents in the area.

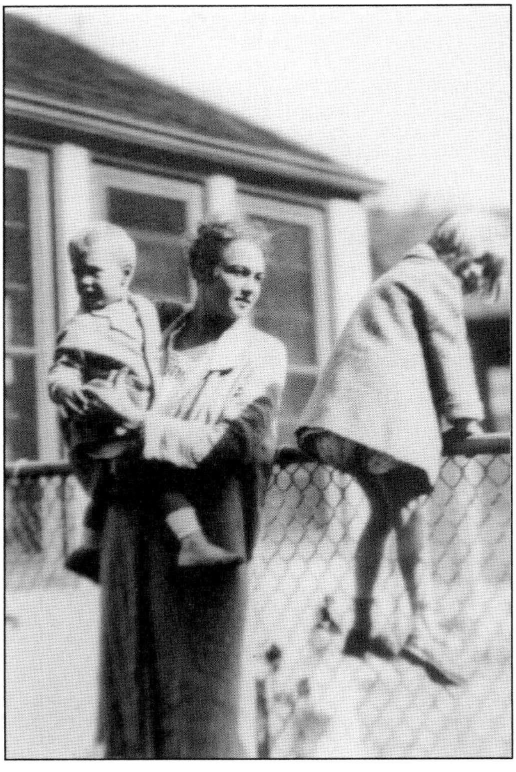

Russell Alger IV and his sister Anne are pictured with their mother, Phoebe Anne Bailey Alger. Phoebe hailed from California, where she married Russell Alger III in Pasadena in March 1926.

The apple of his father's eye, Russell Alger IV stands outside his grandfather's house.

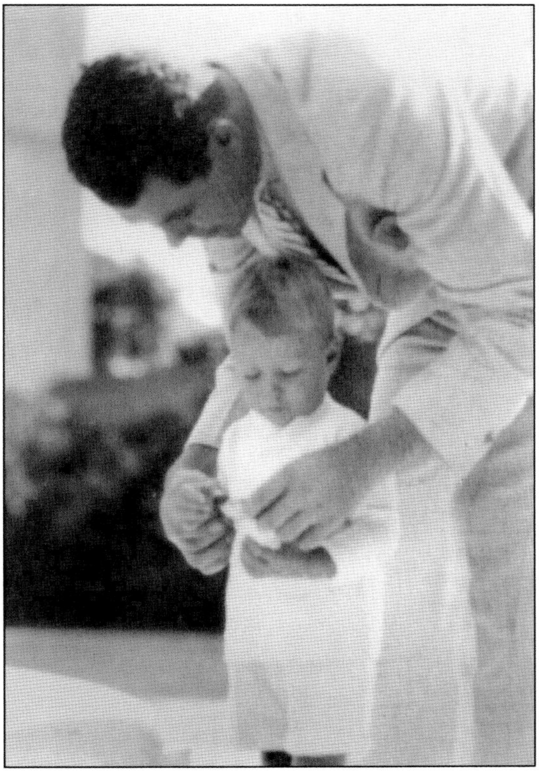

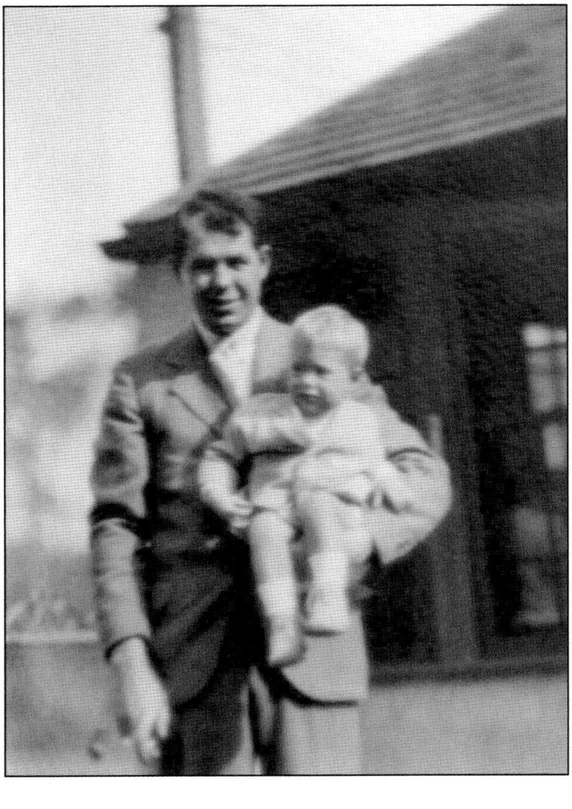

Russell Alger III holds his son, Russell Alger IV. The background looks like the Huron Mountain Club, the private vacation resort in Michigan's Upper Peninsula. The Algers were among the founding families of the association.

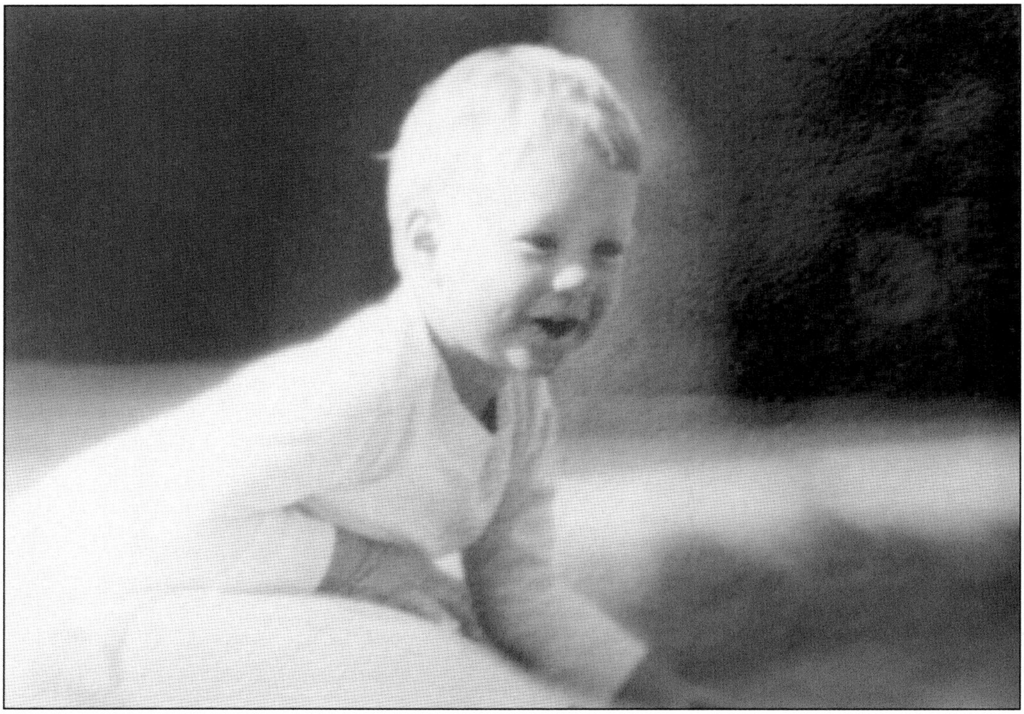

Golden boy Russell Alger IV is shown at his grandparents' house.

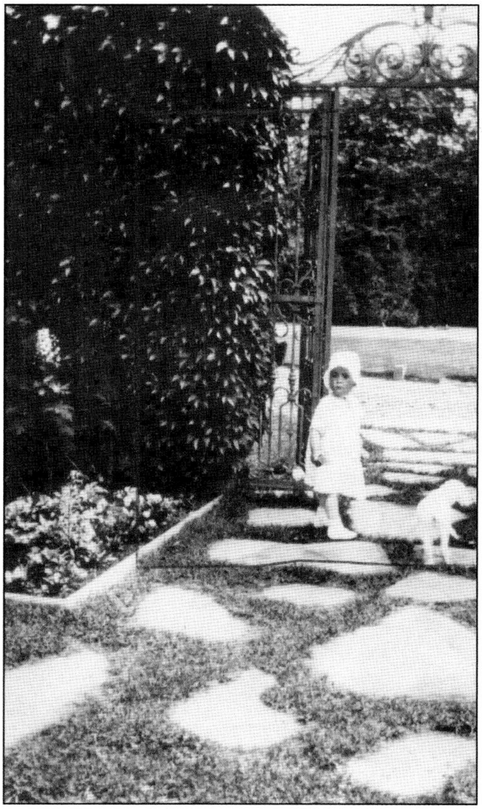

Little Marion Miller is as pretty as a picture as she plays with her puppy while visiting Grandma Marion and Grandpa Rusty. Marion was the daughter of Fay Alger and Sidney Trowbridge Miller. Her grandfather, Sidney "Rusty" Davy Miller, founded Miller Canfield, one of Detroit's oldest law firms. Her father transformed the firm from a small law office to the multidimensional firm it is today.

Marion plays under the shade of the pergola in her grandparents' formal garden around 1925.

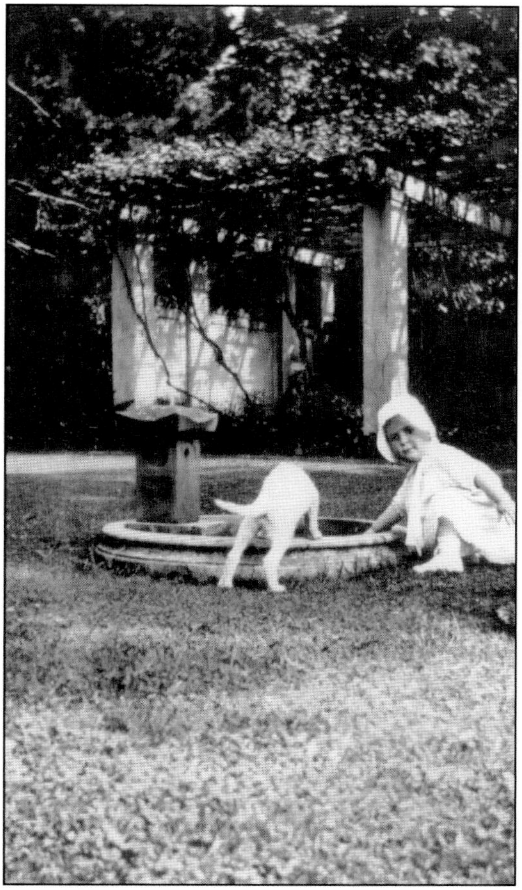

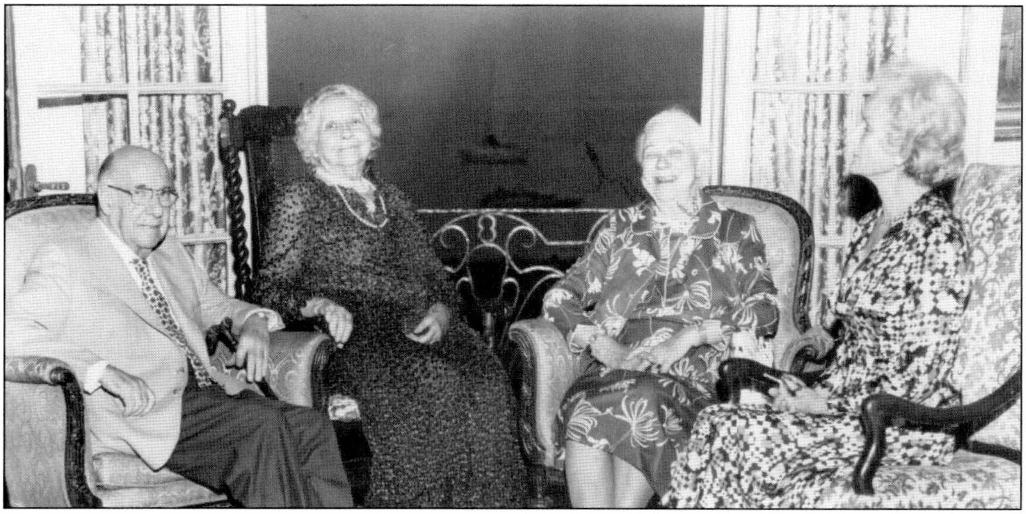

Enjoying a June 1978 Detroit Symphony Orchestra (DSO) concert from the opened doors of the great hall balcony of the Alger House are, from left to right, John B. Ford (chair of the DSO board), Mrs. Allan Shelden, Mrs. Nils R. Johaneson, and Mrs. Ford. Mrs. Johaneson, the former Josephine Alger, was pleased to see so many enjoying the concert evening at the War Memorial, which at one time was her home. Allan Shelden was Josephine's cousin.

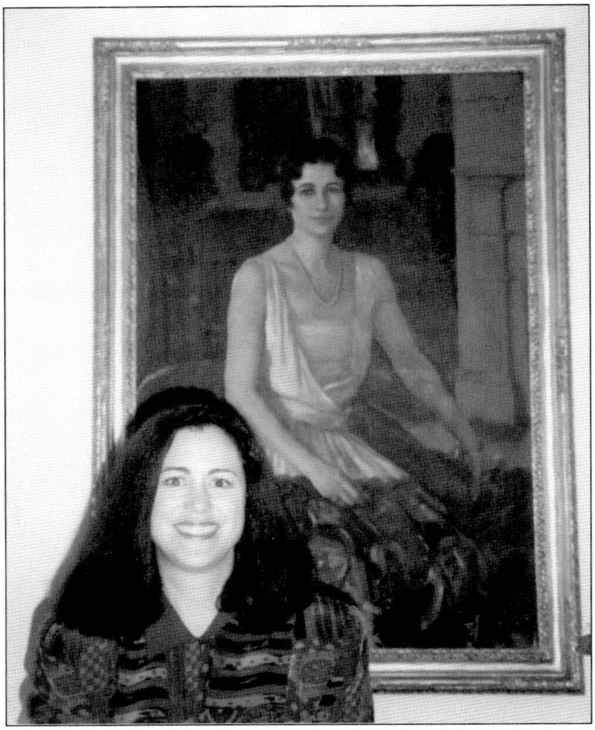

Priscilla Mead stands in front of a portrait of her grandmother, Frances Alger Boyer. Franny, as she was known, was Frederick's daughter and Russell Jr.'s niece. She was a gracious hostess who loved giving dinner parties at the pool house in front of the Lake St. Clair home she shared with her husband, Harold "Bill" Boyer.

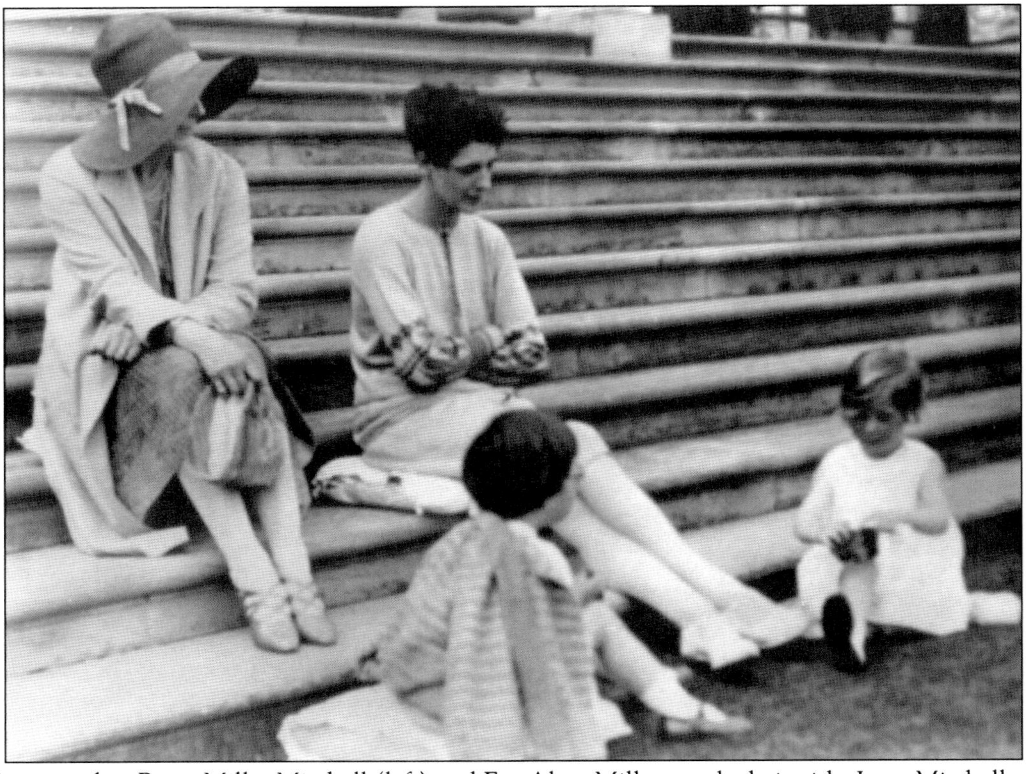

Sisters-in-law Betty Miller Mitchell (left) and Fay Alger Miller watch their girls, Lucy Mitchell (left) and Marion Miller, play on the terrace steps of Fay's parents home around 1928.

Two

At Home By the Lake

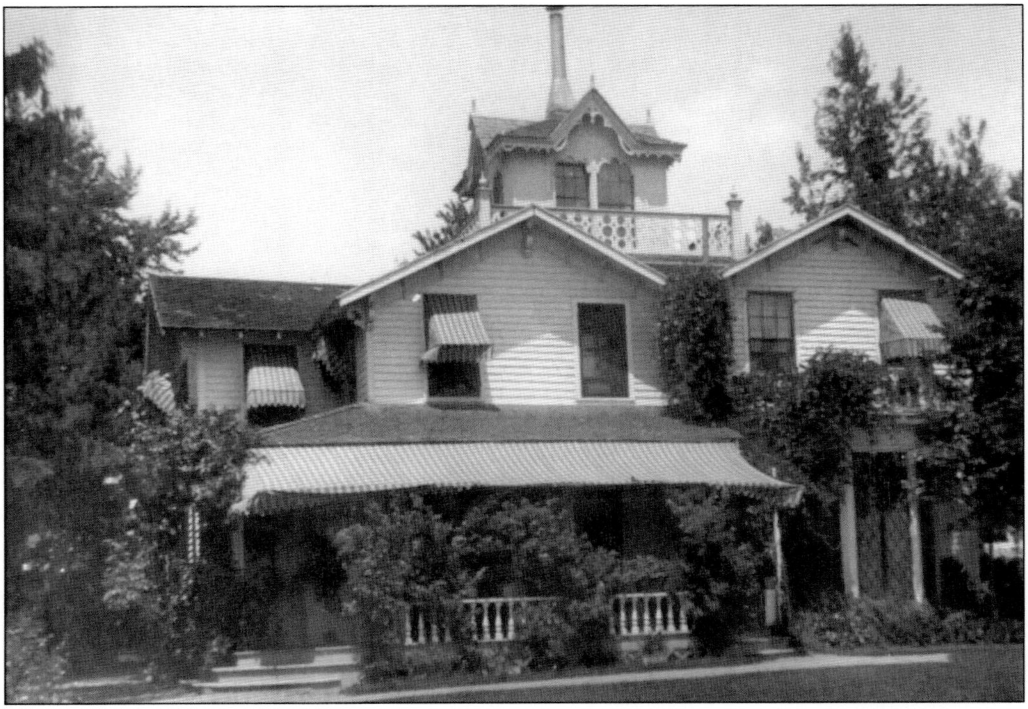

In the early 1900s, the Alger family summered in the old Hinchman home, a charming wisteria-covered clapboard cottage typical of that time. The windows were shielded from the sun by colorful awnings. Vines also helped keep it cool in the summer.

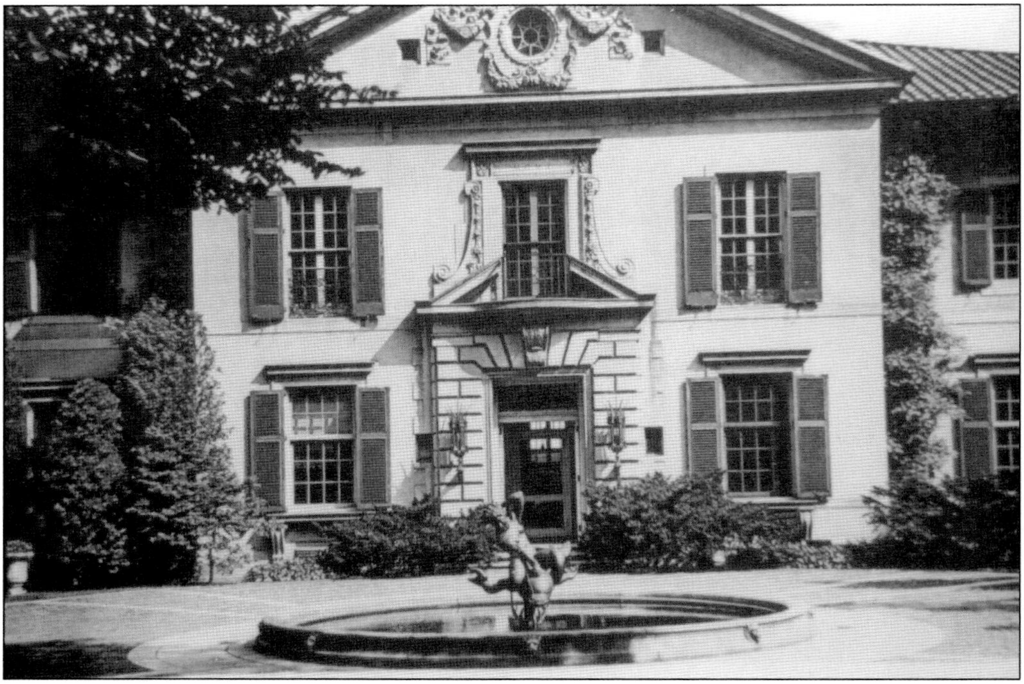

Alger eventually purchased the Hinchman property and tore down the old home to build his dream house. Noted New York architect Charles Platt designed a six-bedroom Italianate villa made of white concrete and limestone with a red tile roof. The home included spacious servants' quarters, a third floor playroom, and a billiard room on the lower level.

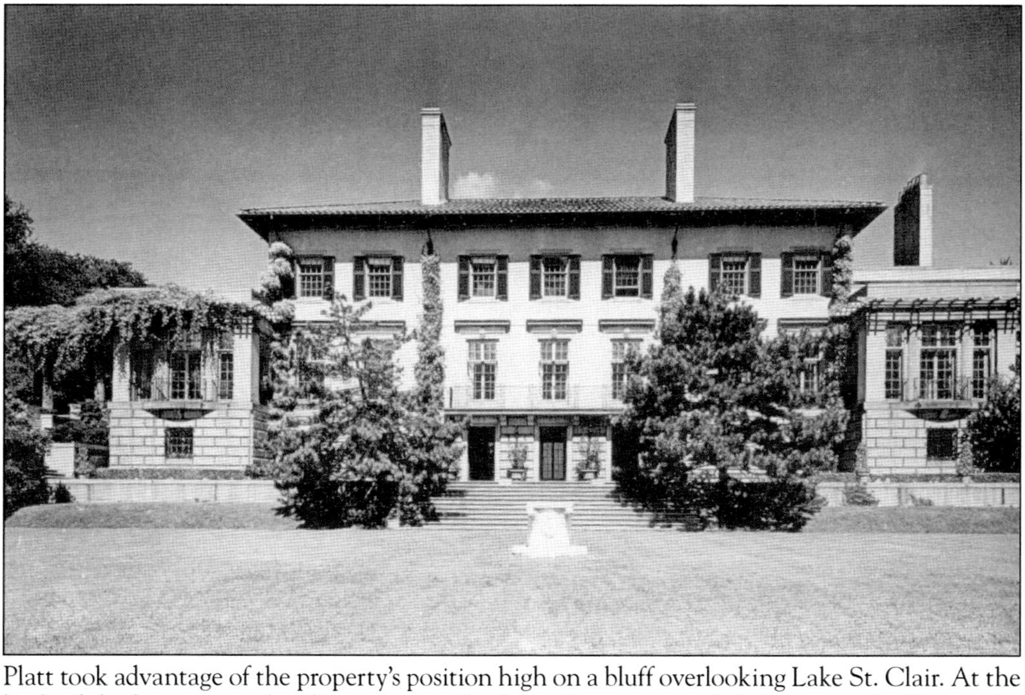

Platt took advantage of the property's position high on a bluff overlooking Lake St. Clair. At the back of the home was a bowling green to the lake. Cement steps led down to a landing at the water with Venetian poles, or moorings, which gave the house its name.

The dining room runs the entire length of the house on the north side. It has a huge Florentine fireplace dated 1625. The chandelier, candelabra, and wall sconces were silver plated by Reed and Barton.

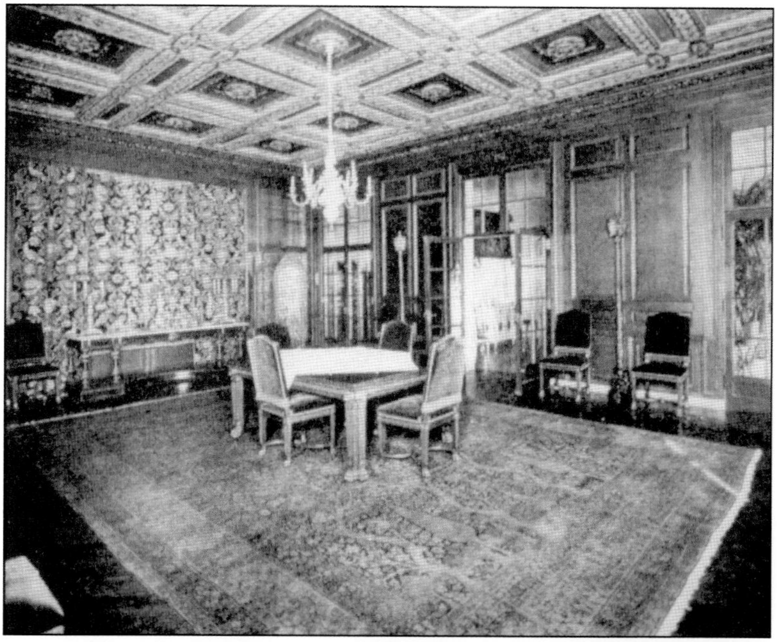

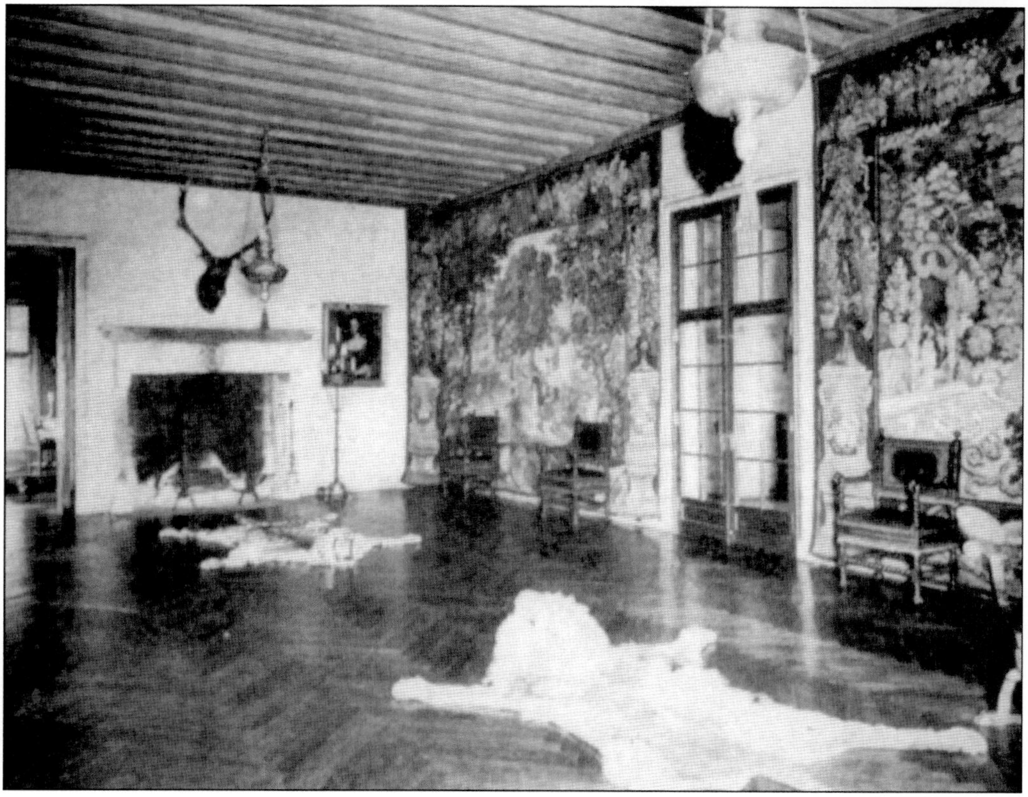

The beams in the great room are made of concrete, painted to look like wood. Alger's first home was destroyed by fire, so he wanted his new home to contain very few flammable materials. The room opens onto a long balcony from which the Algers and their guests could watch the pageant of boats glide by on the lake.

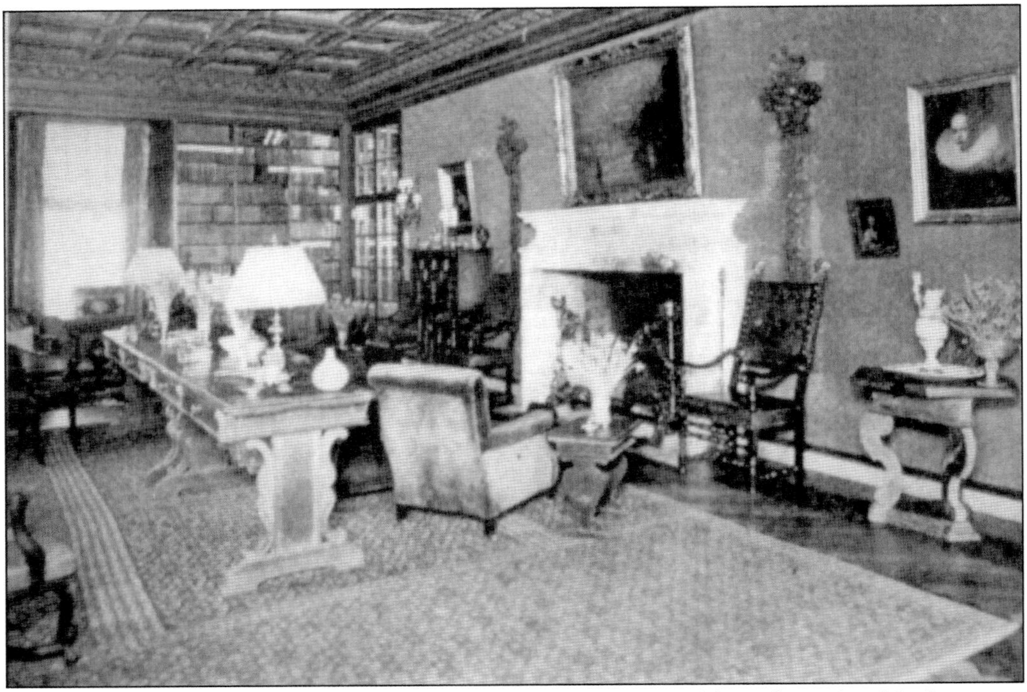

The library served as a family room for the Algers with a large table and comfortable furniture. The intaglio rosettes in the plaster ceiling were hand-carved.

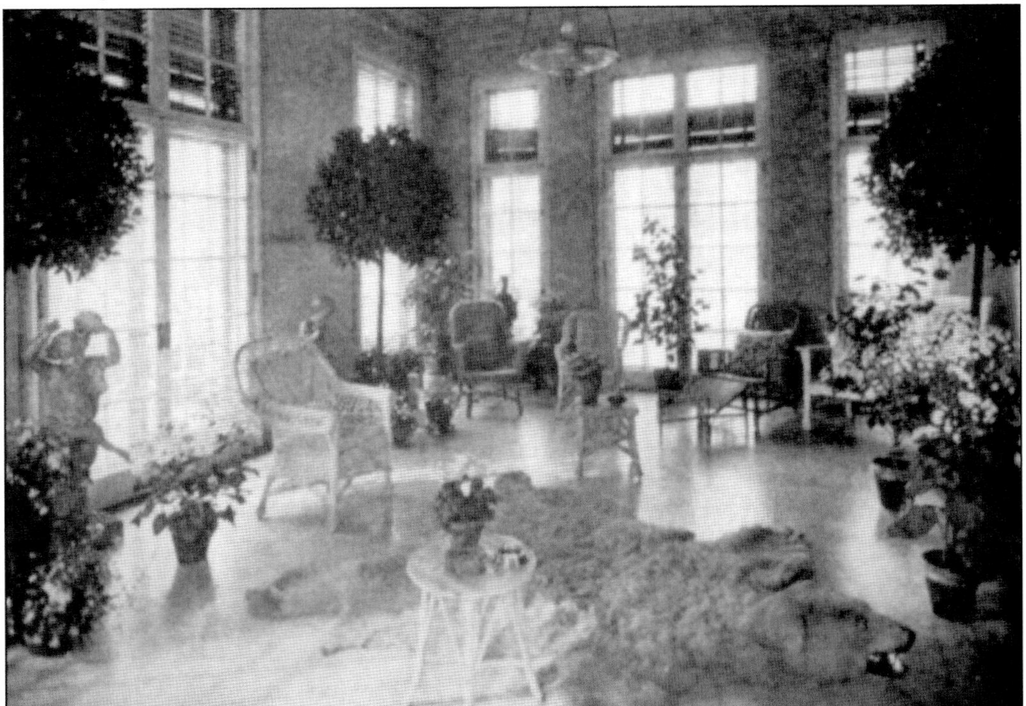

This informal summer room was used for relaxing and viewing the lake. The Algers often had breakfast here. It was furnished in white wicker, Victorian style, with metal Venetian blinds outside to close when the sun was hot. A bearskin rug covered the floor.

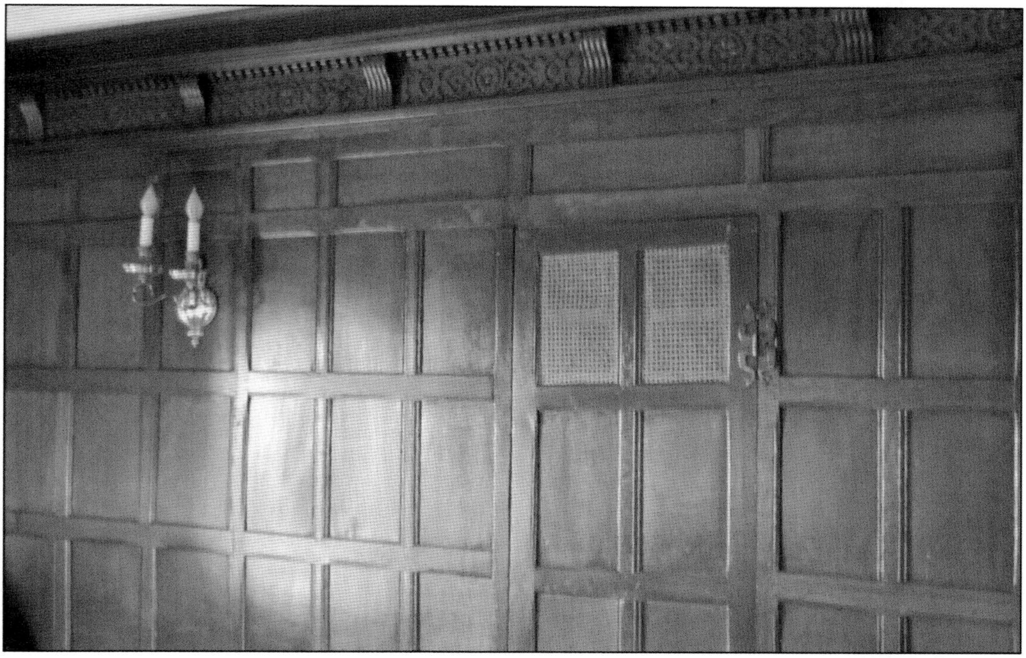

Wood paneling imported from a pub in England lines the walls of the elegant billiard room in the home's lower or lake level, where the gentlemen would retire after dinner. During Prohibition, the room was connected by a tunnel to the lake for clandestine trips to smuggle in contraband liquor. The tunnel was filled in during the construction of the Fries Auditorium. The door to the tunnel is behind a tapestry.

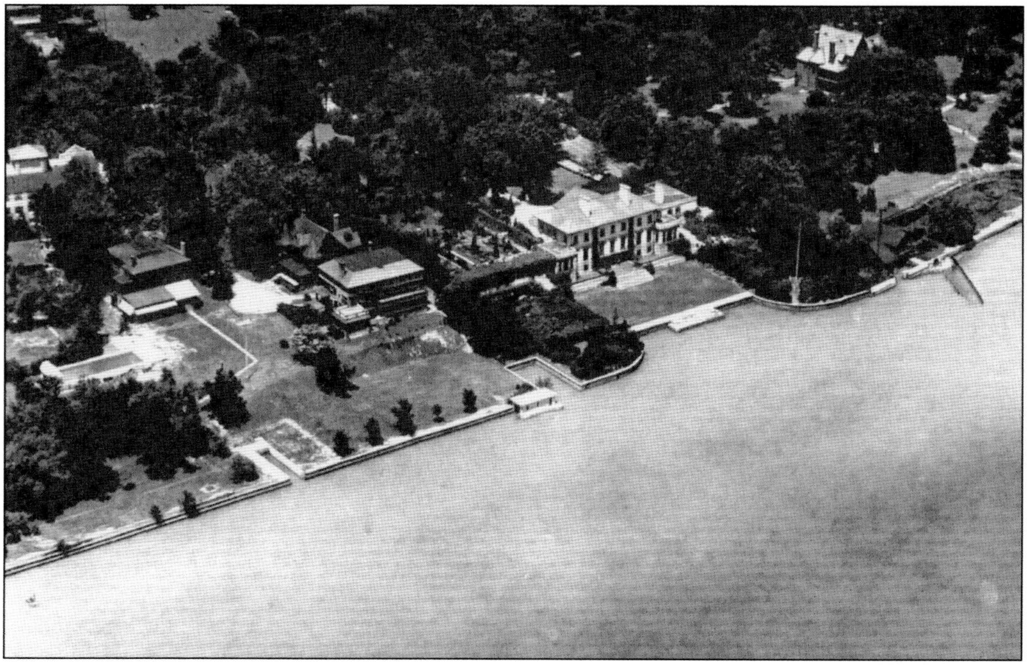

This aerial view shows how wonderfully situated the house was on the water. Josephine Alger tells of her wedding in the home when she and her groom, Henry Cheney, left the reception from the boat well to a yacht that was waiting out in the lake.

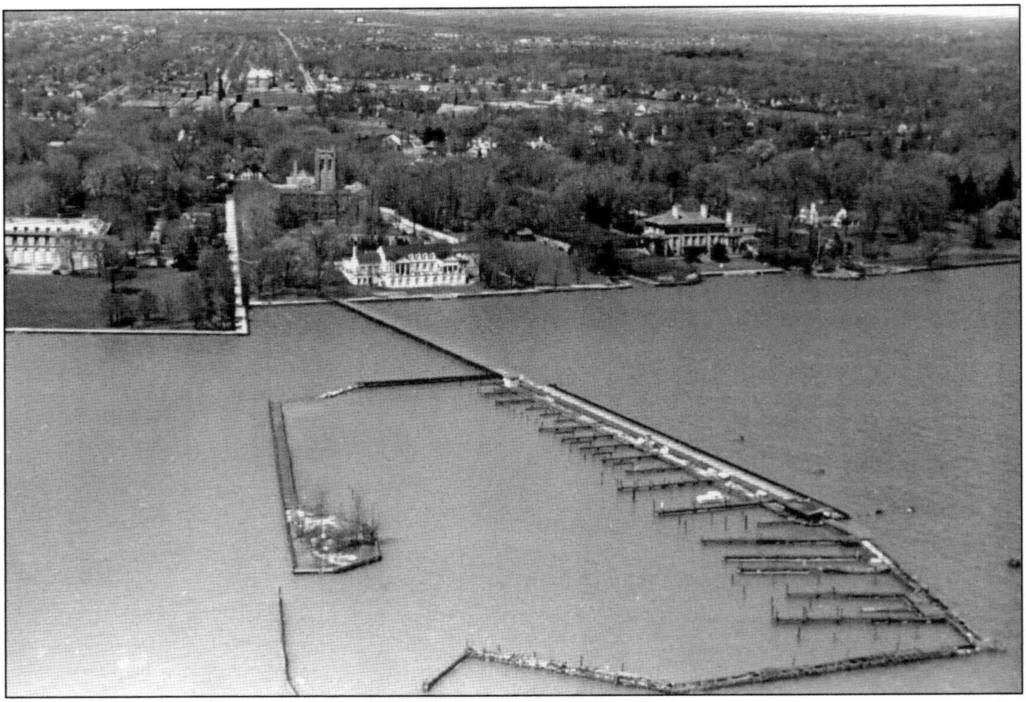

The docks of the Grosse Pointe Club, which was founded in 1923, are directly adjacent to the Alger property. Rose Terrace, the Dodge mansion, can be seen at the far left.

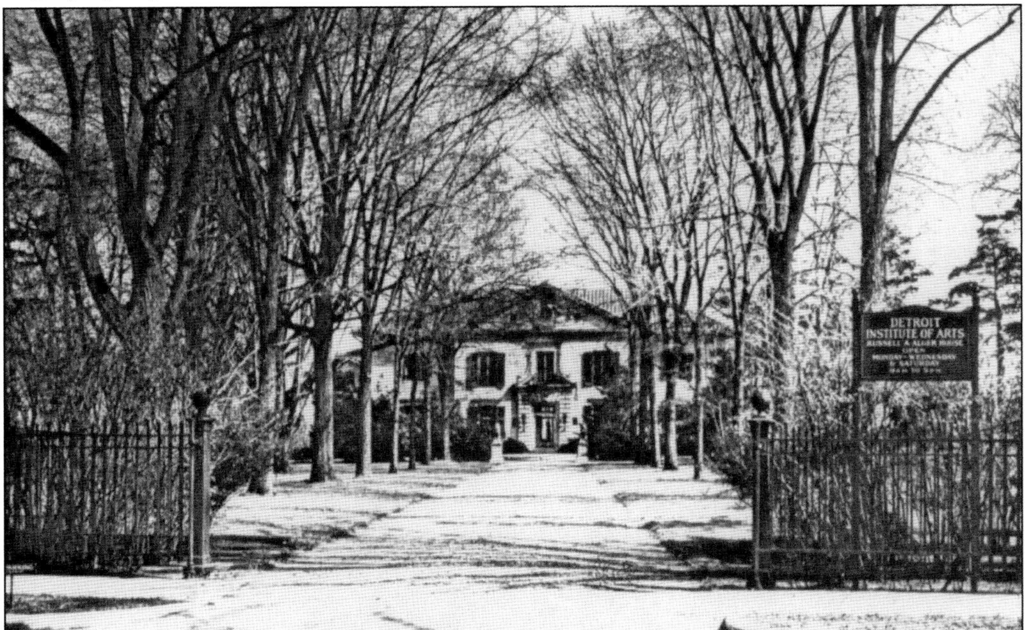

Shortly after Russell II died in 1930, his widow offered the Moorings to the Detroit Institute of Arts. The interior architecture was particularly suited to the needs of an east side museum, especially because of its spacious rooms. On display were a collection of paintings, furniture, and other objects from different eras throughout the history of art, including special loan exhibitions of modern and Egyptian art.

Thomas L. Munson, chairman of the Board of Trustees, announces the addition of the William Fries Auditorium, which was completed in 1962. A bequest from the estate of William H. Fries, former assistant headmaster of the Grosse Pointe University School (now University Liggett) paid for the construction of the large auditorium and meeting center. Walter Buhl Ford II had his staff at the design firm Ford and Earl Associates donate the furnishings for the ballroom, lobby, and downstairs foyer.

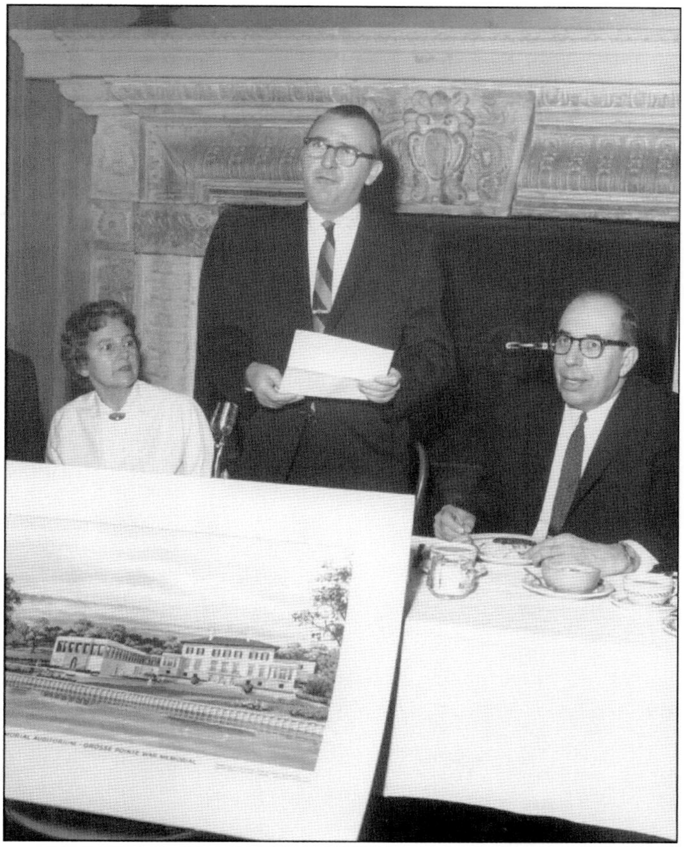

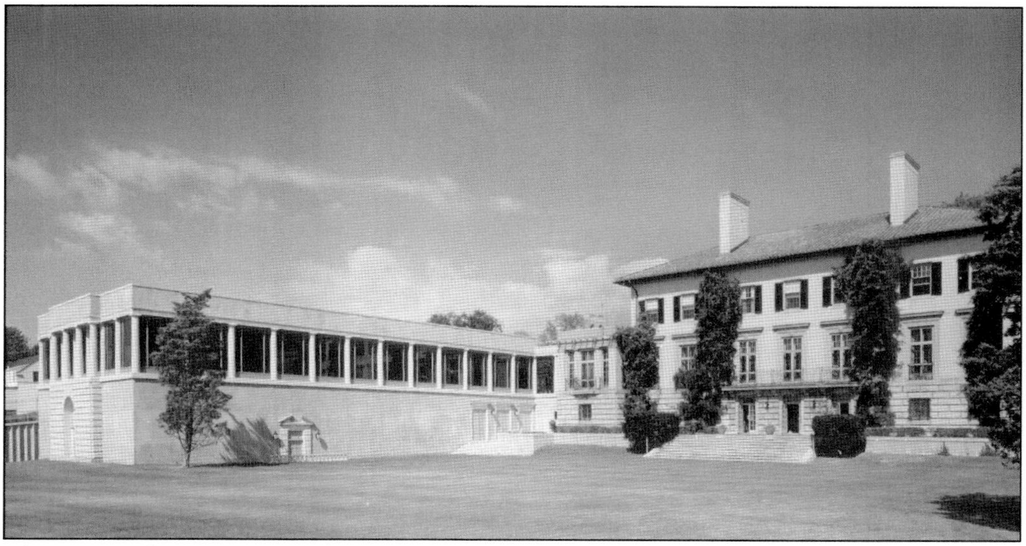

The Fries Auditorium included a banquet hall known as the Crystal Ballroom, a 450-seat theater, and meeting facilities. An inaugural lecture series in early 1963 included Jerome Cavanagh, then mayor of Detroit; Leonard Woodcock, vice president of the UAW AFL-CIO; and Henry Ford II, chairman of Ford Motor Company.

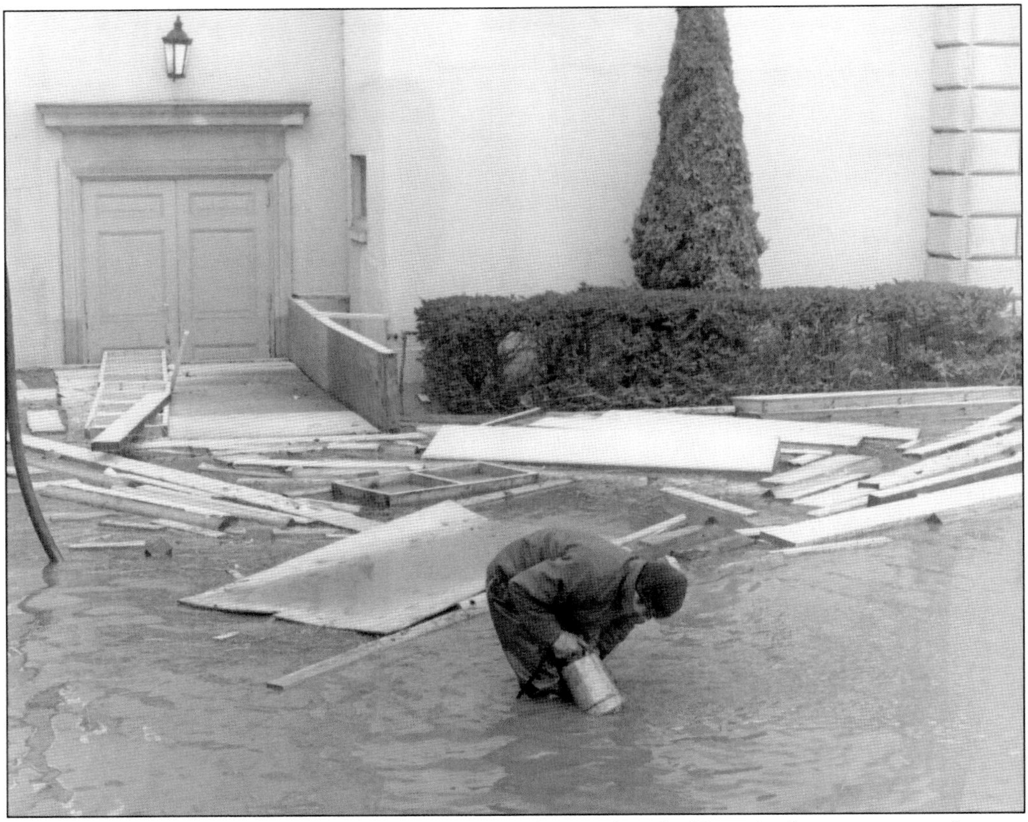

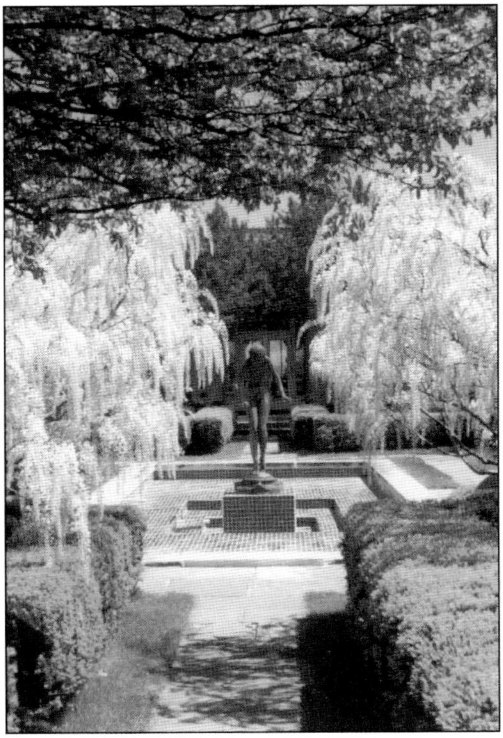

Soon after the Fries Auditorium opened, a tremendous rainstorm occurred the night before the opening of a Grosse Pointe Theater performance. The rain created high waters that crashed over the seawall and into the building, reaching up to the fifth row and causing the piano to float around. Volunteers, including theater members and Mrs. Fred Alger Jr., who was on the board, came in the middle of the night and began to pump the water out and fill sandbags. The show went on the next night, with plastic bags over the first five rows of seats.

The reflecting pool of the formal gardens, right, was graced by *Bronze Nymph*, a beautiful bronze sculpture by Edward McCartan that was originally on the Newberry estate. In 2001, it was stolen from the War Memorial but was discovered accidentally eight years later by divers in the Detroit River.

This iron gate off the entrance courtyard leads to the formal wisteria gardens.

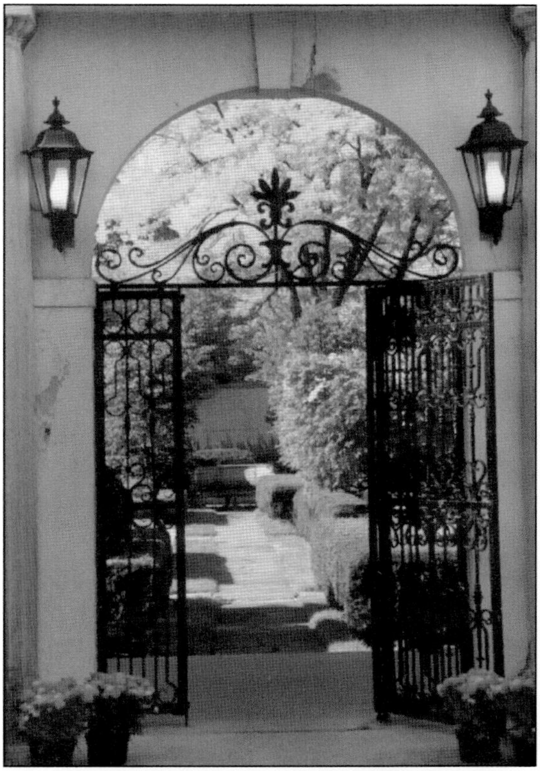

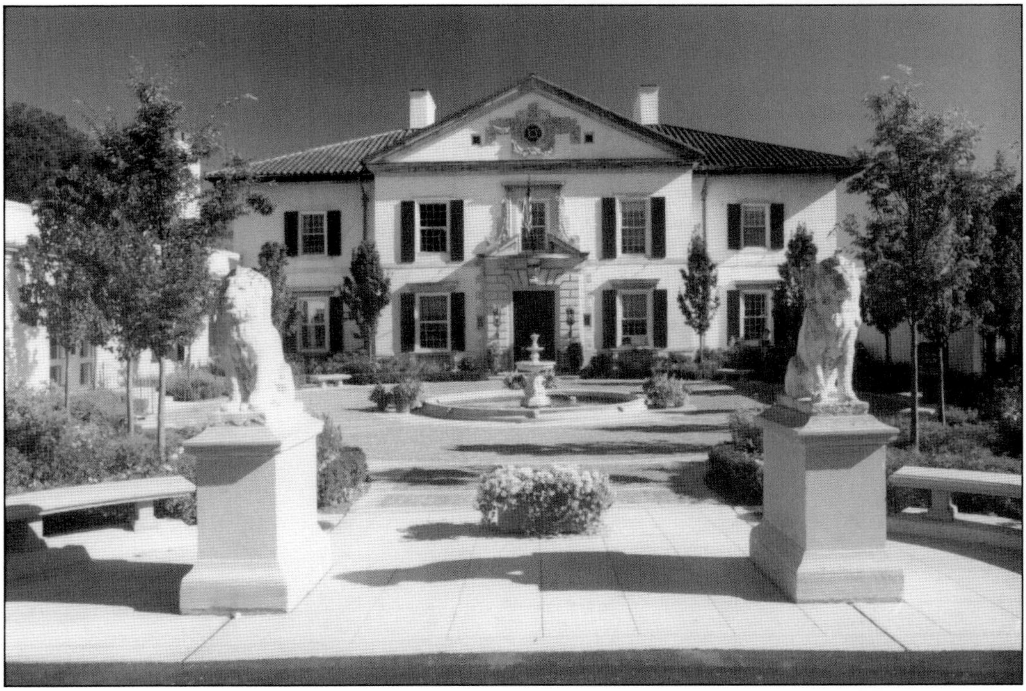

Lions flank the courtyard entrance to the War Memorial. They are replicas of the originals, which were severely damaged by acid rain. The home was placed on the both the Michigan and National Registers of Historic Places.

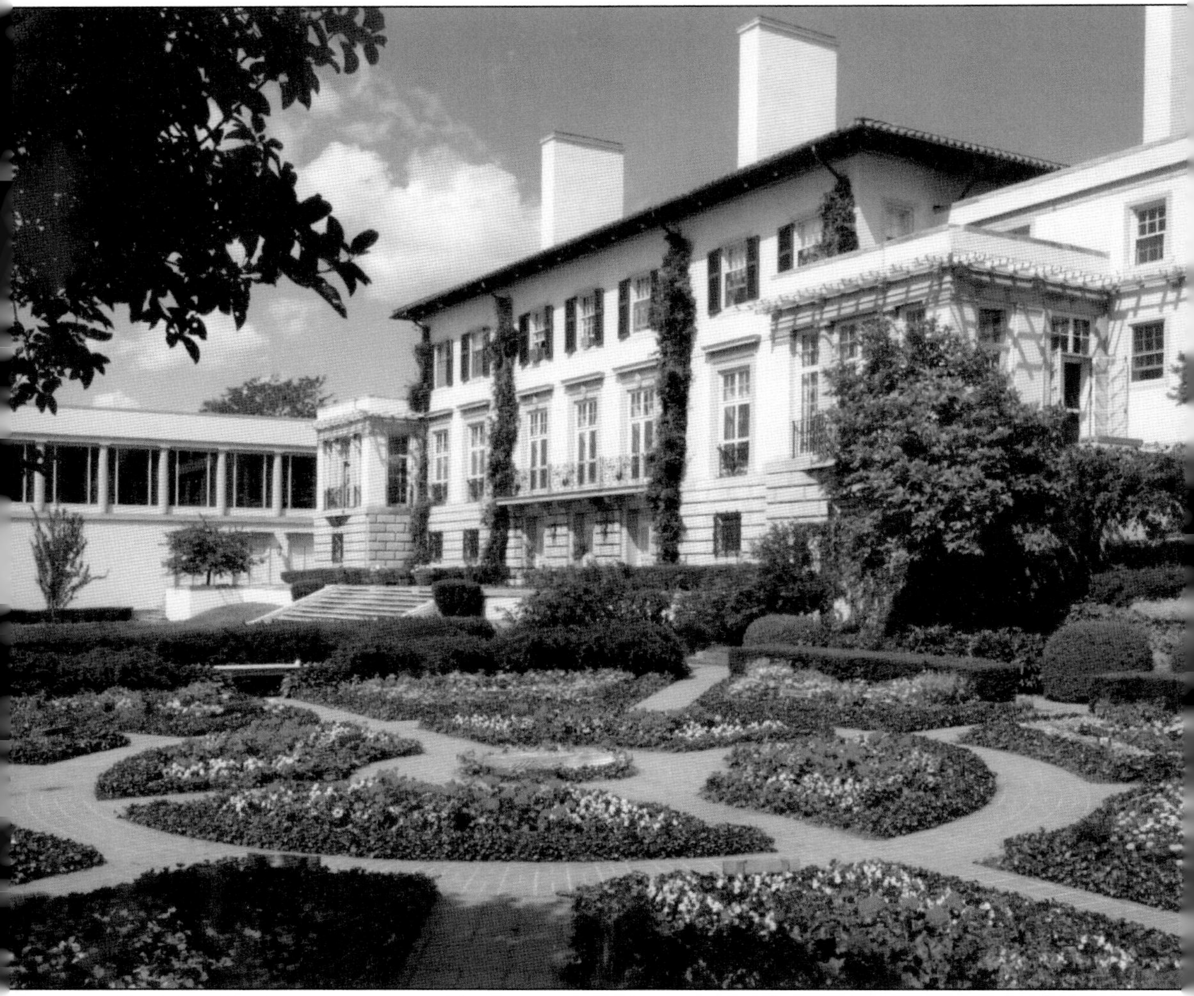

The Trial Garden was so named because it stared out with workers trying to see which different plants and flowers would do well in this climate. It is set in a huge wheel design with an old French millstone at the center, donated by the Lauhoff family. Designed in 1952 by Eleanor Roche, the garden today includes perennials, flowering trees and hedges, and annuals like begonias, dahlias, pansies, sweet peas, verbena and other fragrant and colorful flowers. For a while, Marion Alger's daughter, Josephine, took care of the garden. Today, it is maintained by Grosse Pointe Garden Center members.

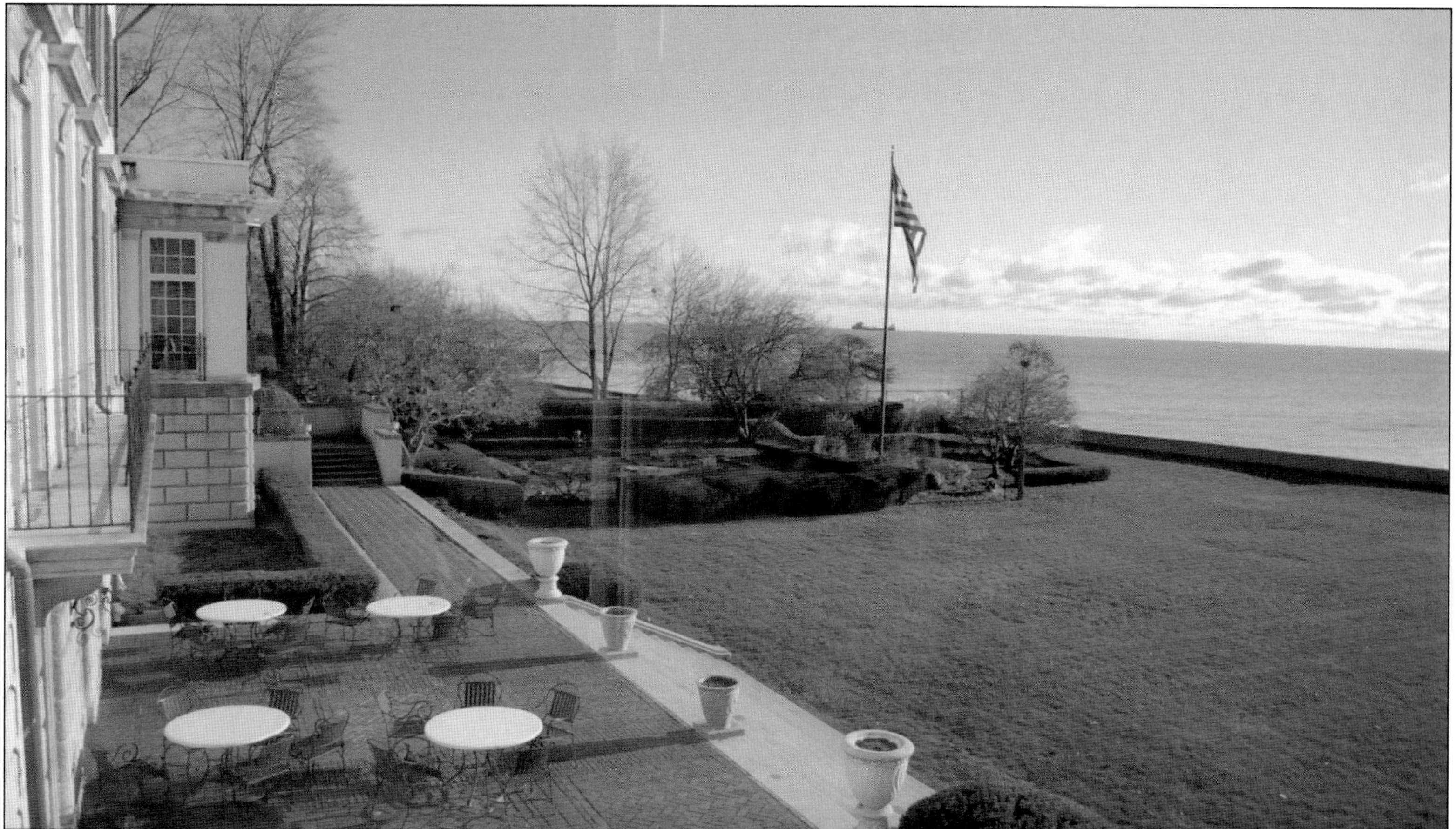

According to the 1913 book *American Country Houses of Today*, which featured the Moorings, "The house is built sufficiently close to the ground to be a part of the natural terrace, to shun the high winds, but enjoy the views. The views are many and very beautiful. Grosse Pointe Lightship is right ahead, looking south when the mists permit; Askins Point of Canada can be seen and the Island of Fishes, when the mirage from the swamp behind is not too thick. Windmill Point is very much in evidence, and at times the well-known Belle Isle."

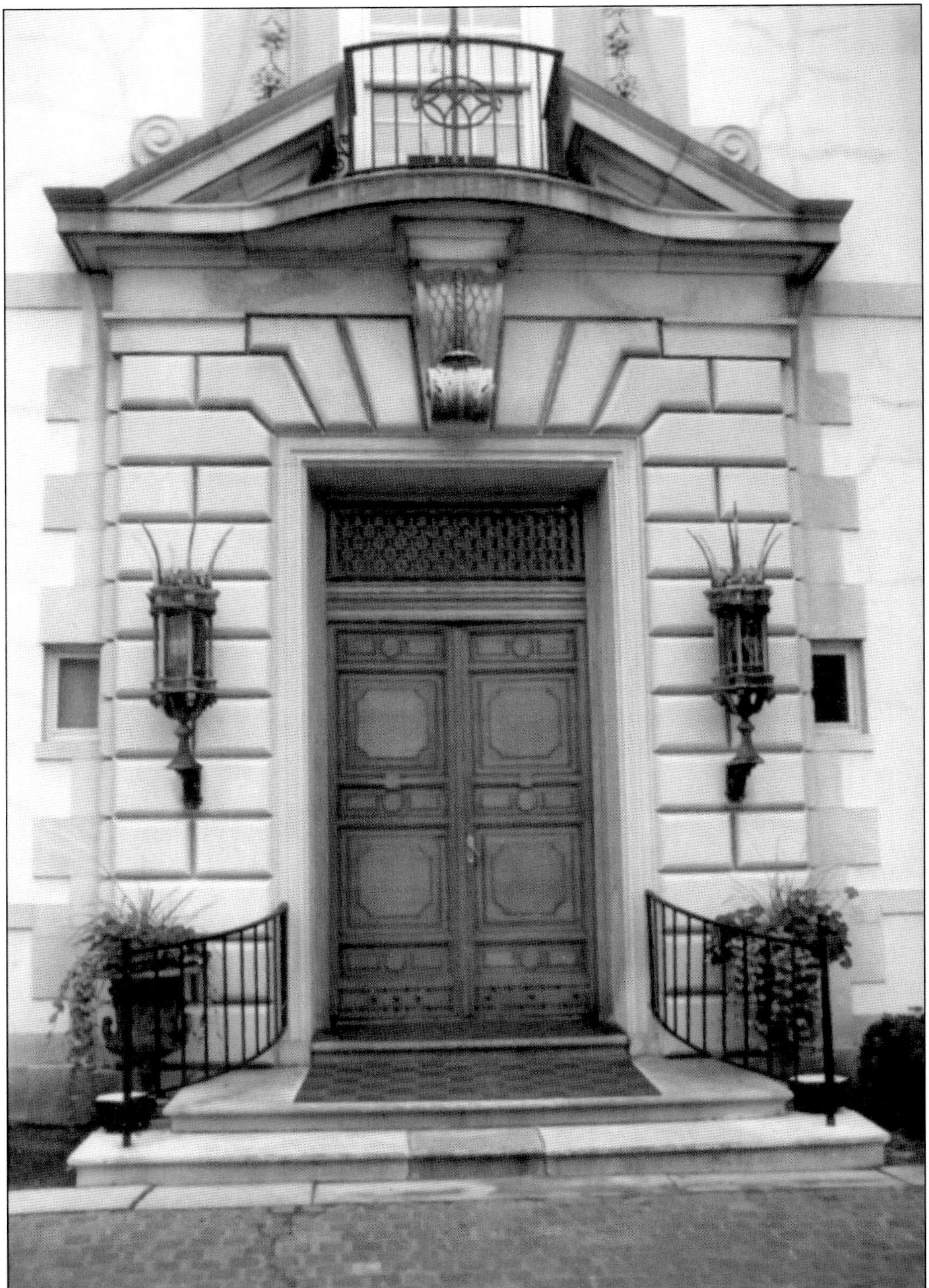

The front door of the Moorings is made of solid wood. Limestone surrounds the iron accents. Architectural critics have praised the vertical lines of the entrance facade of the house as an elegant contrast to the horizontal sweep of the lake facade.

Three

Elegant Eden

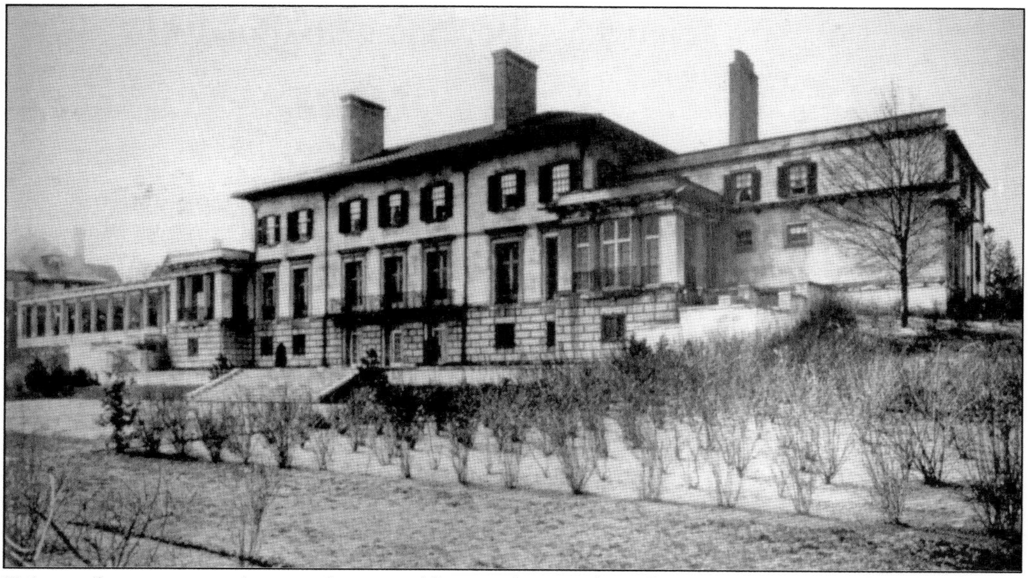

"My mother was an ardent gardener and her gardens spoke of her infinite knowledge of what was right for the right place," Josephine Alger wrote in an open letter to the War Memorial docents. She also said, "The garden became as one with the lifestyle of the house."

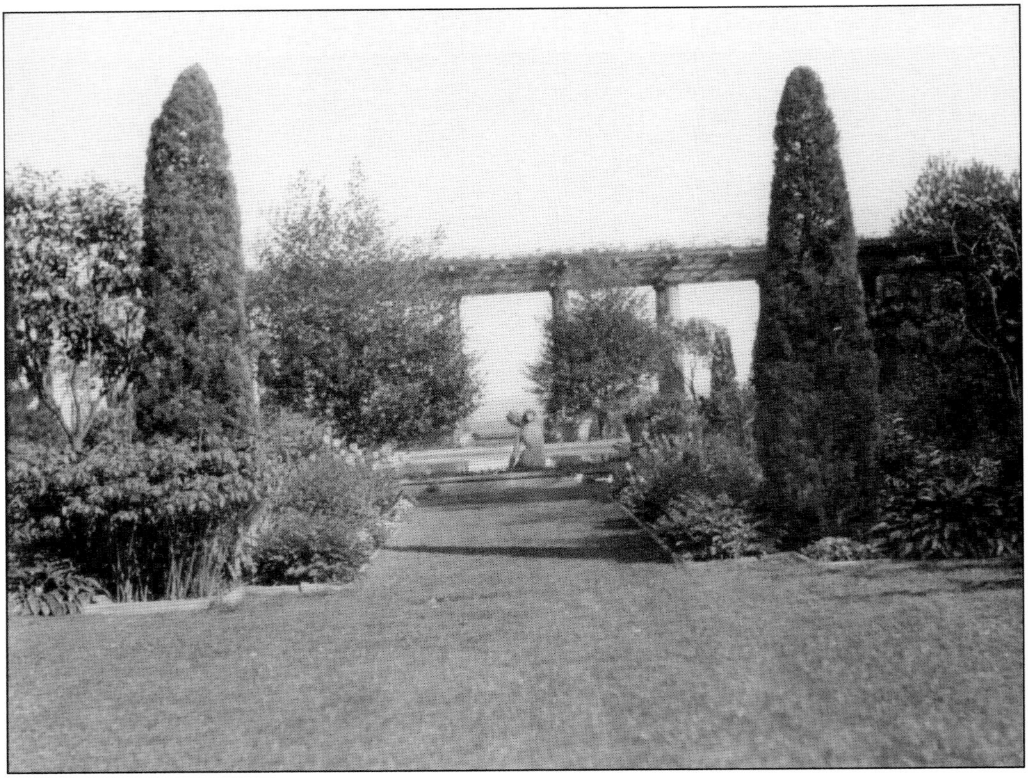

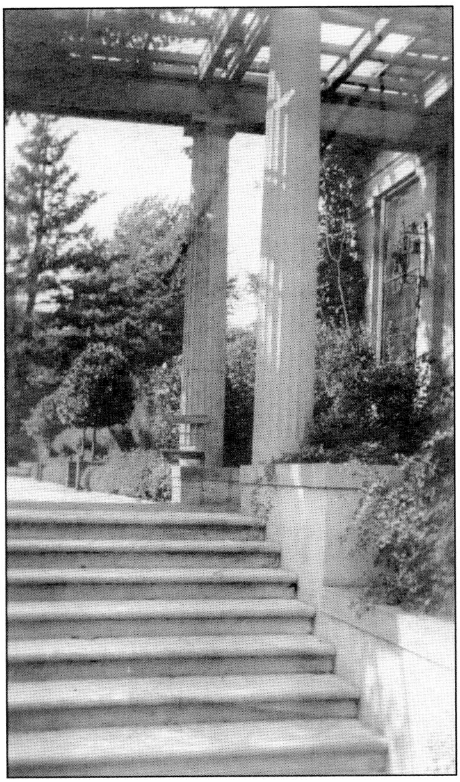

These lovely gardens once extended to Lake Shore Drive and culminated in a wisteria-covered pergola. There was also a stone staircase descending to a lake terrace that overlooked both the water and the spacious backyard.

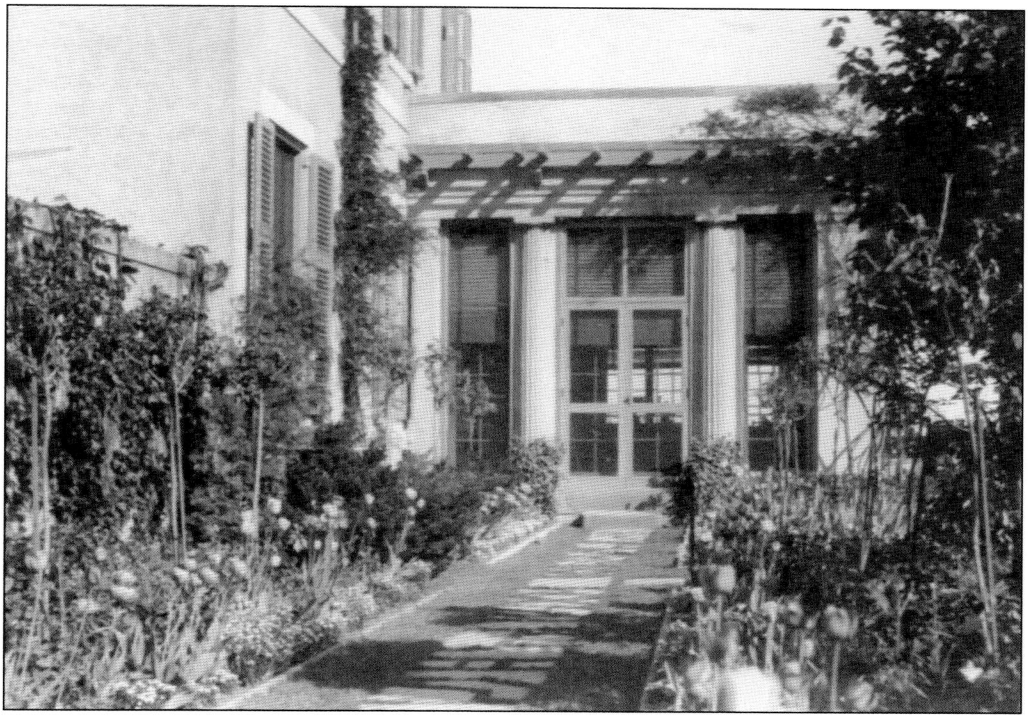

When the Fries Auditorium was added in 1962, the pergola was incorporated into its exterior, thus blending it architecturally with the house. Unfortunately, both the lake terrace and the commanding view of the lake were sacrificed in the process.

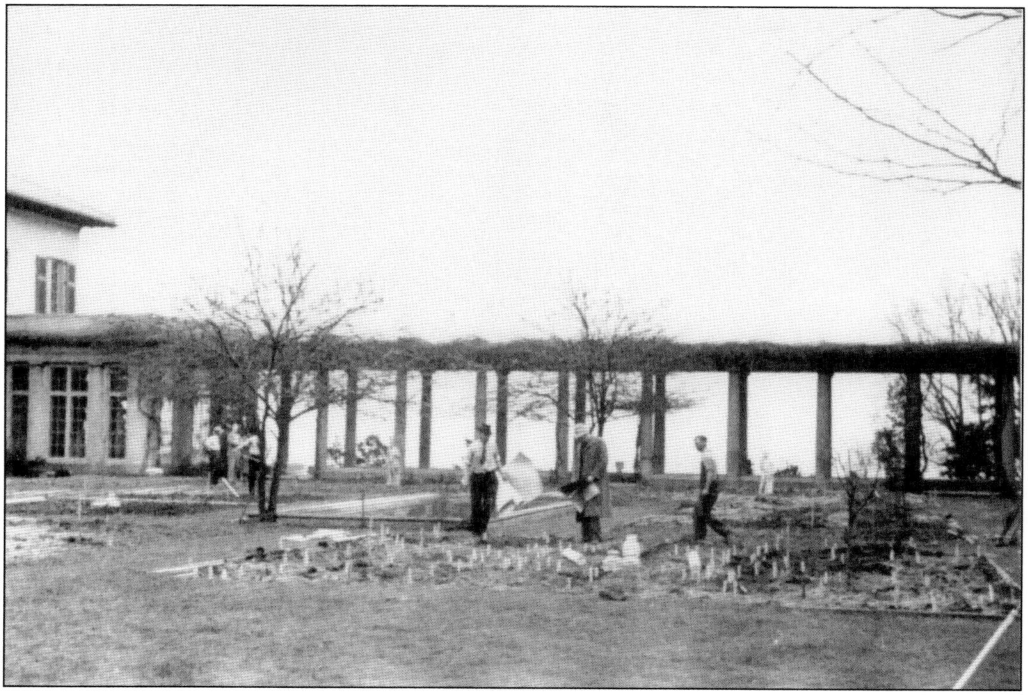

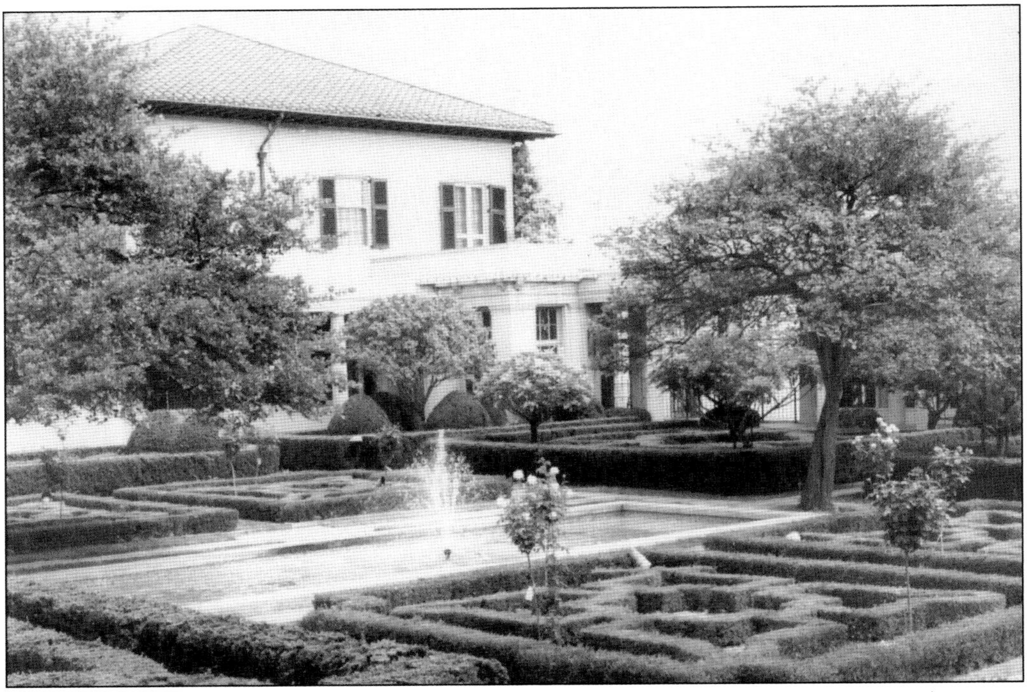

The gardens have been featured in numerous books, magazines, and journals over the years, including the 1924 *Beautiful Gardens in America* by Louise Shelton, the quarterly *Journal of Garden History,* and books about landscape architect Ellen Shipman.

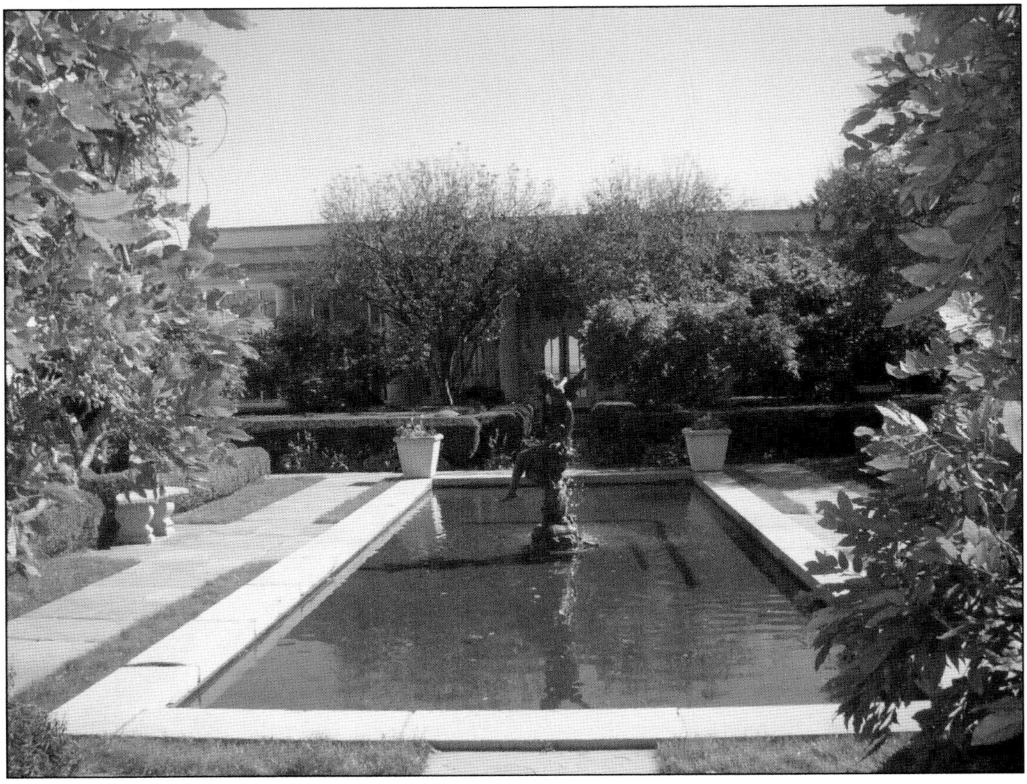

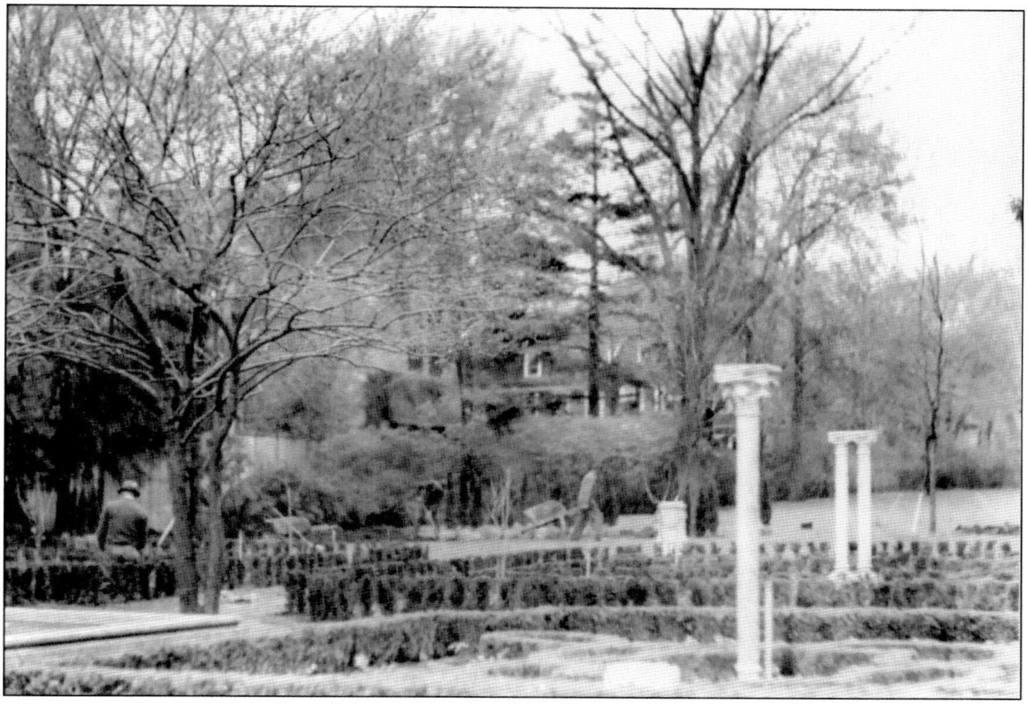

Ellen Shipman was dubbed the "dean of American women landscape architects" in 1938 by *House and Garden* magazine. A prolific artist, she created more than 650 gardens between 1914 and 1946, including 60 in Grosse Pointe. No single community holds more of her public work than Grosse Pointe.

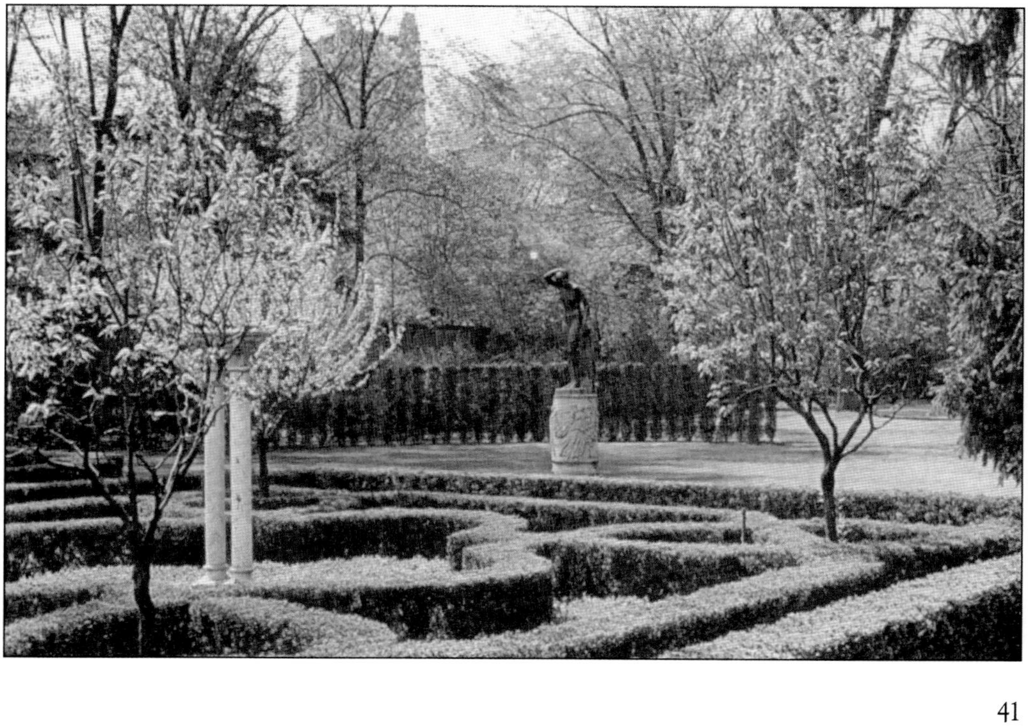

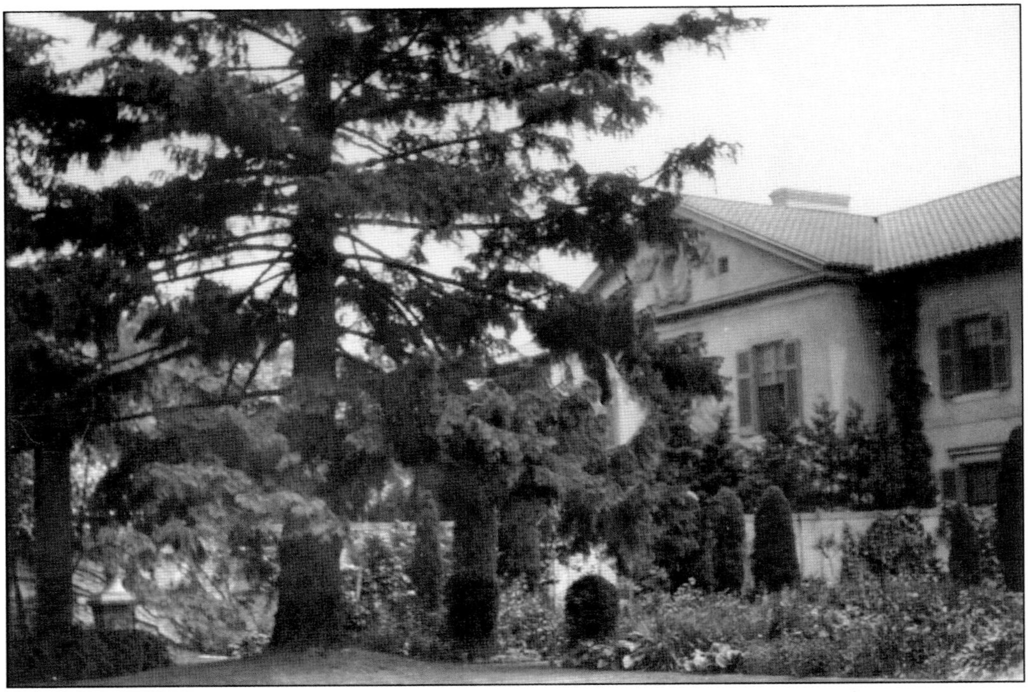

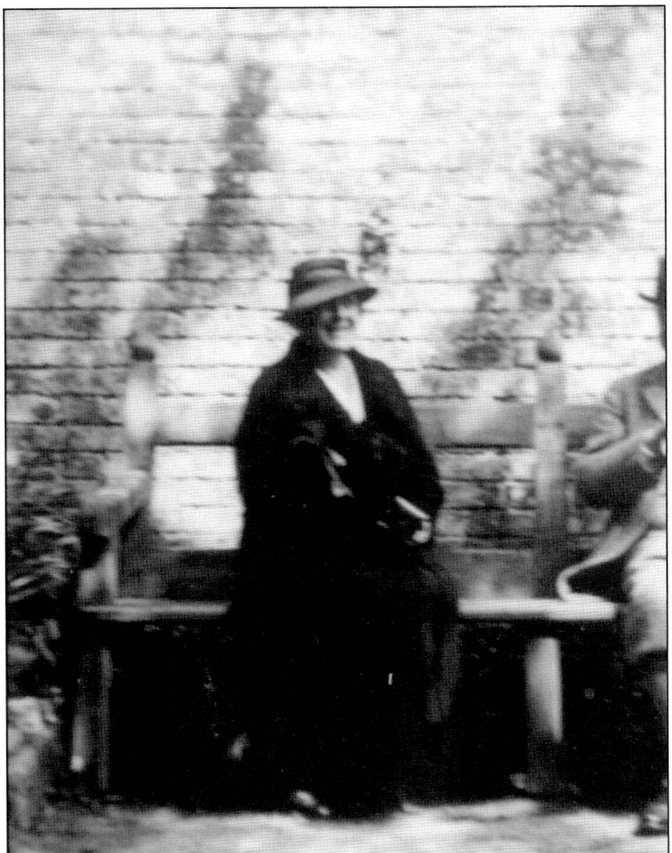

Ellen Biddle Shipman came from a prominent Philadelphia military family. She spent her early childhood on rugged army posts out West. Before entering school, she moved back east with her grandparents. Her grandmother first taught her about gardening.

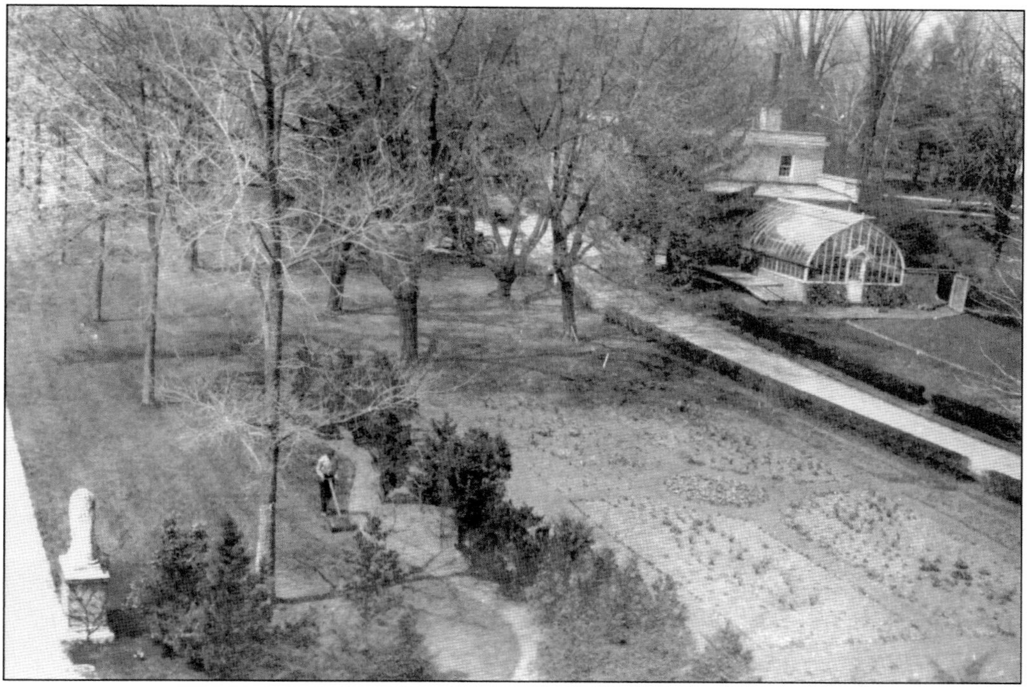

Shipman spent one year at Radcliffe College before marrying Louis Evan Shipman, an aspiring playwright. The couple moved to an artists' colony in Cornish, New Hampshire, a year later in 1893. There she began exploring different styles of garden designs.

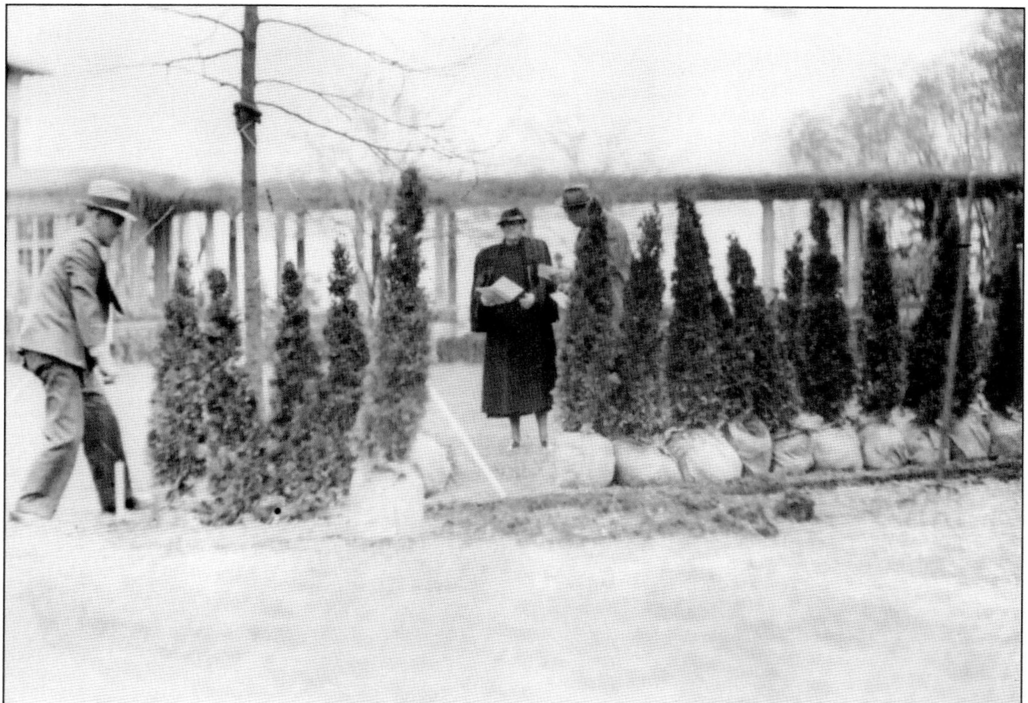

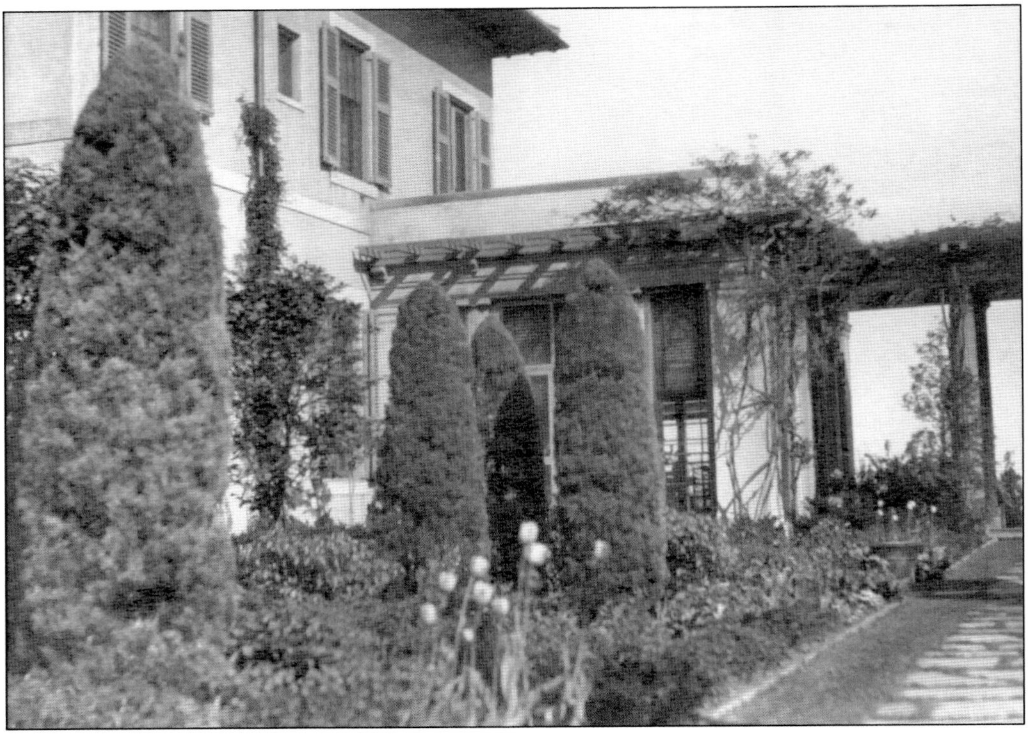

In 1910, Louis Shipman left his wife for another woman and moved to London. Ellen had to raise their three children on her own and began her career as a landscape architect, one of the few design fields open to women at that time.

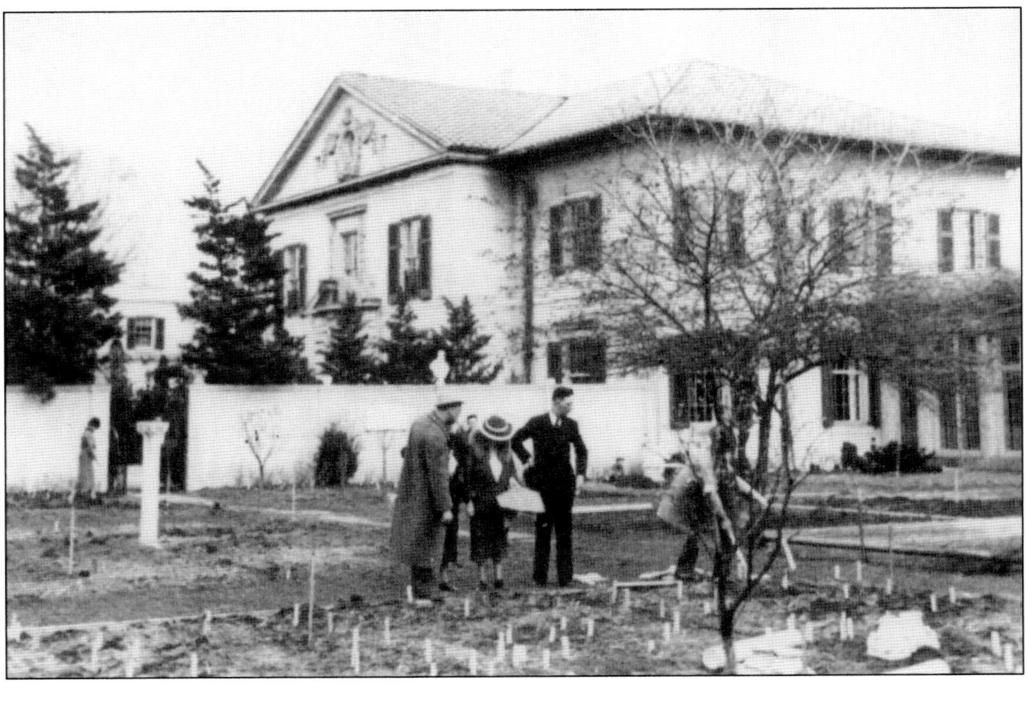

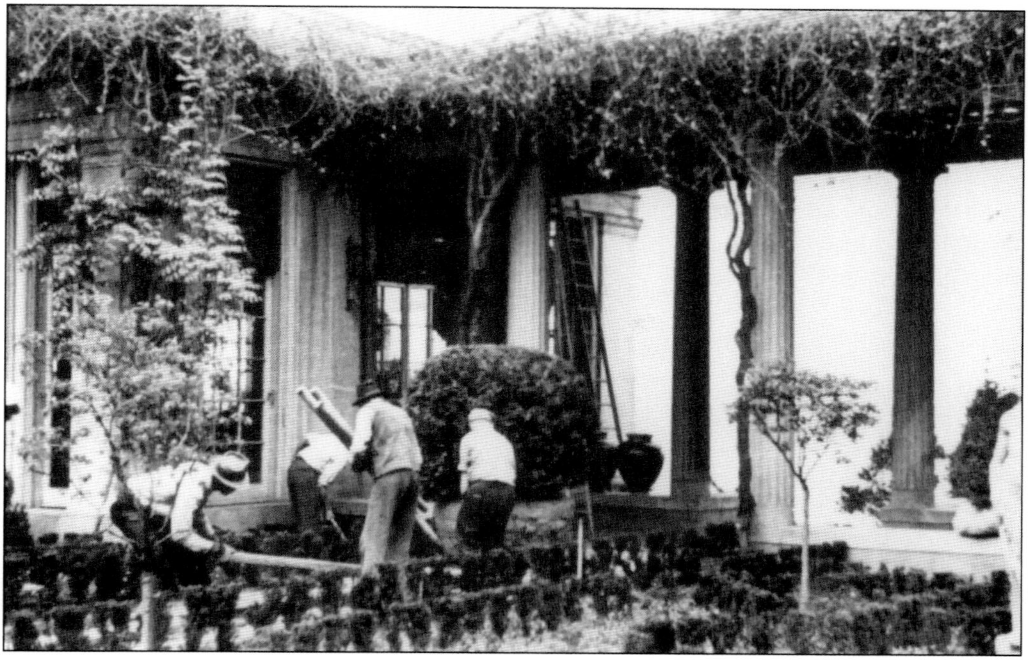

It was in Cornish that Shipman met architect Charles Platt, who would later invite her to design the garden for the Alger house. Platt is credited with creating the modern American garden, which relates directly to the design of the house and is easily accessible from the home.

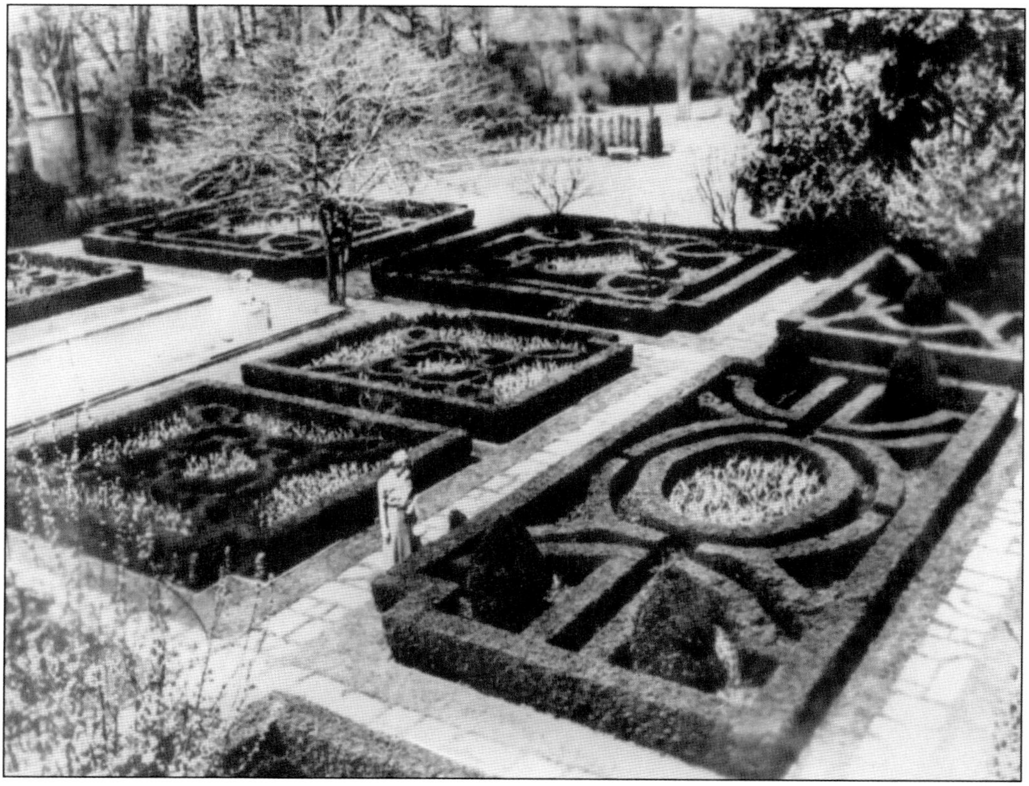

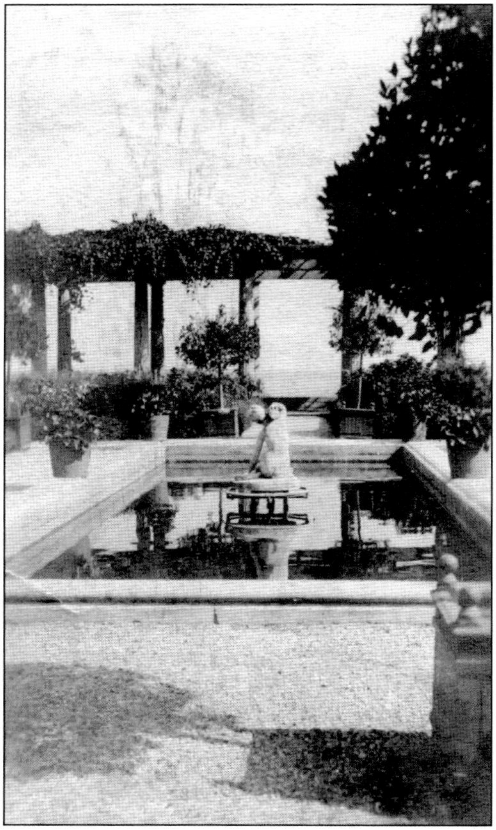

Shipman ran a busy, all-female office in New York City from the 1920s through the 1940s, though business dropped off during the Depression. She and her female colleagues specialized in residential design, probably because female landscape architects were rarely considered for public projects.

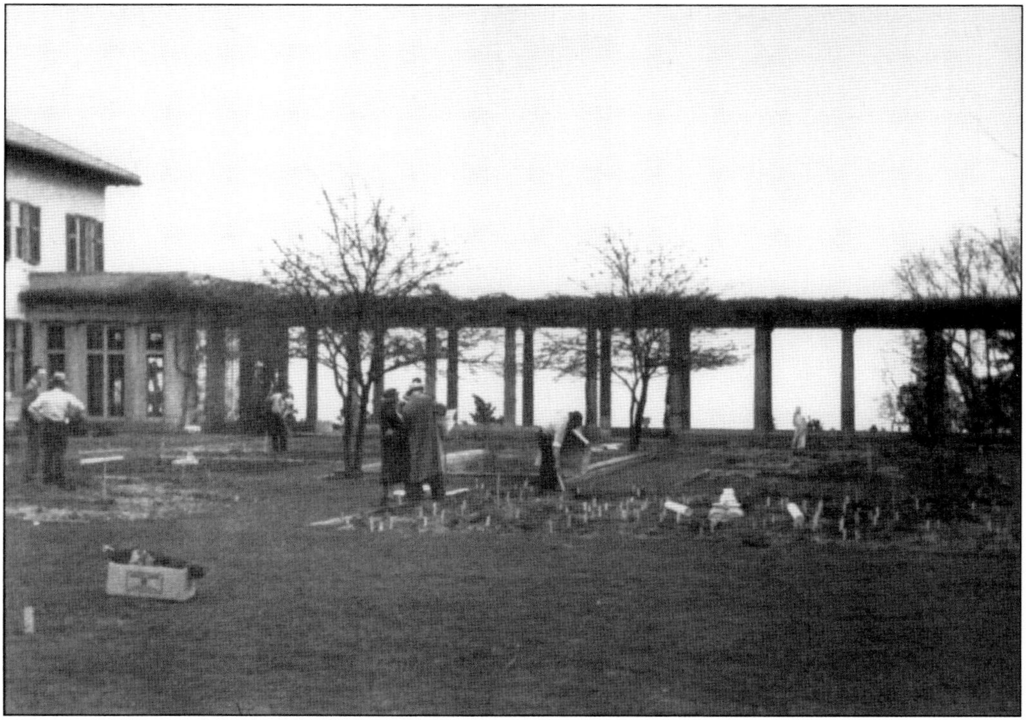

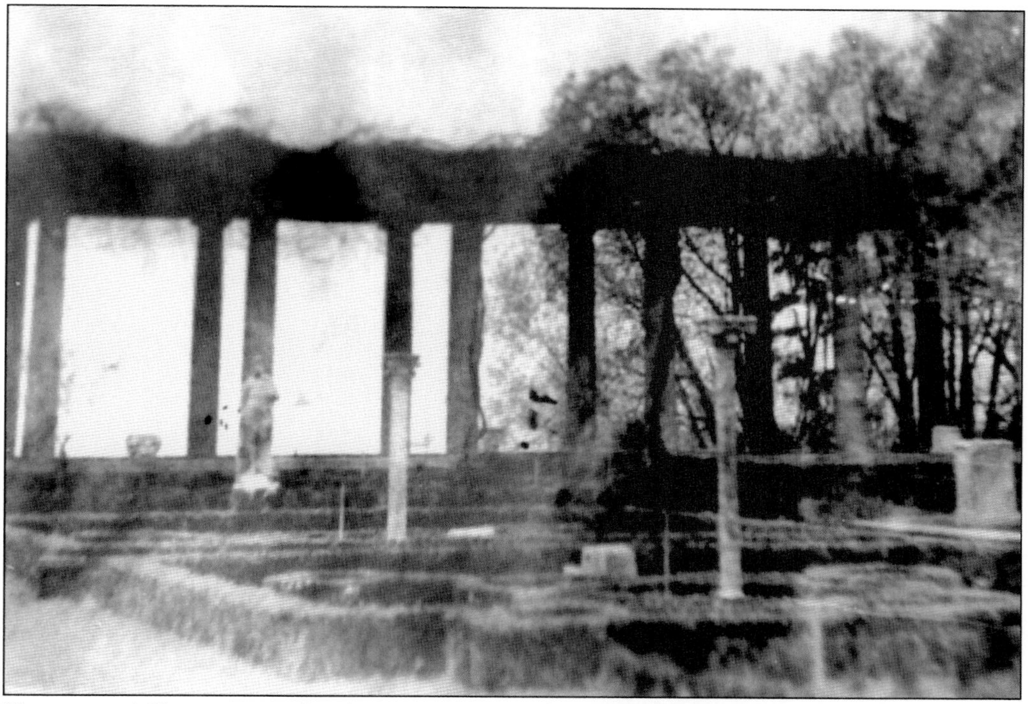

Platt wanted Shipman to refine his planning scheme for the entrance to the court and a small pool garden. He called for a grapevine-covered pergola that drew the eye to a view of Lake St. Clair. She was interested in connecting the garden to the existing landscape by blurring the edge of the designed garden with the surrounding grounds.

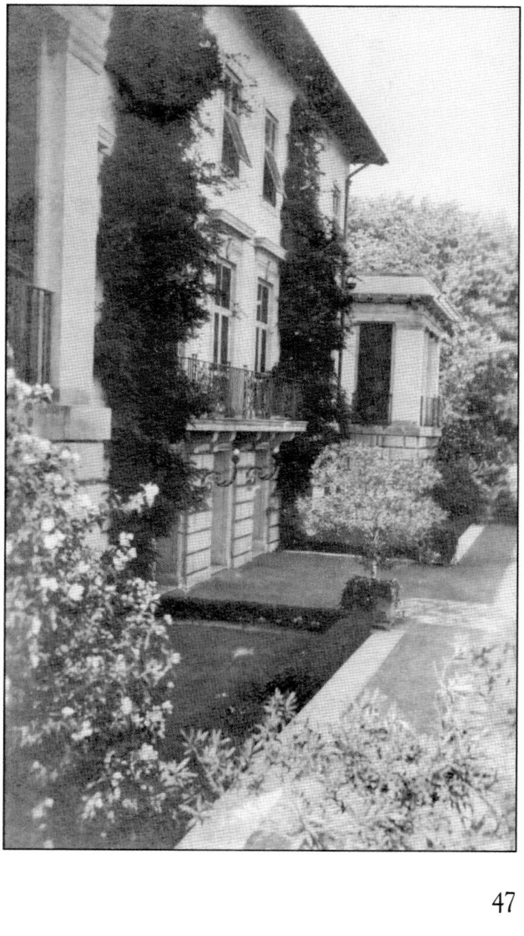

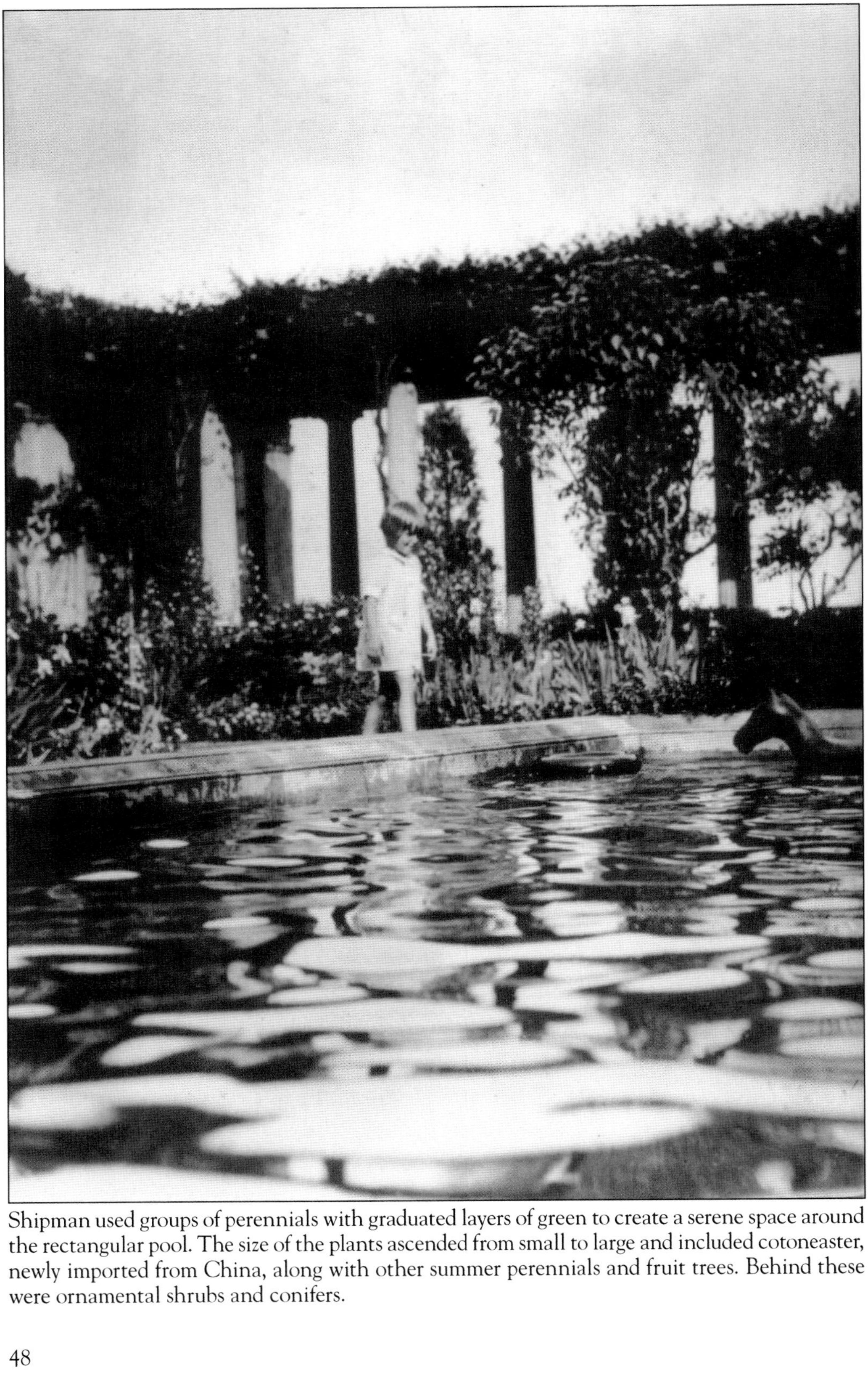

Shipman used groups of perennials with graduated layers of green to create a serene space around the rectangular pool. The size of the plants ascended from small to large and included cotoneaster, newly imported from China, along with other summer perennials and fruit trees. Behind these were ornamental shrubs and conifers.

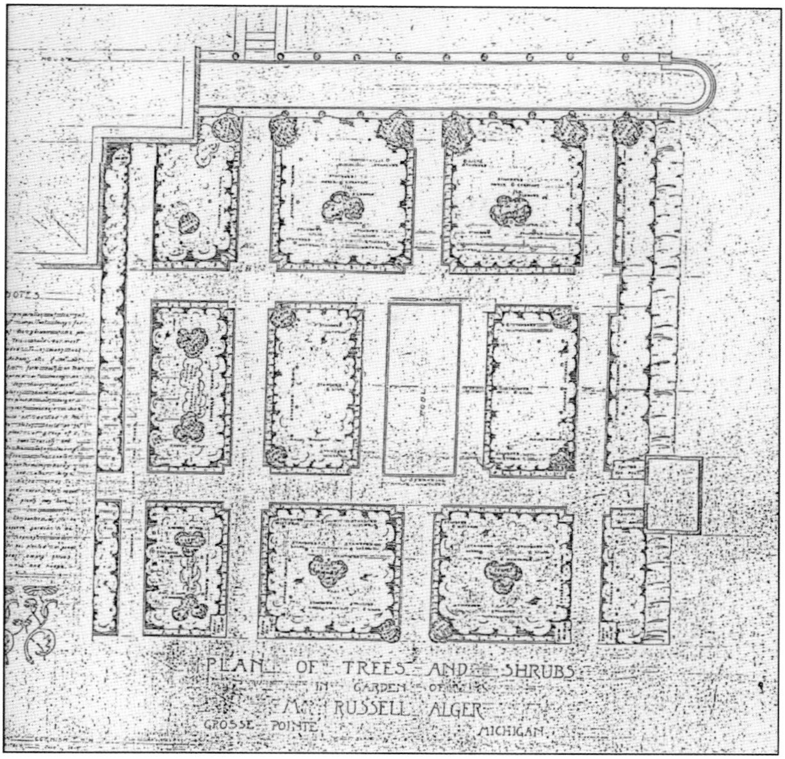

Seen here are Shipman's plans for the garden, which are now housed in the Carl Kroch Library at Cornell University.

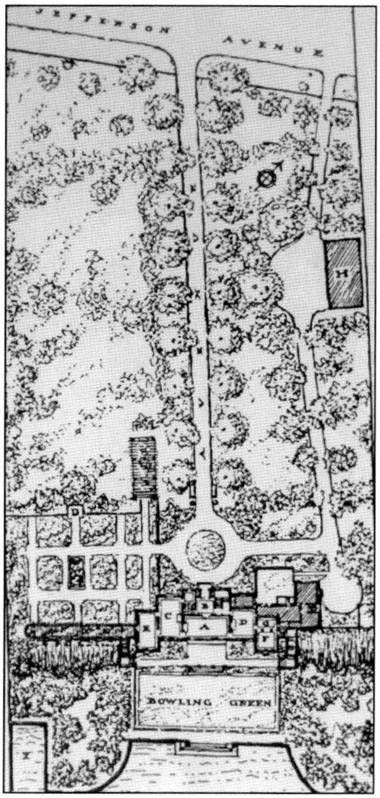

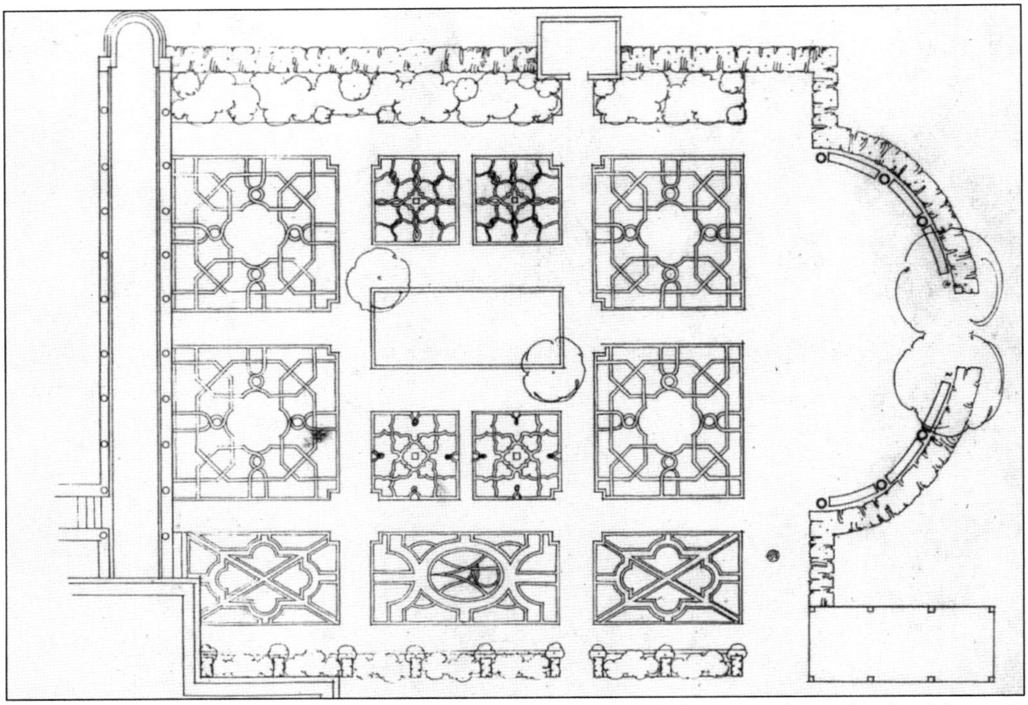

One of Biddle's much loved designs was the knot garden, and she created one for the Algers. A formal layout dating back to 17th-century Europe, the knot garden was often patterned after a rug or tapestry, hence the name. They typically had a square frame containing square compartments with intricate geometric patterns. The gardens traditionally have boxwood borders, fine gravel paths, and include aromatic plants and herbs like lavender, rosemary, lemon balm, and sage.

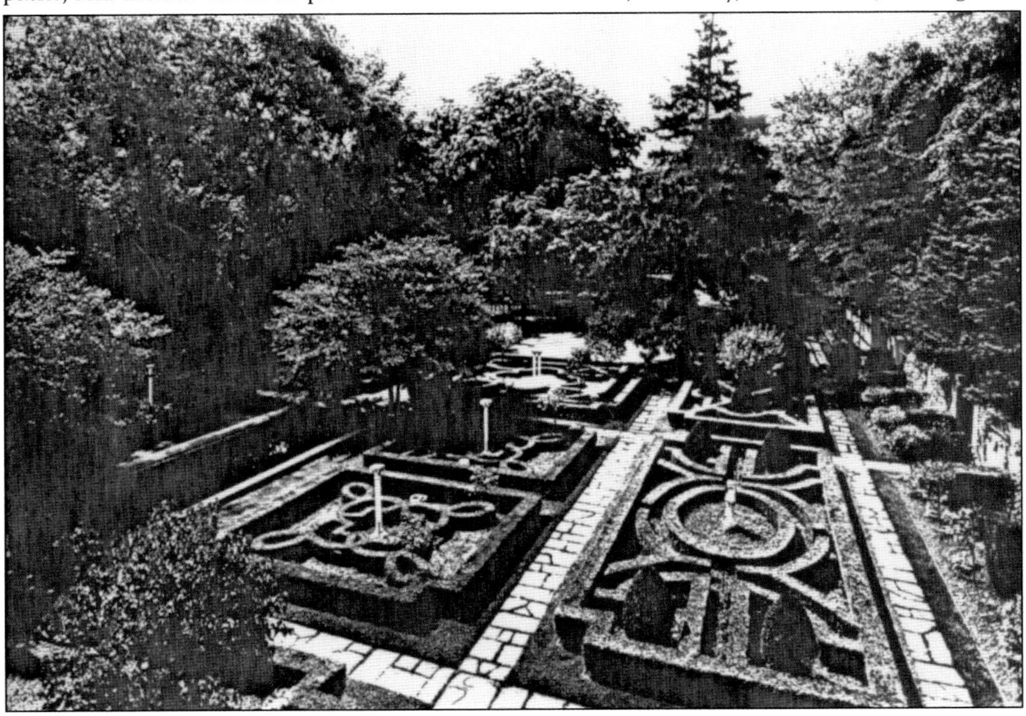

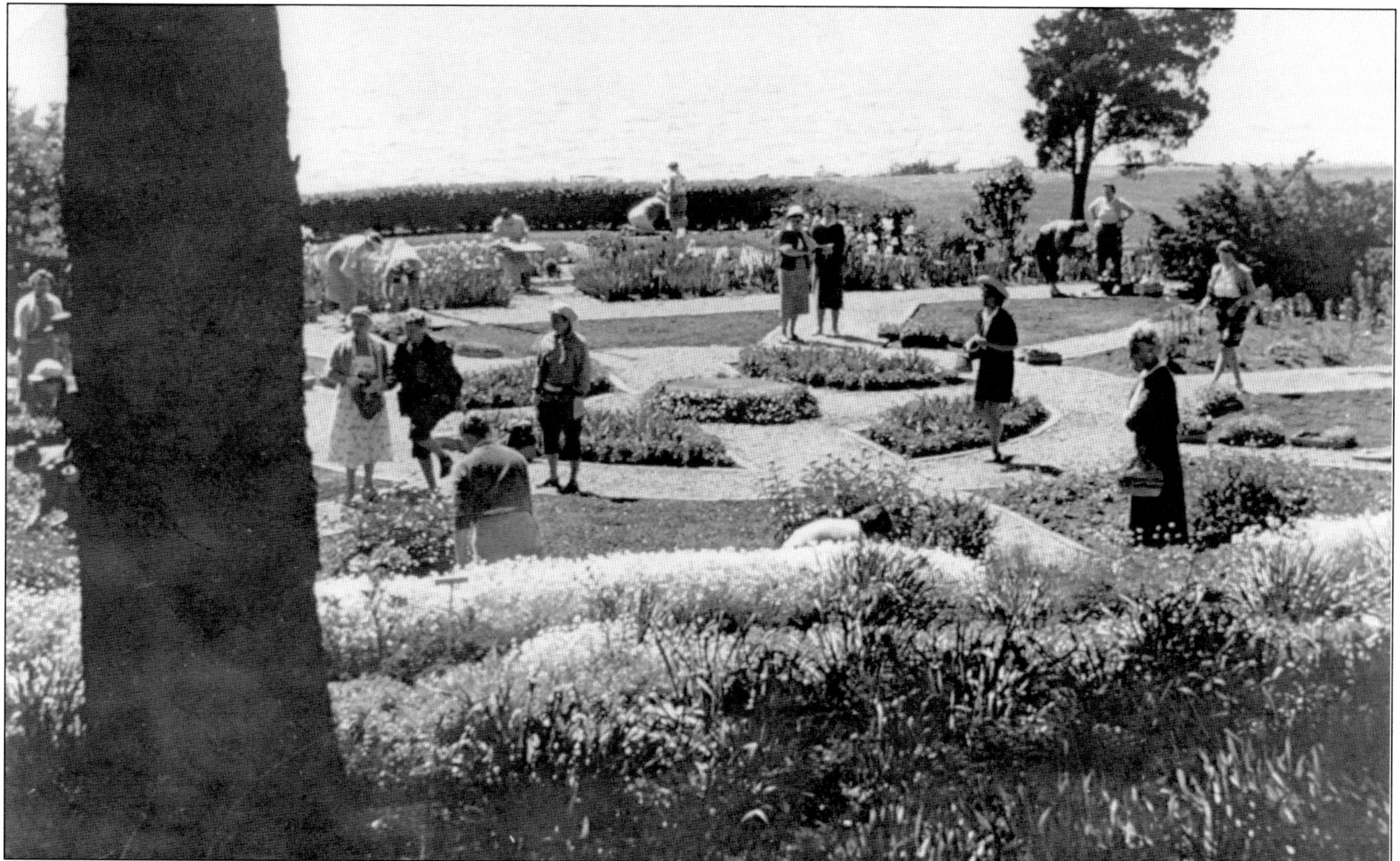

The Grosse Pointe Garden Center used Marion's sitting room and bedroom as an office for a time. The group, representing some 12 or 13 garden clubs in the area, was also given an area for a garden. They created the Trial Garden, so named because they were trying out different species.

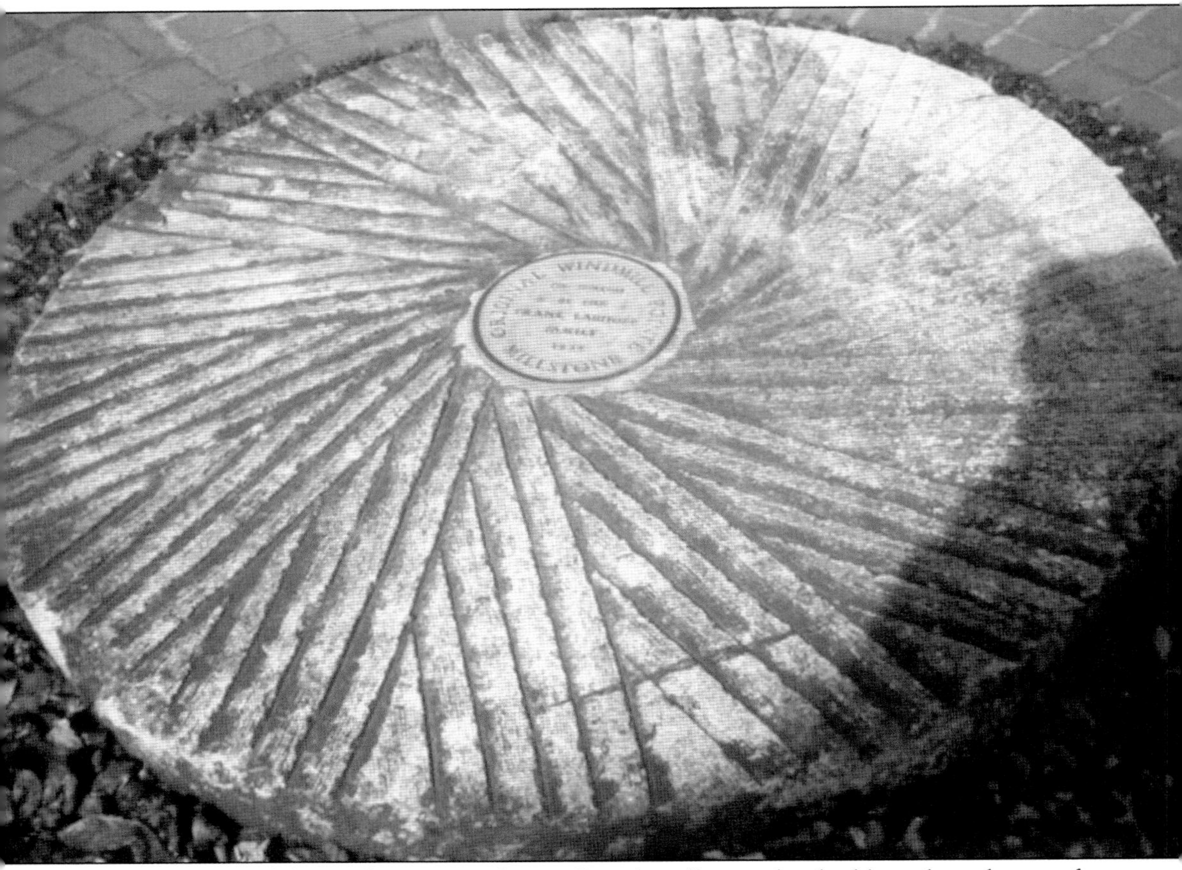

In the center of the garden is an authentic French millstone that had been brought over from France by settlers hundreds of years ago.

Four

THE FINE ART OF LIVING

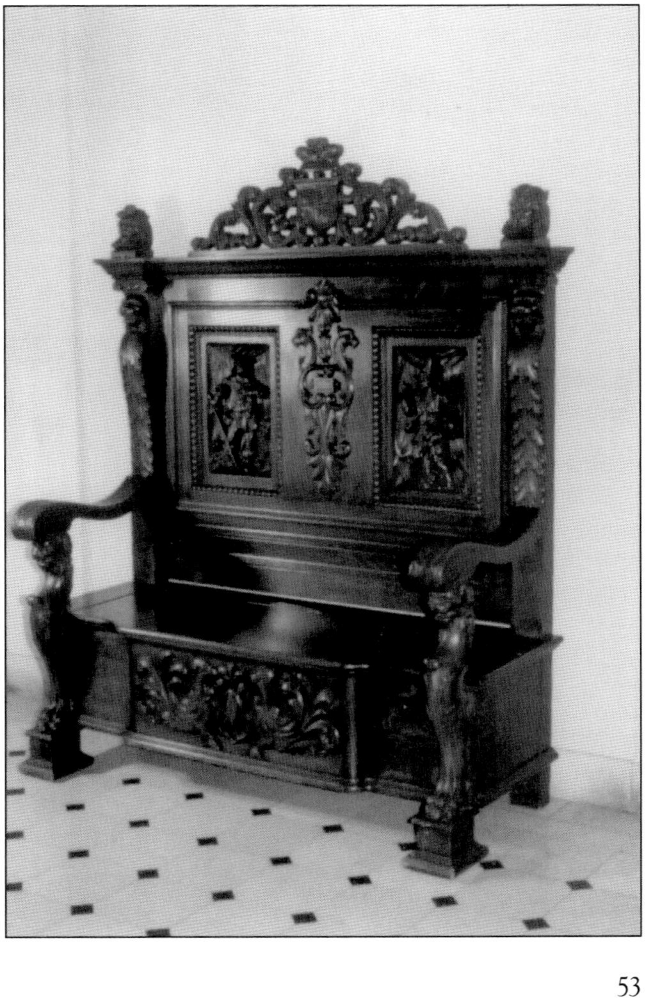

When Marion Alger moved out of the Moorings after her husband died, she took a lot of the furniture with her. Most of the pieces in the house now were purchased later, under the direction of Robert Hudson Tannahill. This Victorian oak settee, which sits in the entry hall, is a prime example. It dates from 1870 and depicts Renaissance-style Italian soldiers.

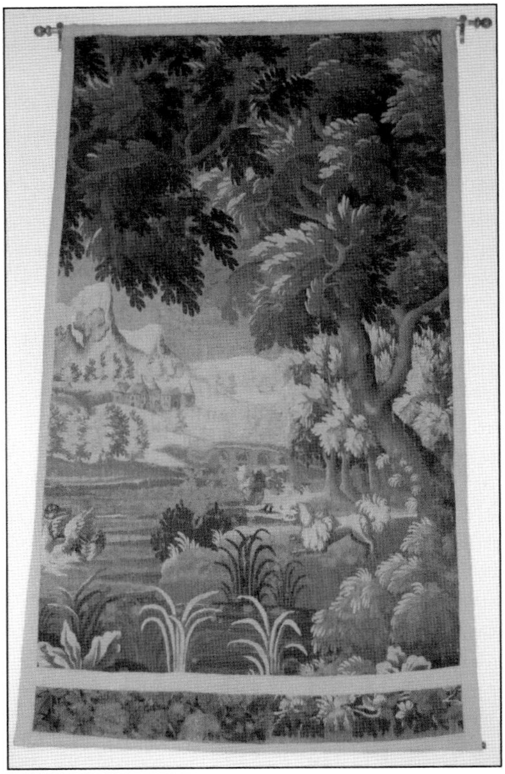

Tannahill bequeathed money to create an art wing for the Grosse Pointe War Memorial, which was established in 1978. One of the first projects that took place there was an extensive tapestry restoration. The first piece to be refurbished was *The Dog and the Pond.* The face of the dog had been entirely obliterated. The work is framed by a light tabby (narrow strip) woven by Lois Robertson on looms at the War Memorial.

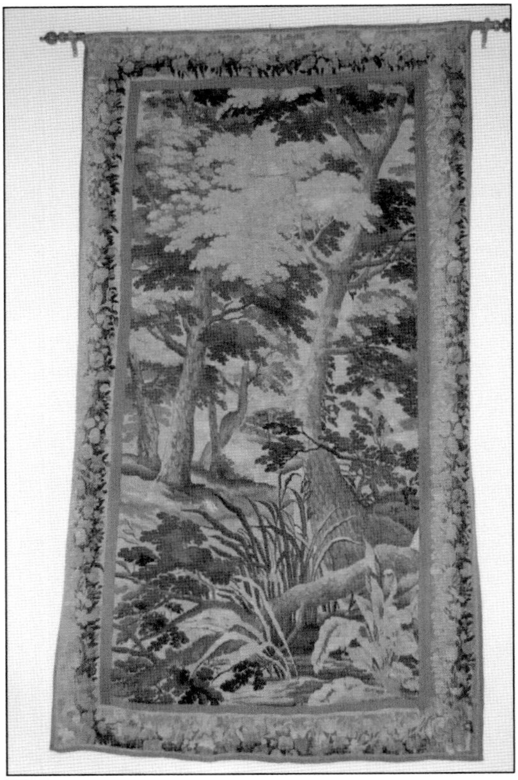

This 17th-century Flemish tapestry hangs in the reception room. It is especially notable because it is marked with the initials or name of the artist. Because it was so fragile, the restorers started their repair work at the bottom while it was hanging.

This 17th-century Flemish piece, which also has the artist's name on it, hung in the reception room but is now in the library. It was diligently restored by the Tapestry Guild, who had a tapestry expert from the Art Institute of Chicago come in and give a workshop. The projects were funded in part by local Questers.

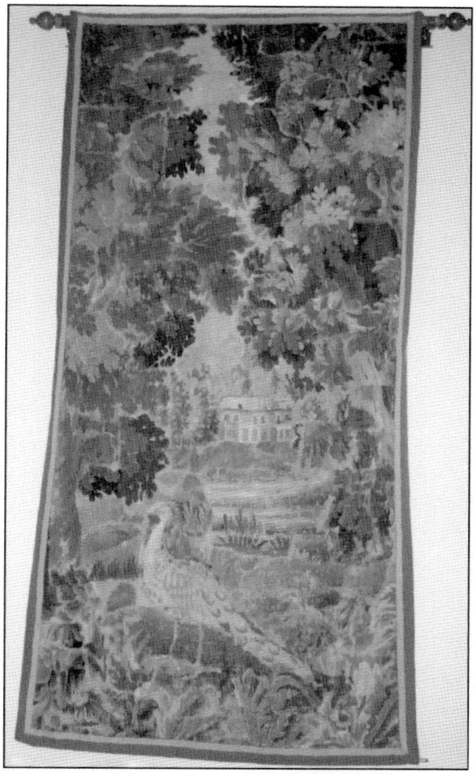

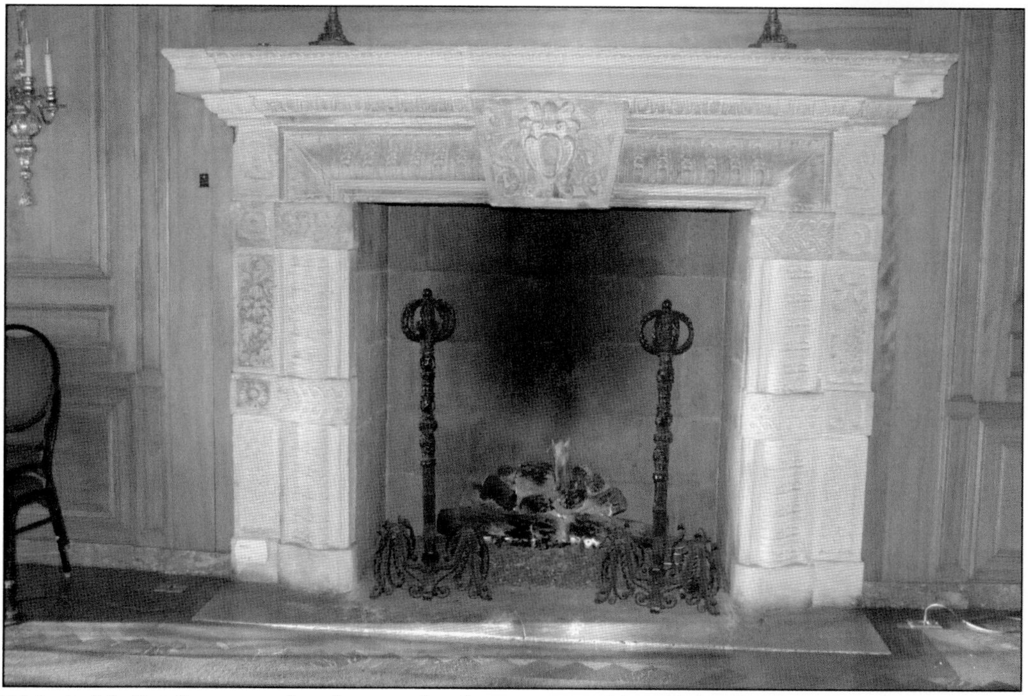

This de Medici limestone fireplace in the dining room, like all the fireplaces on the first floor, was imported from Italy. Marion Alger so loved the one in the library that she took it with her to her new home. The rest, including this one, which dates from 1650, are original.

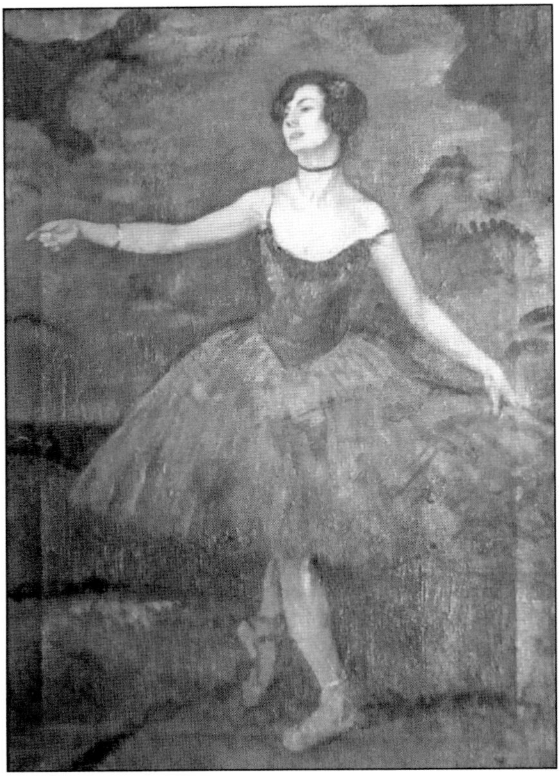

Two oil paintings of ballerinas by American artist Louis Kronberg hang in the house. Kronberg was often referred to as the "American Degas." He was born in Boston in 1872 and studied at the School of the Museum of Fine Arts, Boston. He was fascinated with the theater and especially with dancers on the stage. These paintings are especially beloved by the hundreds of young dancers who have studied ballet at the War Memorial since the program began in the 1950s, headed by the inspiring Mary Ellen Cooper.

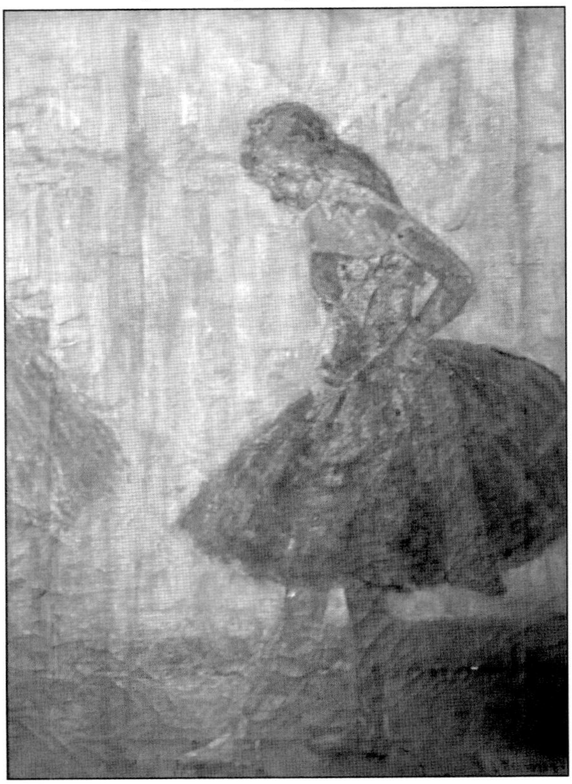

This console table and mirror sit in the dining room between two tall windows that overlook the lake. The mirror is 14th century blown glass from Venice.

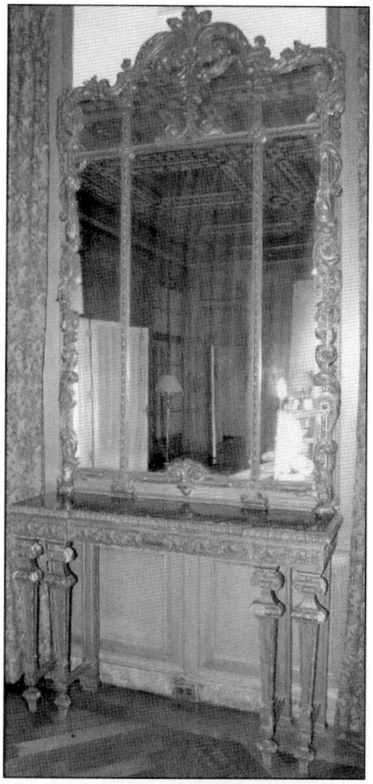

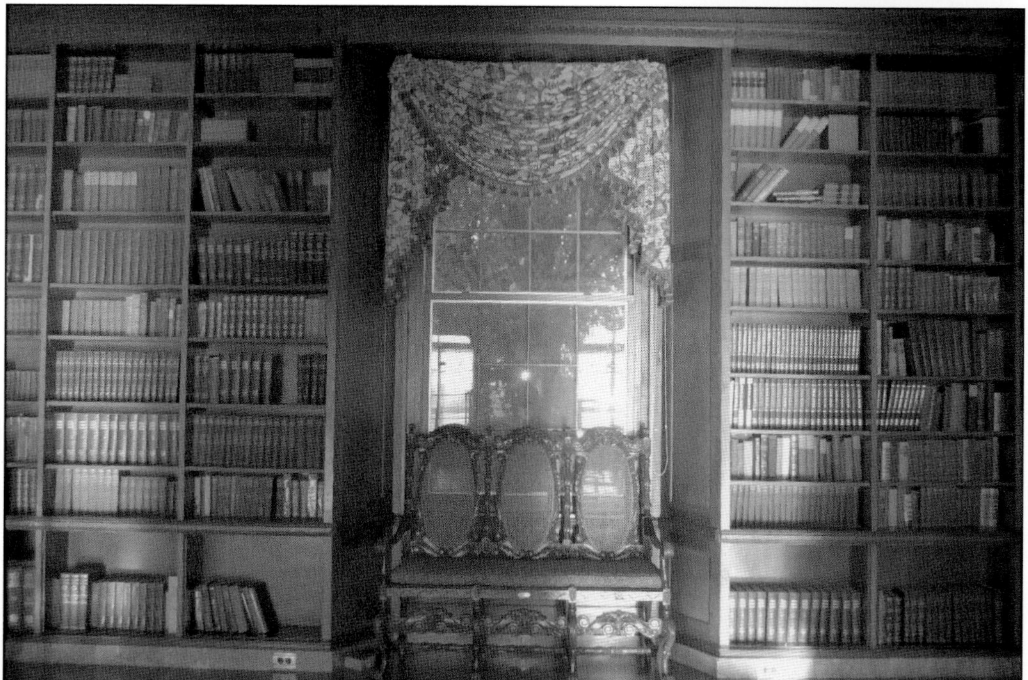

Bookcases in the library flank a window looking out over the entrance courtyard. They were covered up during the Detroit Institute of Arts years and uncovered by accident. The chair—a Tudor-style, open arm, three-back settee—was a gift of Paul and Linda Marino in memory of Ralph E. Marino, a World War II veteran.

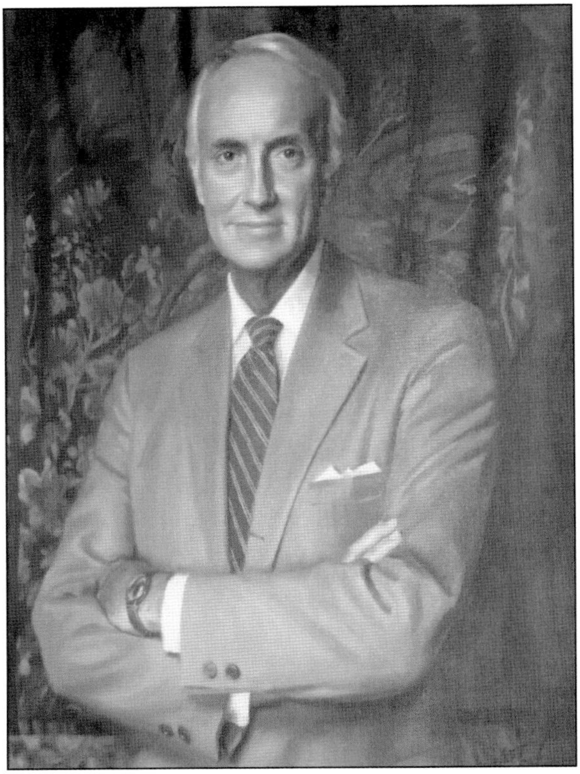

A portrait of John Lake hangs in the library. Lake was the beloved first director of the War Memorial. A native of St. Louis, he came to Grosse Pointe in 1947 to teach history at Grosse Pointe High School. Five years later, he was asked to be the first director of the War Memorial by Alger Shelden, a nephew of Russell Alger Jr. who was president of the board. For 30 years, Lake led the center through tremendous growth and expansion. He died in 1984.

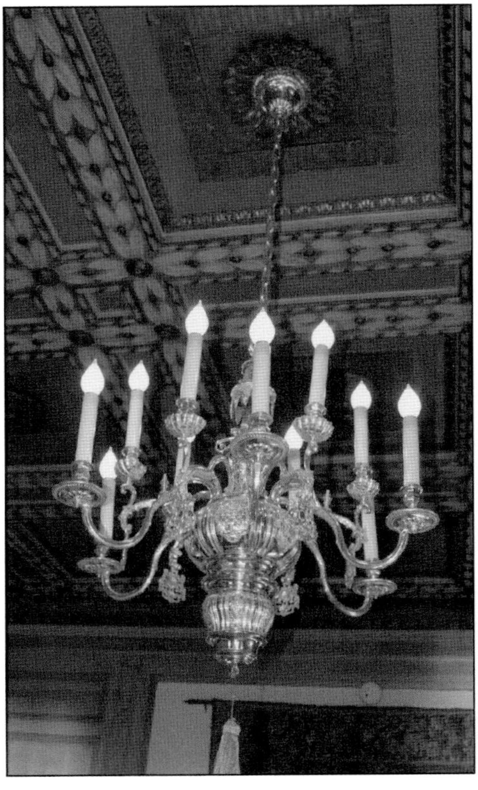

The Reed and Barton silver chandelier hanging in the dining room is original to the home, as are many of the lighting fixtures. The room also includes Reed and Barton silver candelabra and wall sconces.

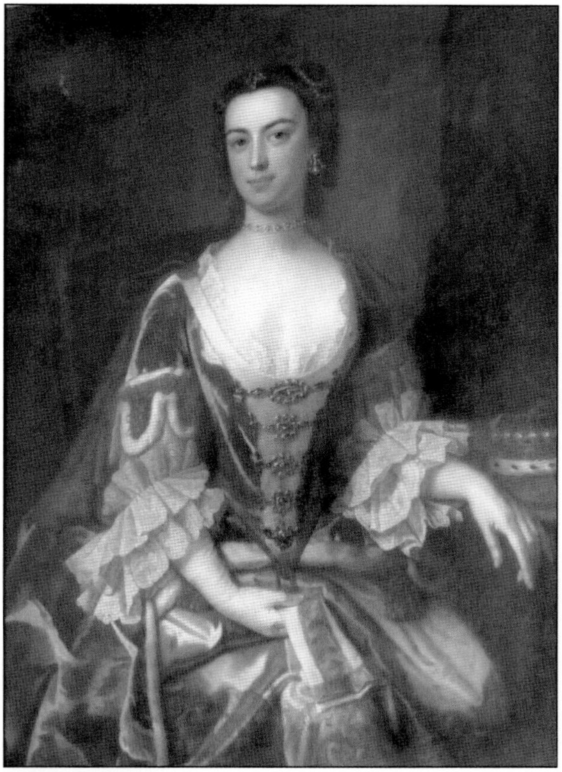

These portraits of Robert Walpole, prime minister of England from 1721 to 1742, and his wife, Lady Catherine, hang next to one another in the library. They were restored in 1981.

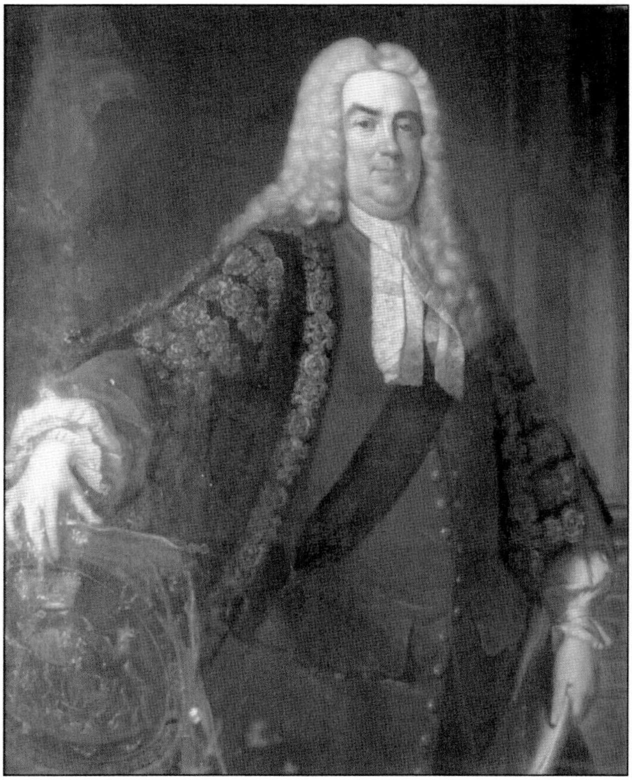

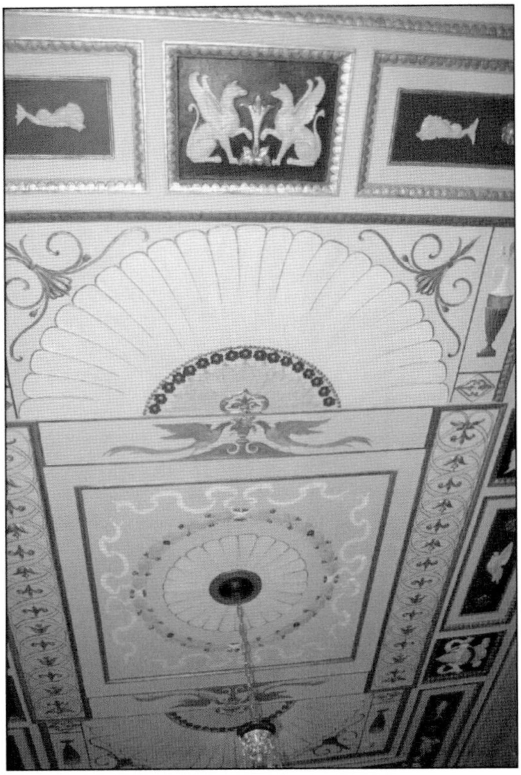

The ornamental ceiling in the entrance hall is molded plaster. When the Detroit Institute of Arts had its branch here, its administrators had the ceiling painted over. In the 1980s, the ceiling was restored to its original design by artist Joan L. W. Hendrix, using an illustration from the architect's drawings. Hendrix spent the summer on her back on a scaffold, Michaelangelo-style, to finish the project.

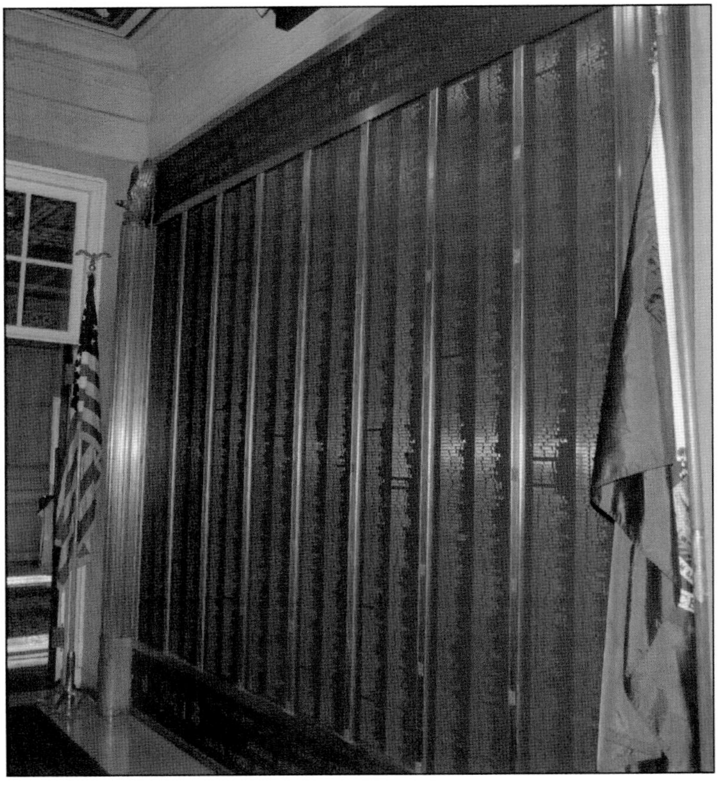

A bronze plaque off the entrance hall lists the names of all Grosse Pointers who served and died in World War II. It was installed in the late 1940s.

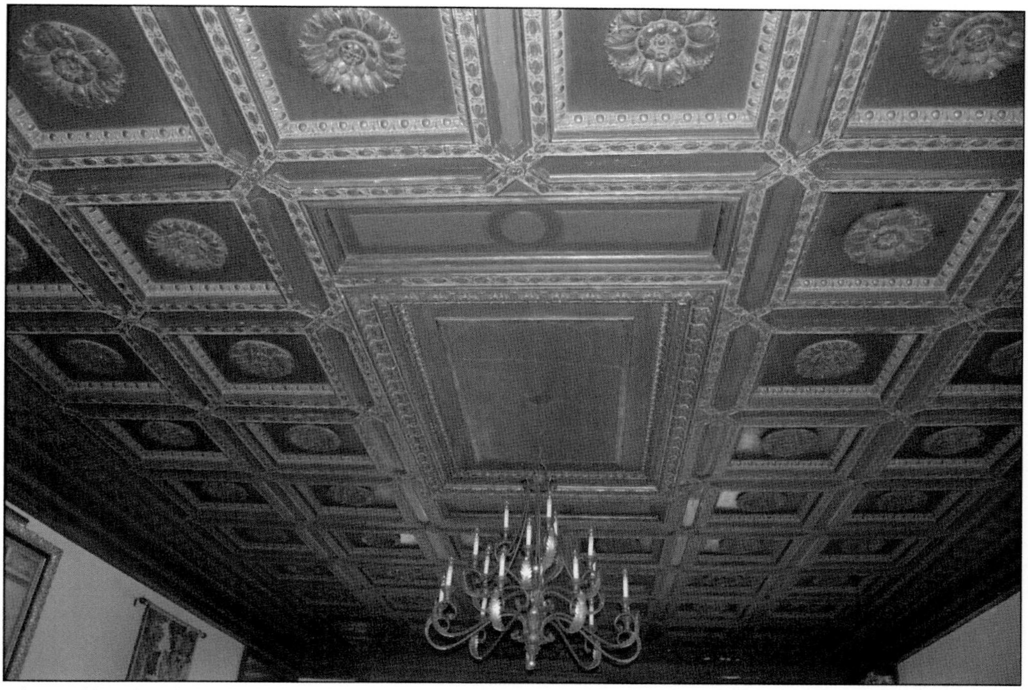

The coffered ceiling of the library looks like wood but is actually molded plaster with a repeating Tudor rose pattern. It was entirely handmade using the intaglio process.

This piece, called *Four Workers in the Country* is believed to have been woven in Oudenard or Brussels in the 16th century. It is probably the oldest tapestry in the War Memorial and the most colorful of the tapestries that was restored. Its restoration took five years to complete. The subject is probably one of the labors of the months and was used as calendars are used in modern times. It now hangs in the dining room.

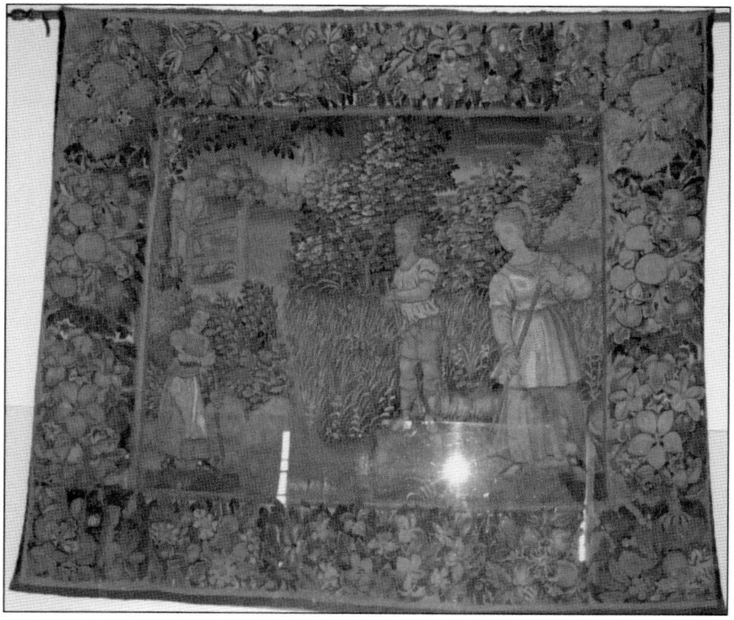

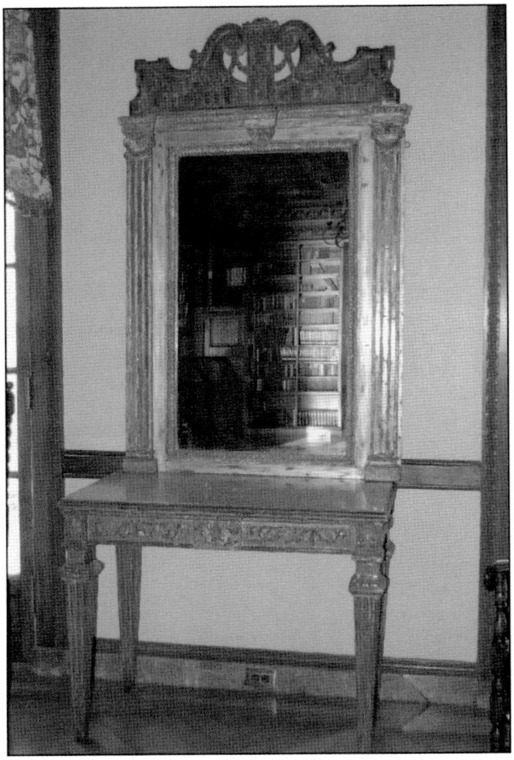

This French-imported gilded console and mirror set is original to the home. It first stood in the front hall, and is in the library today.

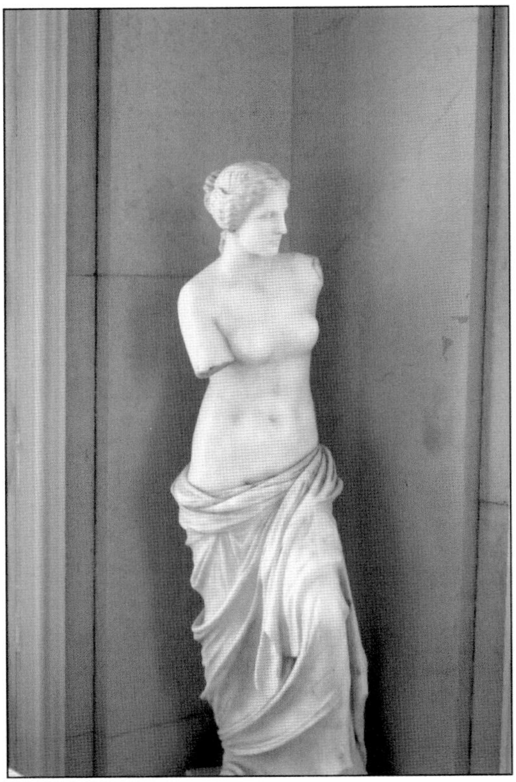

A marble replica of the Venus de Milo stands today in the Palm Room. Though this statue is not original to the home, the Palm Room did have a number of statues to add to its charm.

A jadeite vase/Majolica urn for oil reportedly dates from 15th-century Florence from the Medici and Orsini families. The house originally had two and they were located in the garden. This one is on the landing going to the second floor.

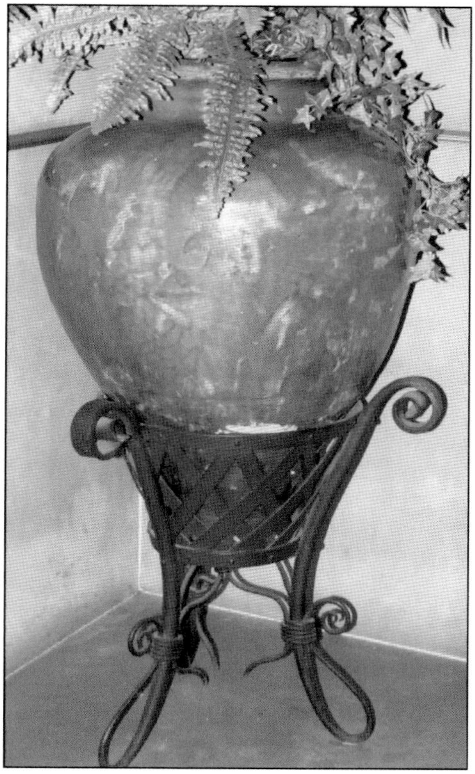

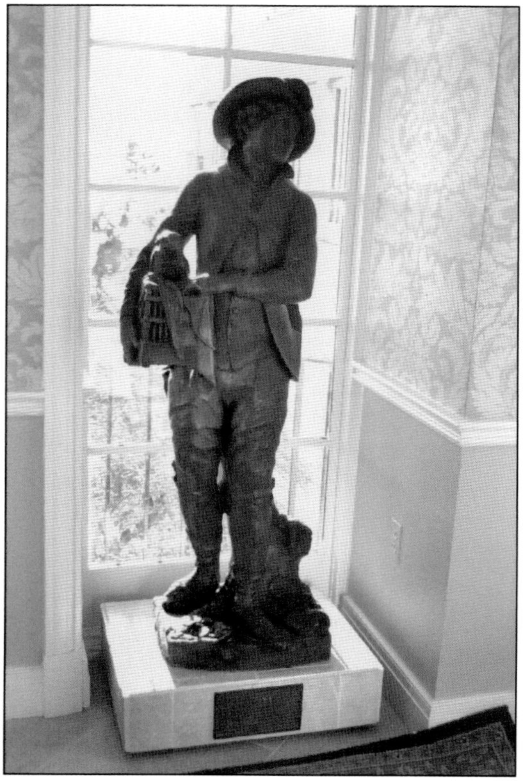

The Falconer was given to the War memorial in 1972 by Roy Chapin Jr. in honor of his mother. A plaque on the bronze statue reads, "In loving memory of my mother, Inez T. Chapin, who appreciated beauty."

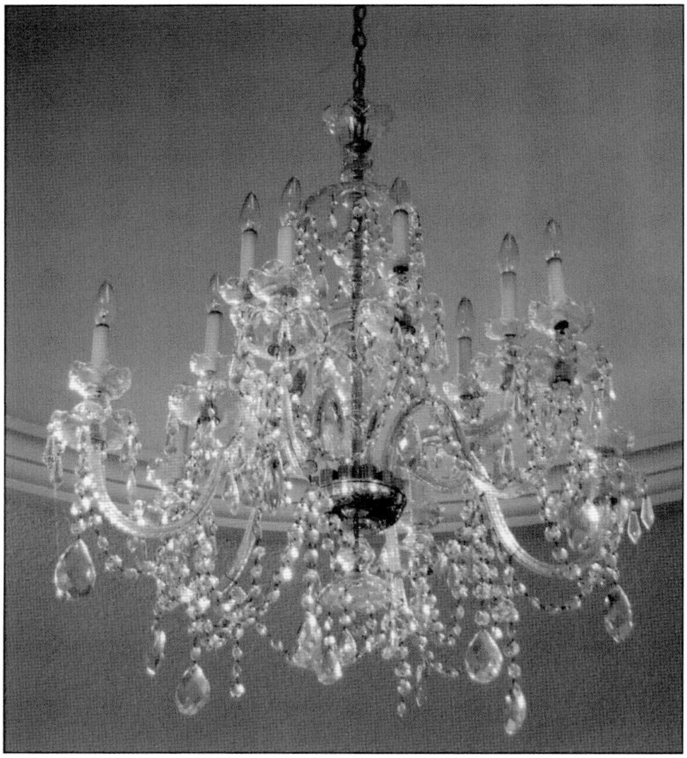

Four crystal chandeliers hang in the appropriately named Crystal Ballroom in the Fries Auditorium.

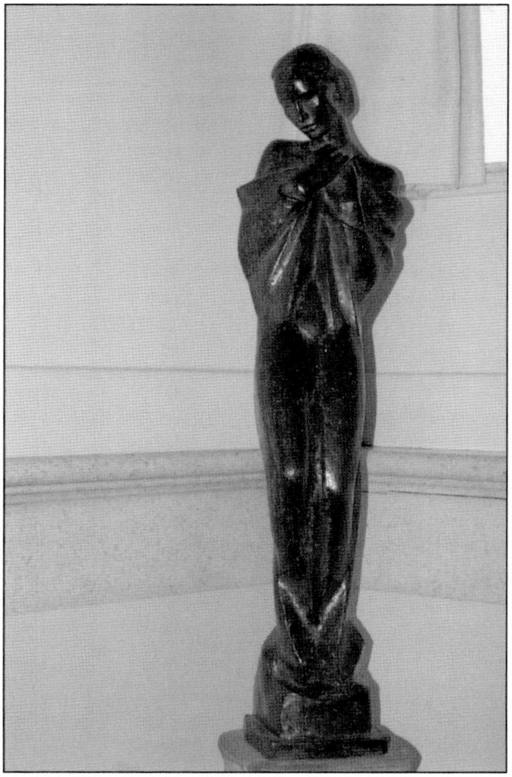

The inscription at the base of this lovely bronze statue, *Adagio*, reads, "All the beauty of the place is in thy heart." A gift of Esther Longyear McGraw Murphy and the Garden Club of Michigan in 1934, it originally stood in the garden and today is on the landing of the stairs going down to the Fries Auditorium. The artist is Georg Kolbe, a leading German sculptor of the late-19th and early-20th centuries.

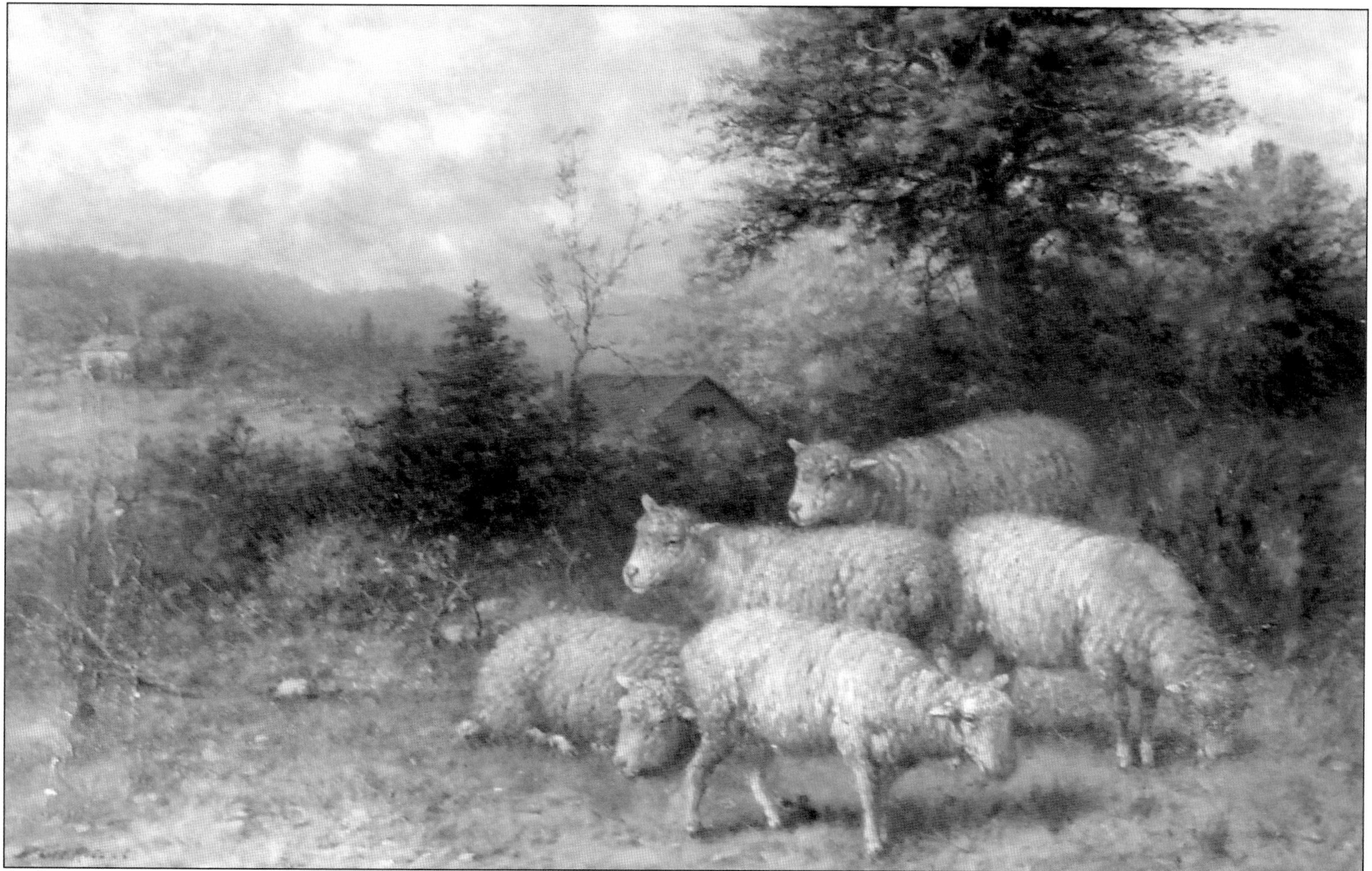

A charming pastoral scene by rural landscape artist George Riecke hangs in the Terrace Room.

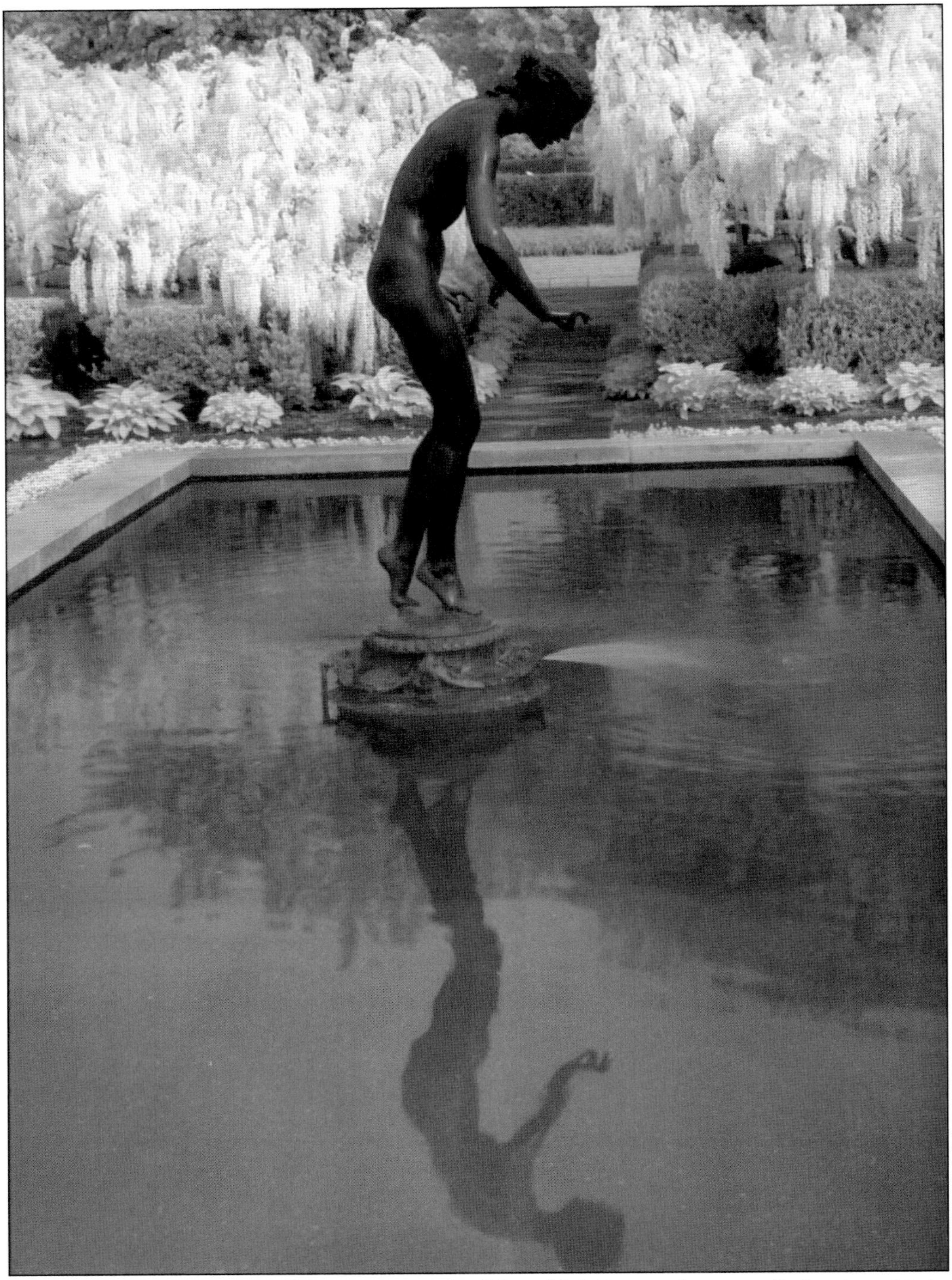

Bronze Nymph, a six-foot tall bronze statue by Edward McCartan, has travelled quite a bit in its day. Originally on the John Newberry estate, it was given to the War Memorial in 1947 for the reflecting pool in the garden. There it stood for more than 50 years until, to everyone's astonishment, it was stolen. (The bolts that held her in place were cut.) In 2009, a Detroit police dive crew on a routine training exercise discovered the statue in the murky waters of the Detroit River. She has been returned to the War Memorial for refurbishing.

Five

Yare Yachts and the Wright Stuff

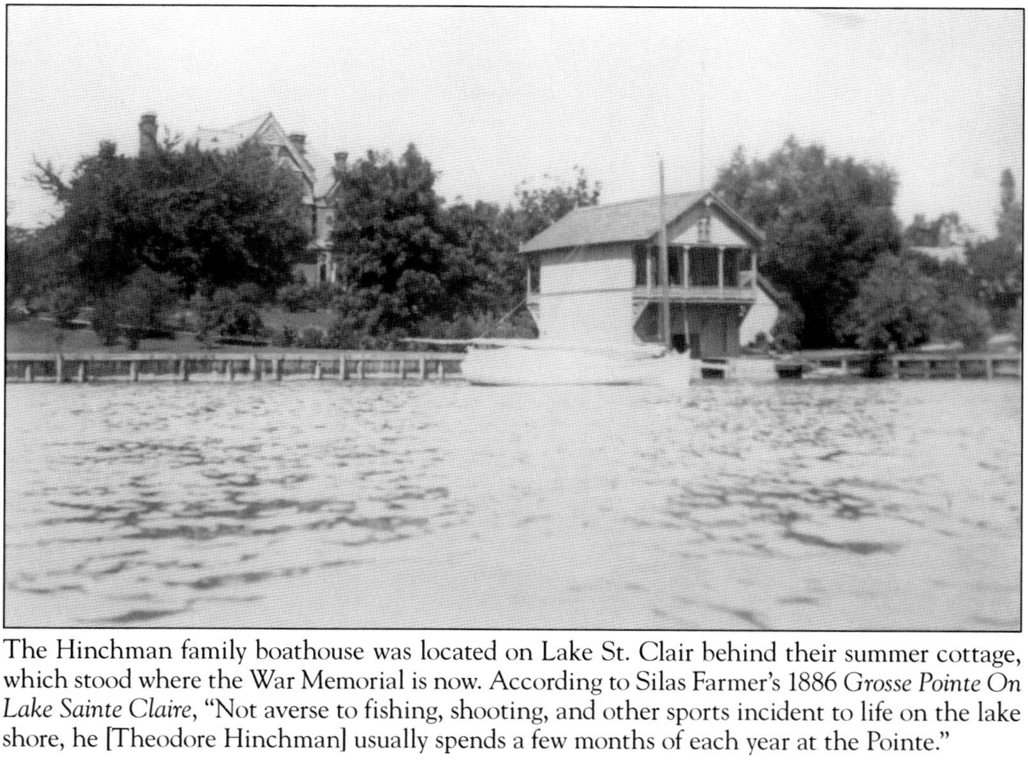

The Hinchman family boathouse was located on Lake St. Clair behind their summer cottage, which stood where the War Memorial is now. According to Silas Farmer's 1886 *Grosse Pointe On Lake Sainte Claire*, "Not averse to fishing, shooting, and other sports incident to life on the lake shore, he [Theodore Hinchman] usually spends a few months of each year at the Pointe."

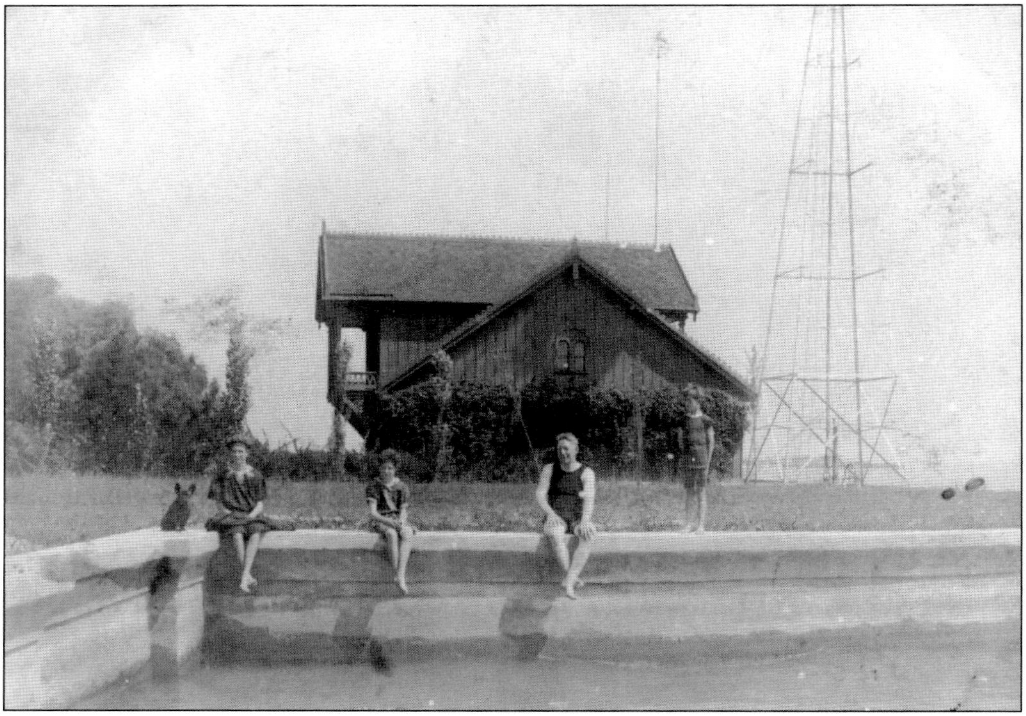

Russell Alger Jr. is shown with his three children, Josephine (left), Fay, and Russell Alger III. Russell Jr. was a devoted family man who loved to spend time with his children. They took great pleasure in their life on the water.

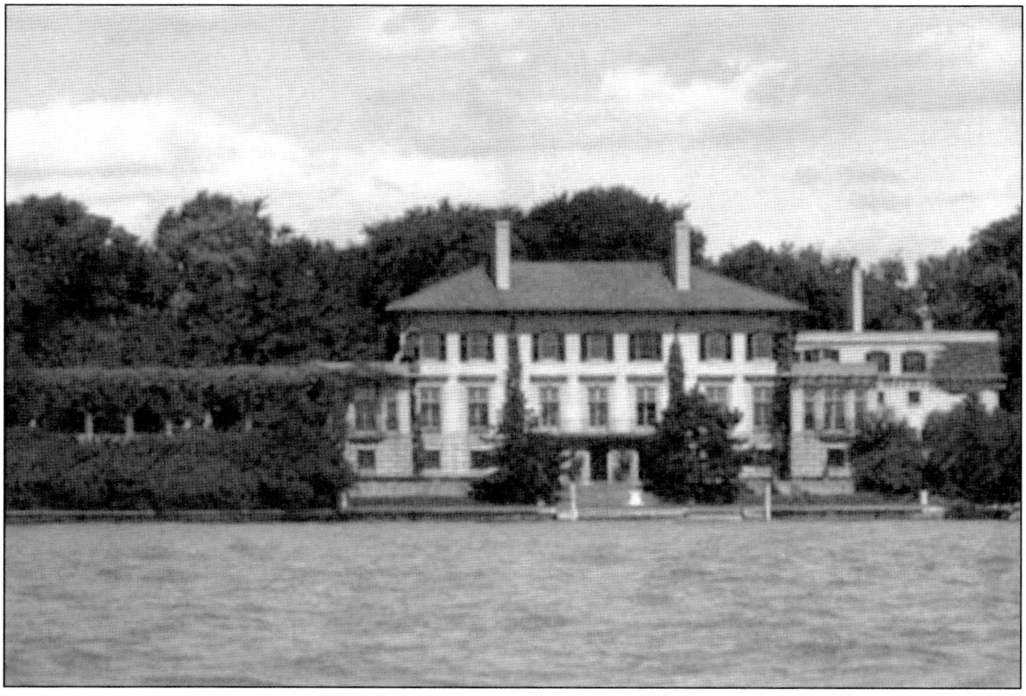

In this view of the Moorings from the water, the Venetian-style mooring poles that inspired the home's name are visible in front of the boat landing in the center of the green.

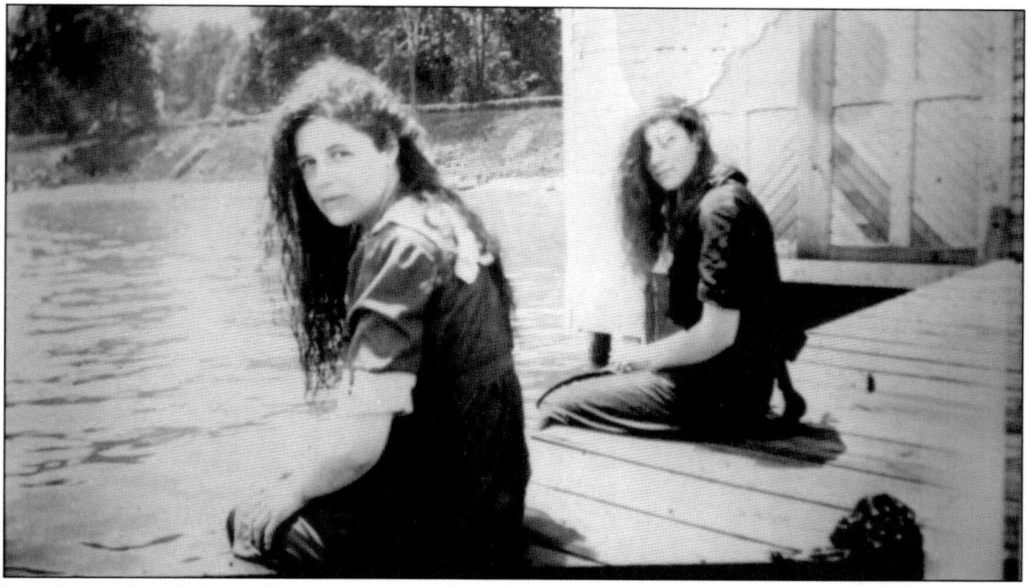

Josephine Alger (left) and Marion Scherer dry off on the dock of the Scherer's summer home, which was just down the road from the Moorings. Marion's father, Hugo, was a successful businessman who owned a thriving pharmacy. His firm, H. Scherer and Company, also made carriages for automobiles. In 1902, he founded the Detroit Automobile Company.

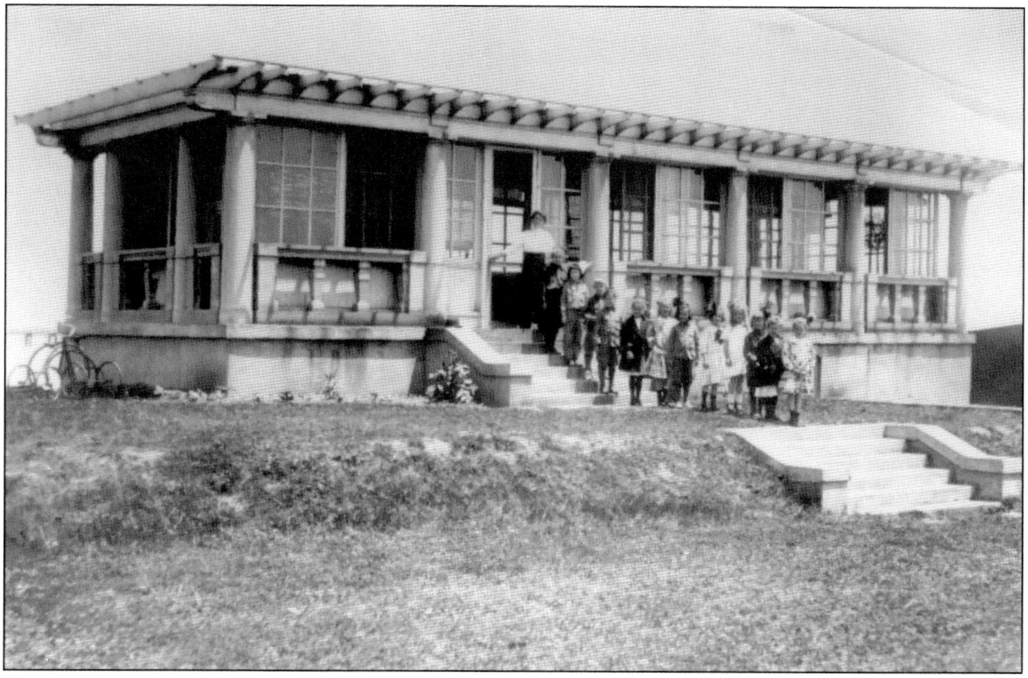

Around 1914, an outbreak of typhoid fever that prompted a citywide quarantine left the children of Grosse Pointe with nowhere to go to school. Fred and Mary Alger transformed their boathouse, at the foot of Island Lane, into the Grosse Pointe School. It served boys and girls from kindergarten through ninth grade. In 1916, the school moved to a larger building nearby and was later named Grosse Pointe Country Day School, which in turn merged with the Detroit University School to become today's University Liggett School.

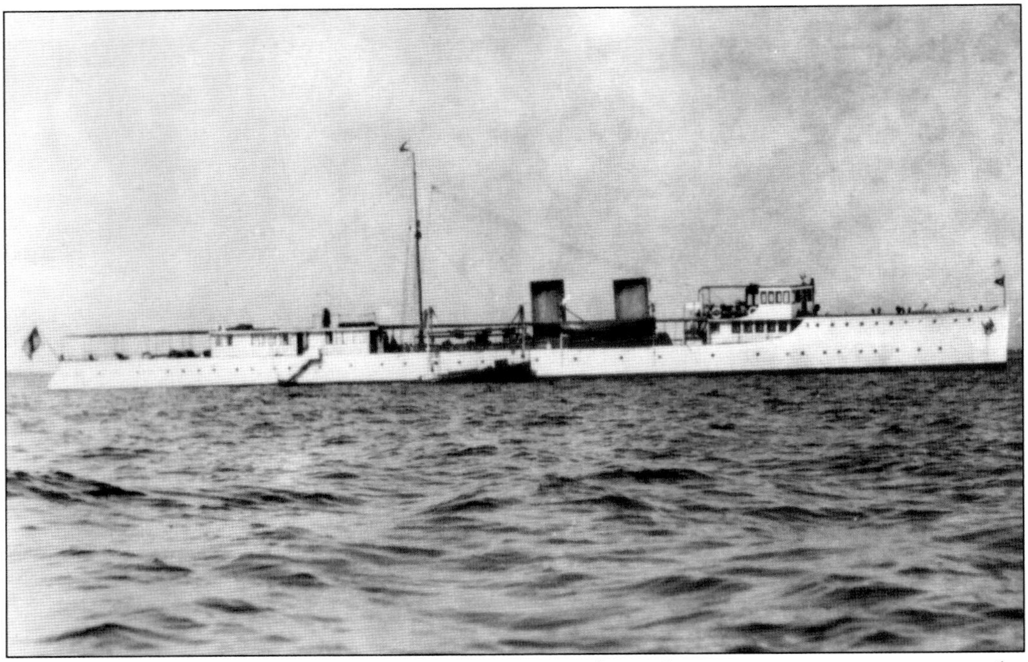

Russell Alger Jr.'s yacht, the steel-hulled, steam-powered *Winchester*, spent two years serving the U.S. Navy, from 1917 to 1919. The vessel was initially employed by the navy on patrol duty in the Long Island Sound area, between New London, Connecticut, and Chatham, Massachusetts. It was sent to Norfolk, Virginia, early in 1918 as a test ship for minesweeping equipment and, after that, to City Island, New York City. It also served the Royal Canadian Navy. Over the course of its naval career, the boat carried one 6-pounder gun, two machine guns, one Y-gun and two 21-inch torpedo tubes.

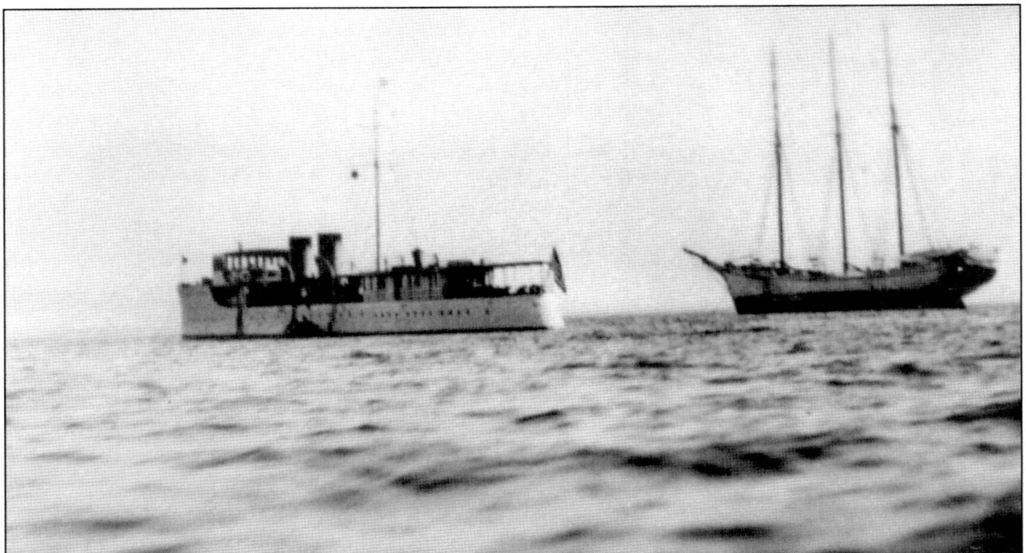

The *Winchester* was built in 1916 by the Bath Iron Works in Bath, Maine. It weighed 399 tons and was 225 feet long. Its first owner was Peter Winchester Rouss. After its service to the navy, it became a bit of a celebrity boat, being sold to Vincent Astor, then Alger, and after that to Cornelius Vanderbilt.

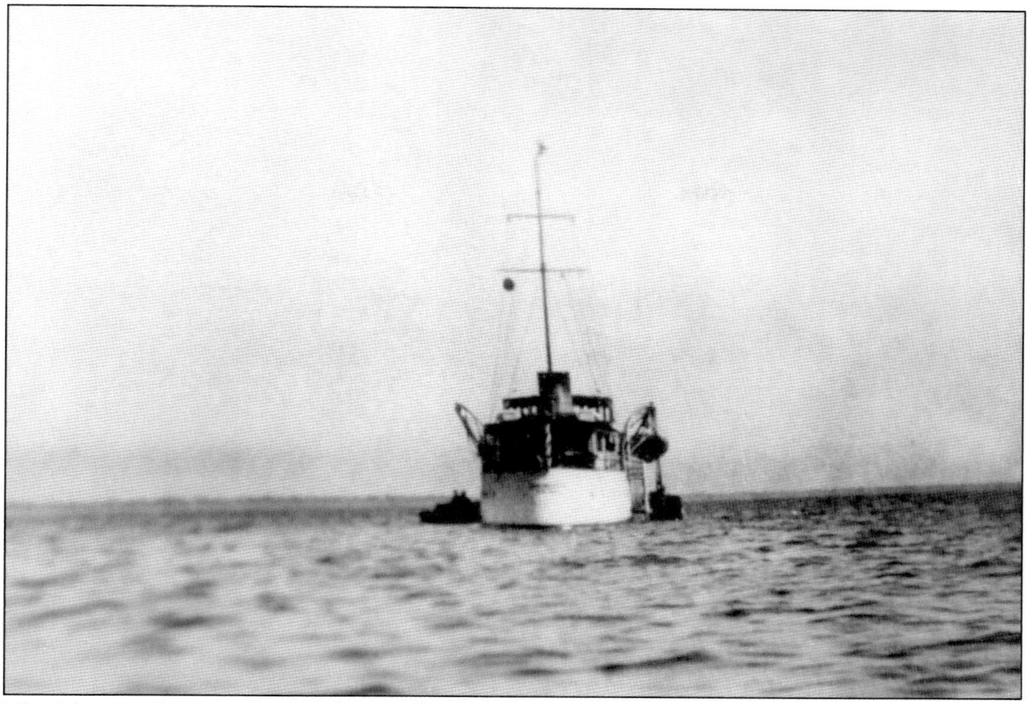

The Algers took many trips on the *Winchester*, sailing to Florida and the Caribbean, often traveling with family and friends. It was on one of these trips, in 1928, that Russell suffered a debilitating stroke, dying two years later.

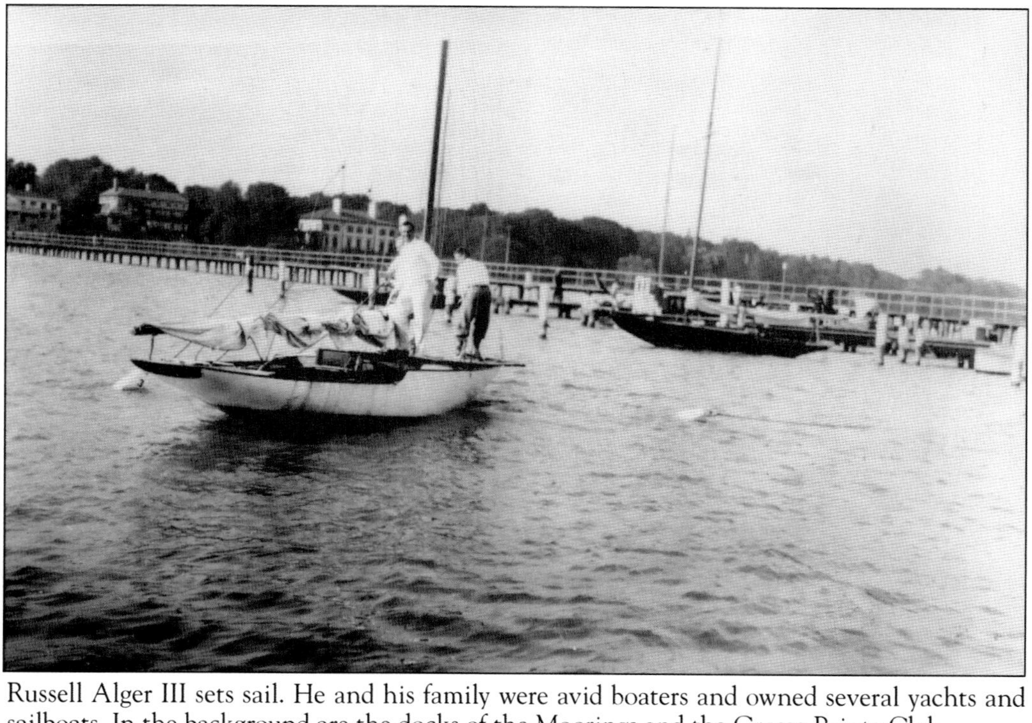

Russell Alger III sets sail. He and his family were avid boaters and owned several yachts and sailboats. In the background are the docks of the Moorings and the Grosse Pointe Club.

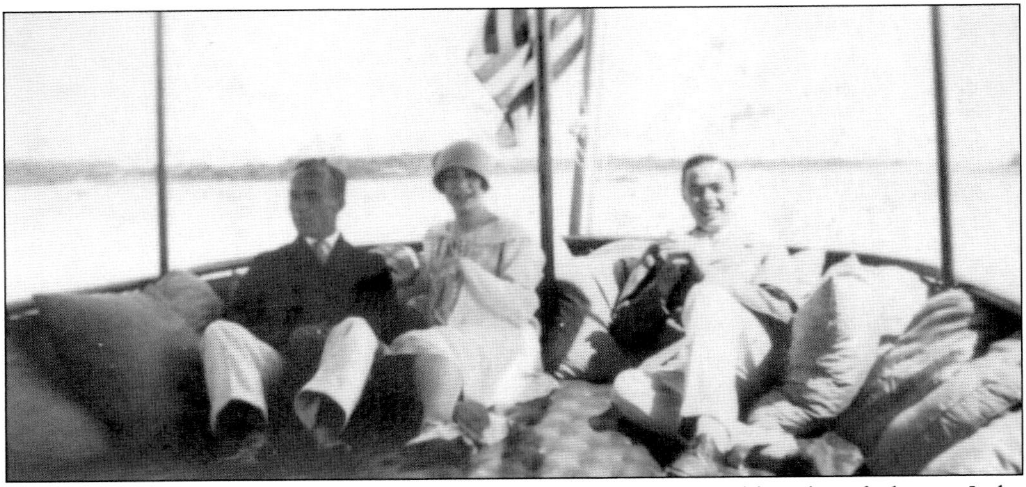

Lang Hubbard (left), Franny Alger Boyer, and her brother Freddy Alger frolic on Lake St. Clair aboard the *Winchester*.

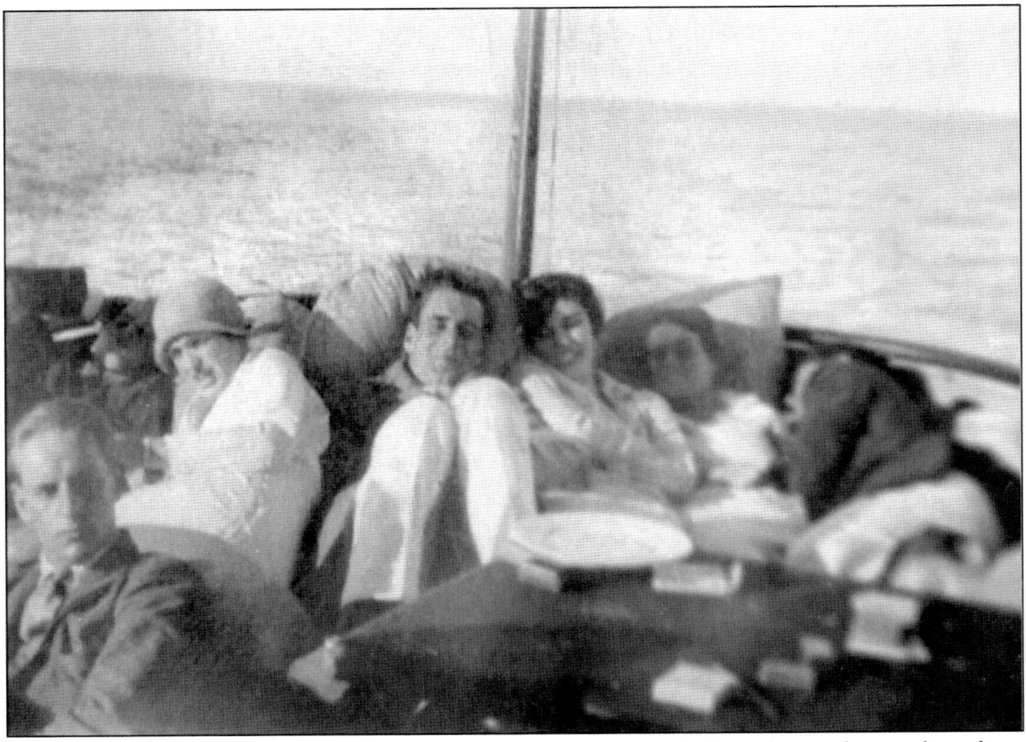

Pictured from left to right, Lang, Franny, Freddy, and a few of their friends are a bit tired out from their boating excursion on the *Winchester*.

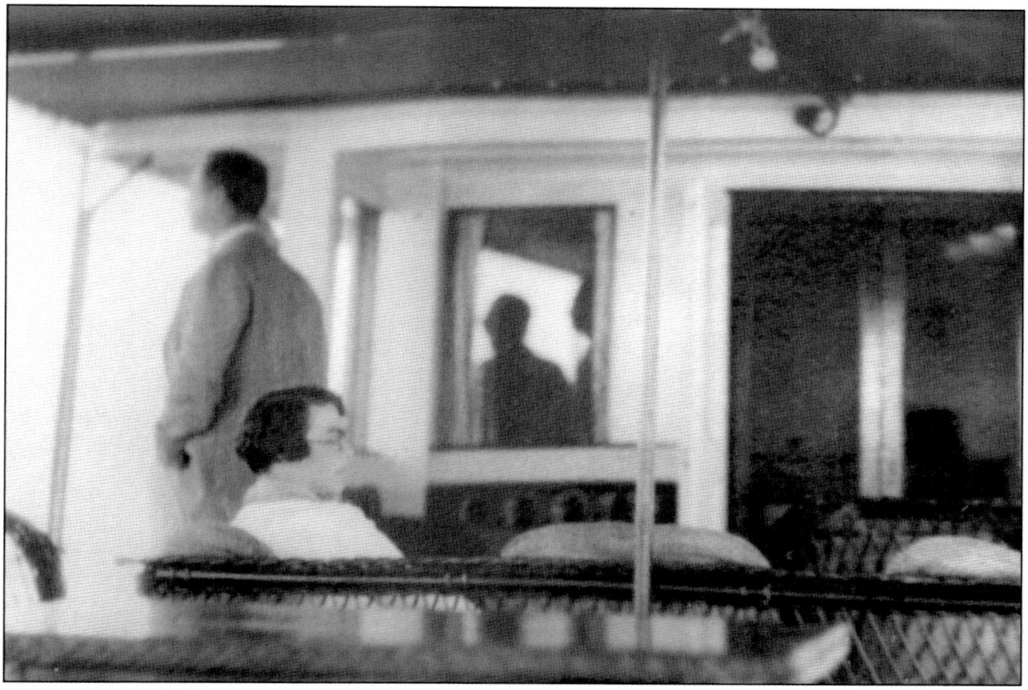

Marion Campbell, daughter of well-connected Detroit lawyer Samuel Douglas (named for his uncle, Judge Samuel Douglas), enjoys a trip on the *Winchester*. She and her husband were frequent guests of the Algers.

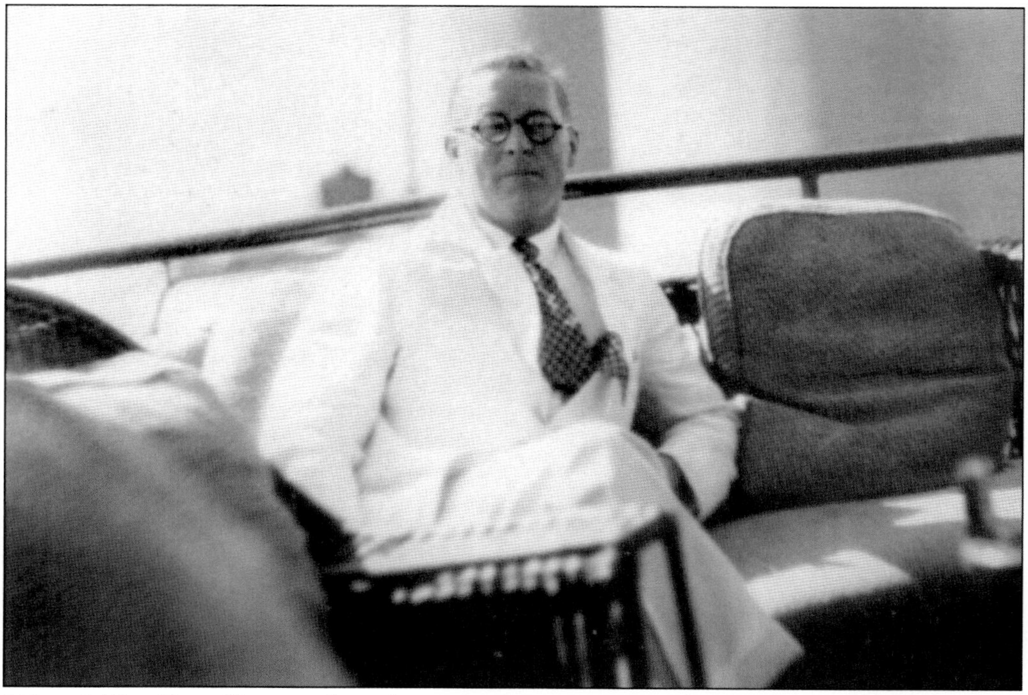

Sidney Miller, Russell's son-in-law, also enjoyed many trips on the *Winchester*. He was with the Algers when Russell was stricken in 1928 while vacationing in Cuba. Russell was reported taking a cruise of the West Indies on the yacht *Winchester* for his health. He was not yet 57 years old.

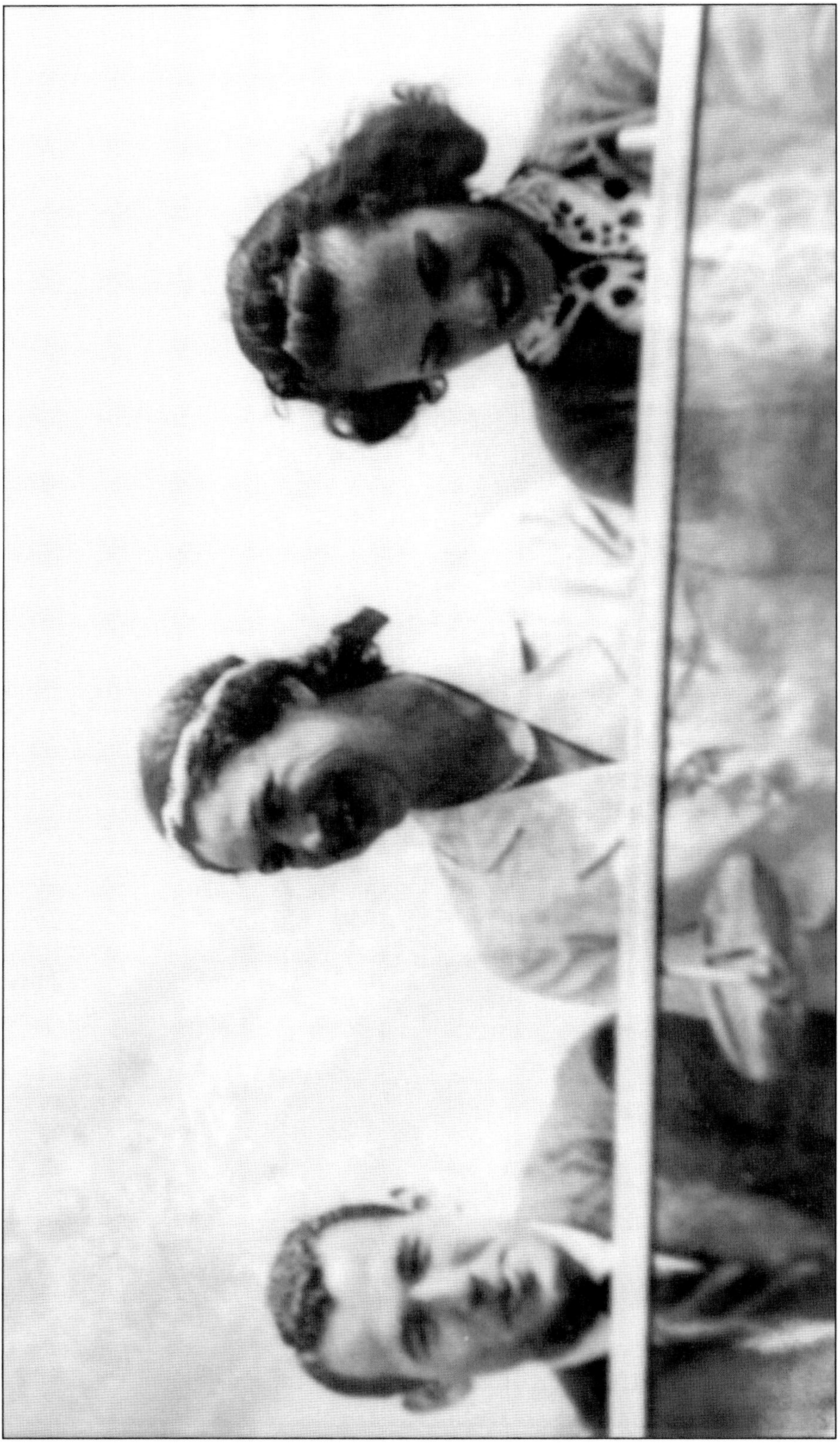

Russell Alger III and his sister Josephine (center) are out for a boating excursion with an unidentified friend.

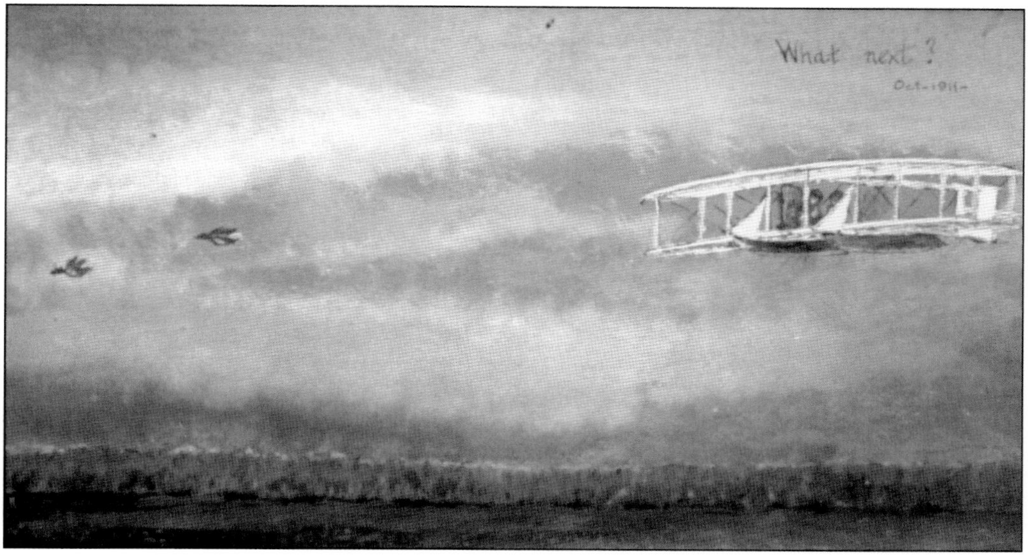

The October 19, 1911, log of the Duck Club of Walpol Island, St. Clair Flats Shooting Company lists an airplane trip depicted in these paintings, which still hang in the club: "At 4:12 p.m. we were much surprised to see the air ship come flying up the river with Messrs R.A. Alger and Frank Coffyn on board. They made a beautiful landing along side of the clubhouse and will spend the night. This is the first time an air ship has made the trip from the United States and landed in Canada." The airplane they flew was a seaplane that Alger built by putting pontoons on a Wright brothers No. 6 biplane. It was one of the first seaplanes ever built and the flight from the United States to Canada was one of the world's first international flights.

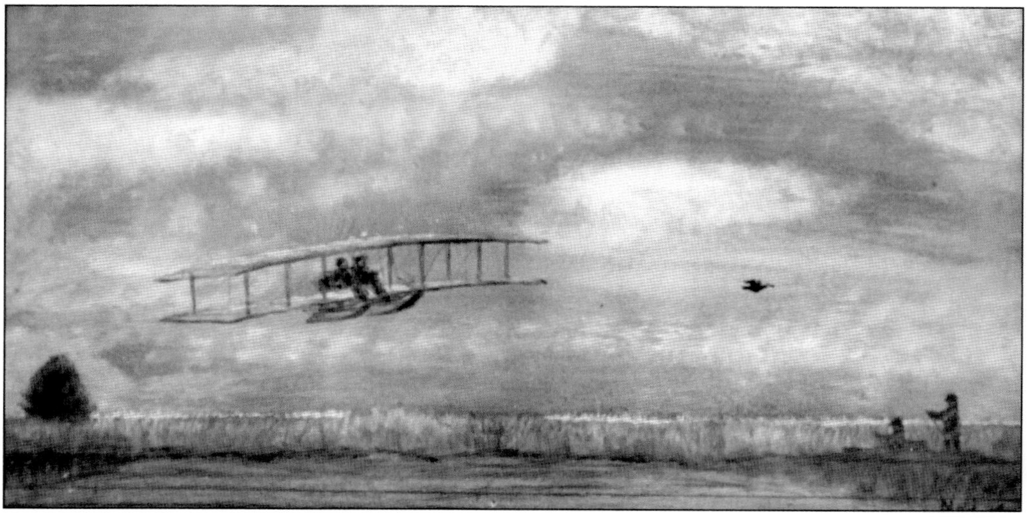

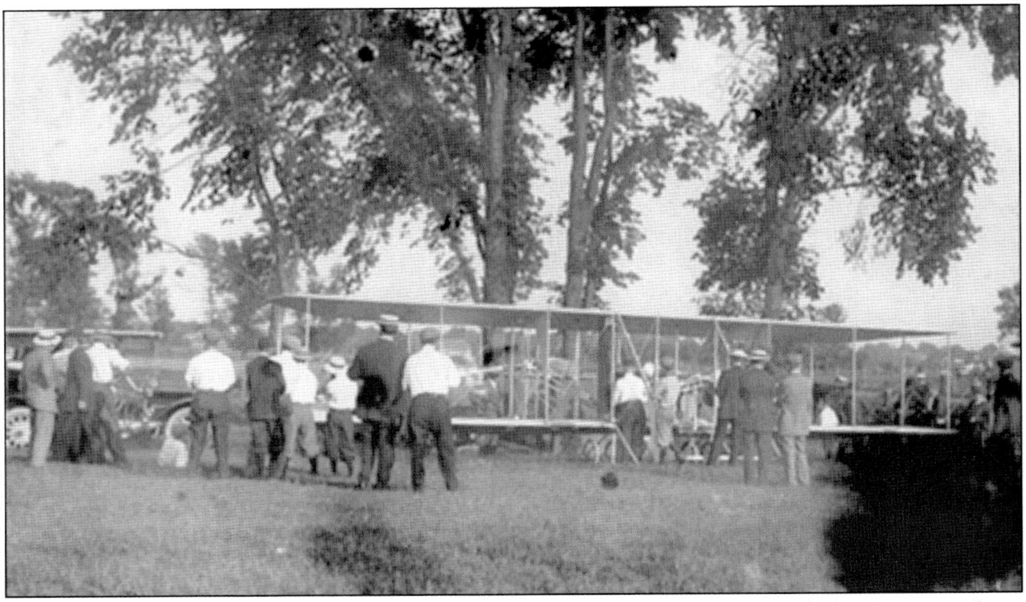

Russell Alger Jr. had many interests beyond lumber and automobiles, and chief among them was aviation. Alger was an early investor in the Wright brothers' airplanes. To generate some interest in the business, Alger arranged for a Wright Flyer airplane to come to Grosse Pointe to give demonstration rides on June 19, 1911.

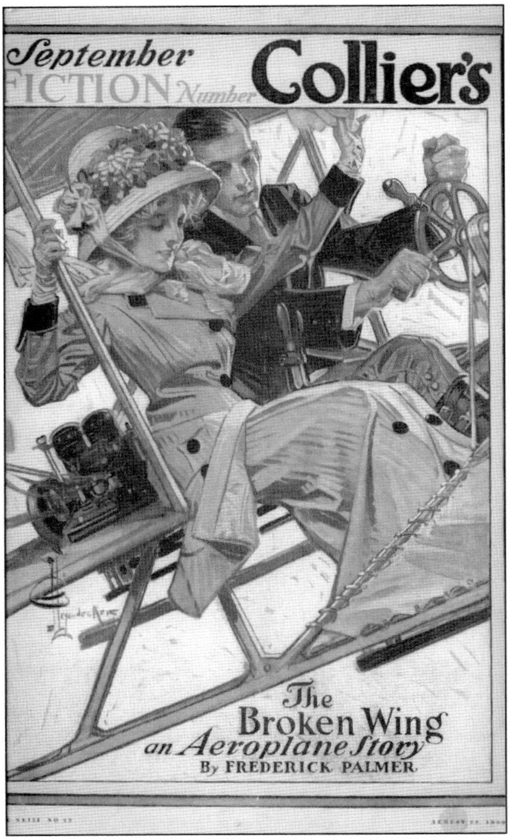

The editors of *Colliers* commissioned renowned artist Joseph C. Leyendecker to illustrate the cover of this magazine, which featured a short story about an airplane ride in 1909. Publisher Robert Collier was a friend of Alger's and an investor in the Wright brothers' company. He certainly knew stories of Alger's young daughter, the daring Josephine, who had accompanied her father up in the air. In fact, at 12 years old, she was the youngest person in the United States to ride in an airplane.

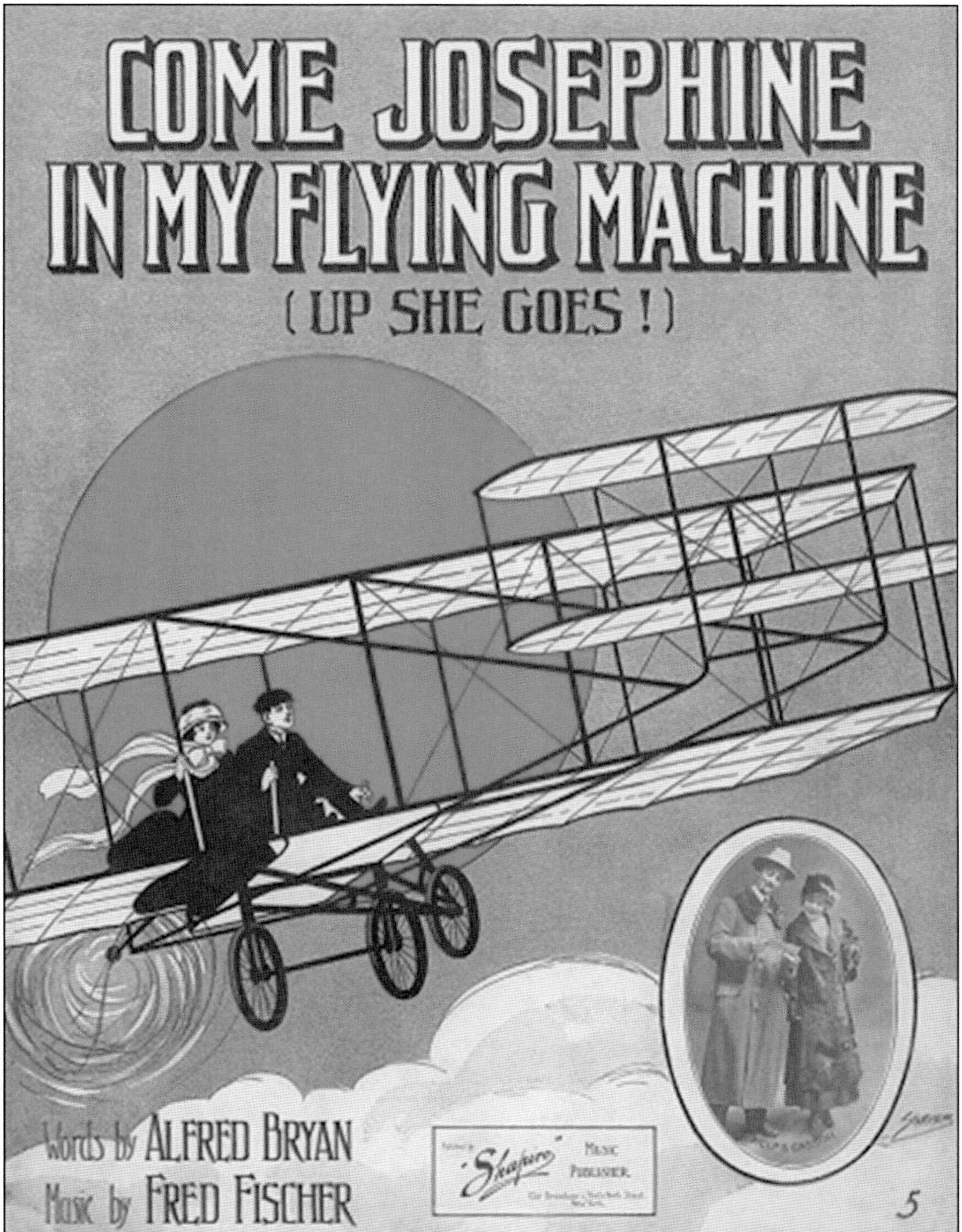

No doubt that same Josephine and the magazine cover also inspired Tin Pan Alley songwriters Fred Fisher and Alfred Bryan to compose "Come Josephine In My Flying Machine." According to family letters, the song was written about Josephine Alger's early flight experiences. The song was made famous again when it was used in the 1997 blockbuster movie *Titanic*.

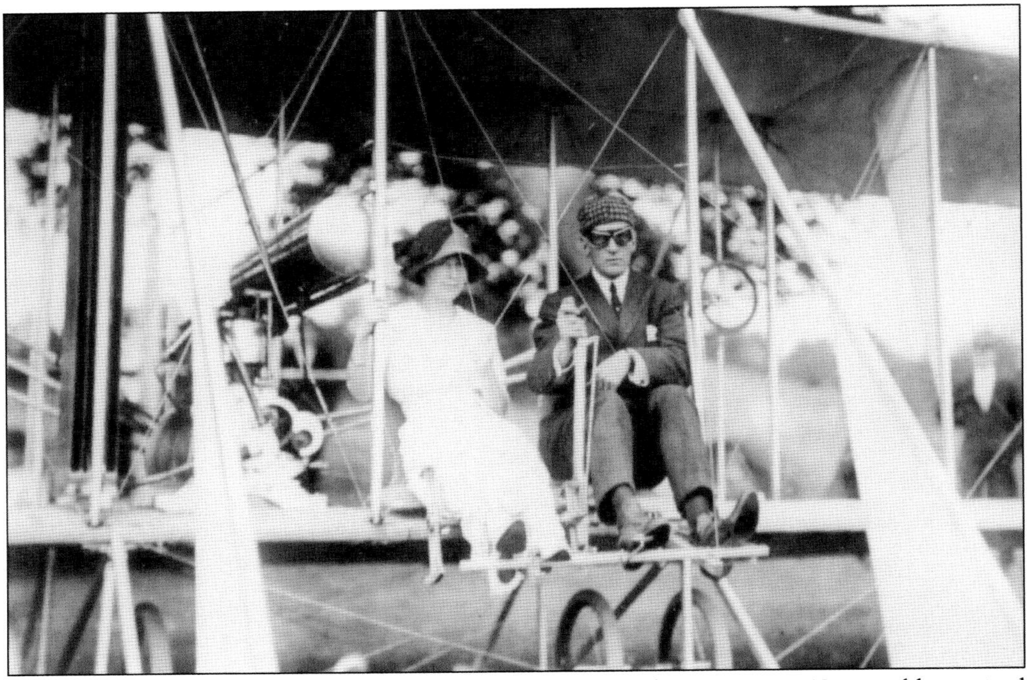

One of the lucky passengers was society girl Beth Loomis. The precocious 18 year old surprised onlookers by "suddenly appearing on the scene and jumping into the aeroplane, mother to the contrary," according to a note on the back of this photograph written by her mother. Frank Coffyn, right, piloted the airplane in this and the following photographs.

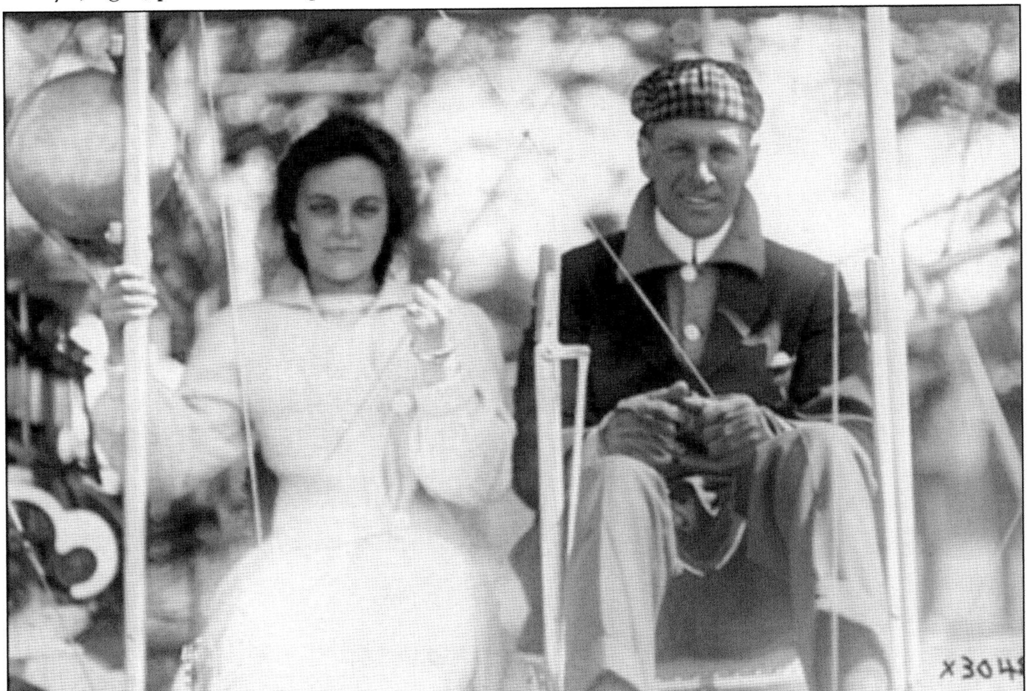

Helen Wadsworth was the daughter of Frederick E. Wadsworth, who founded Detroit Engine Works with Hugo Scherer and was president of the Michigan Steel Boat Company.

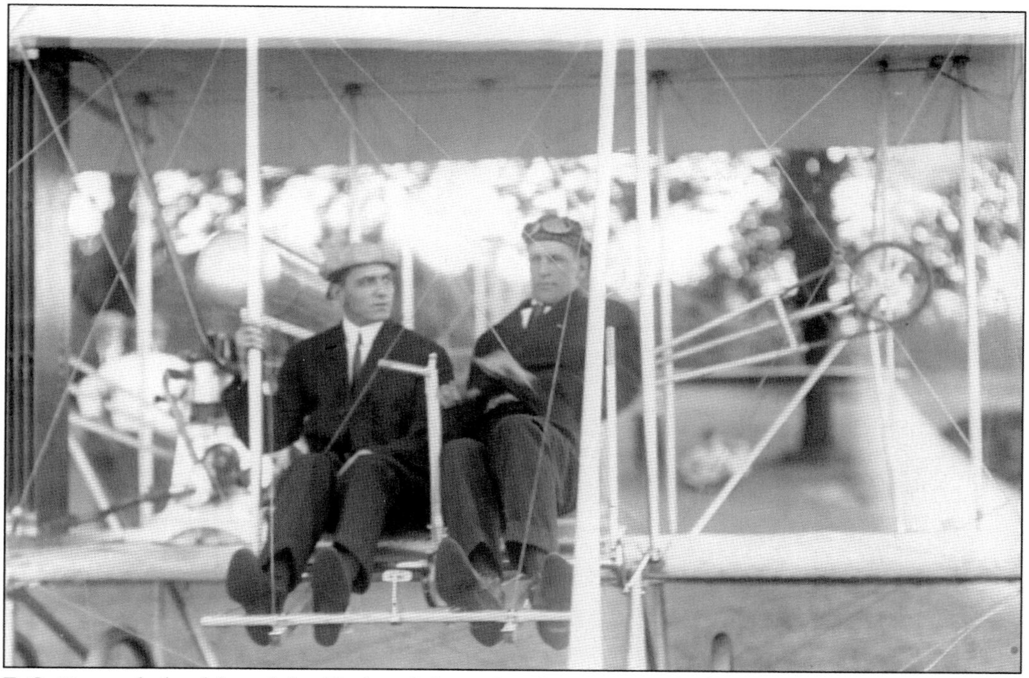

F. O. Bezner helped found the Hudson Motor Car Company with department store entrepreneur Joseph L. Hudson, Roy Chapin, and others. It became one of the leading car companies in the country, known for its innovation and design.

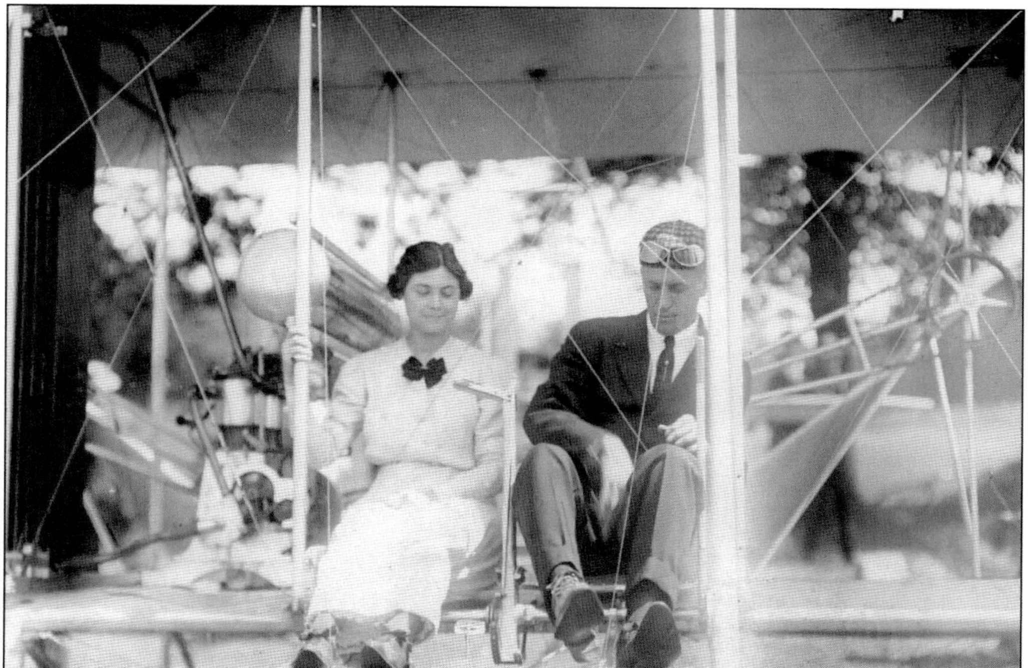

Virginia Brush was a member of one of Detroit's most prominent families. She was the granddaughter of Edmund A. and Eliza Cass Hunt Brush, who were among the first Detroit families to summer in Grosse Pointe.

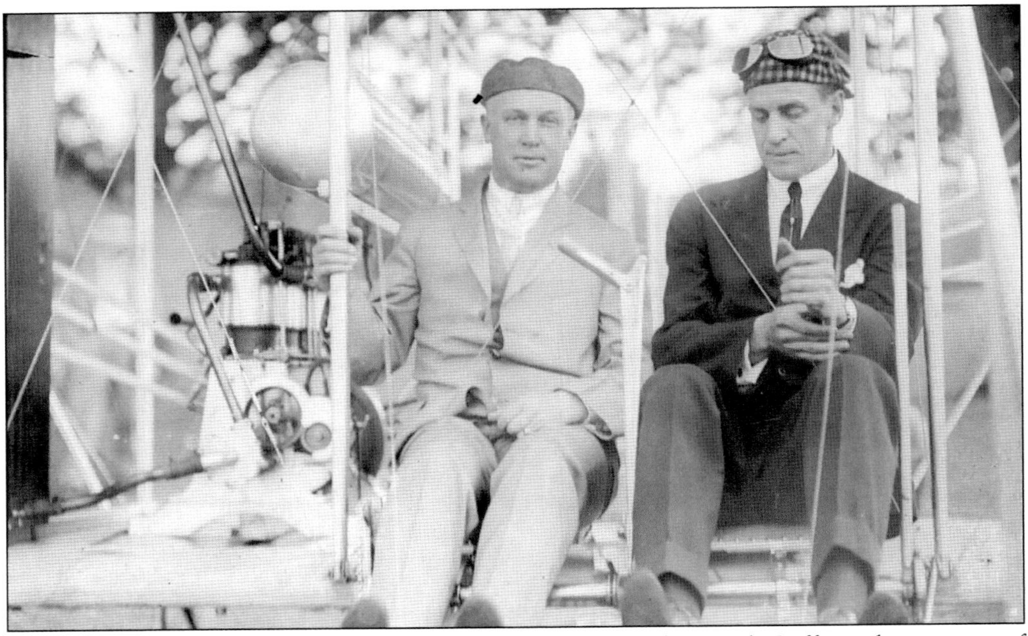

An unidentified passenger prepares to take to the air with pilot Frank Coffyn, who was one of the five original members of the Wright brothers exhibition flying team. According to an article about the Grosse Pointe event in the *Winnipeg Free Press* on July 12, 1911, "Coffyn has made himself a name all over the continent as the steadiest of the bird men—witness the fact that last month at Detroit he carried in three days as many as 45 passengers, 12 of them ladies."

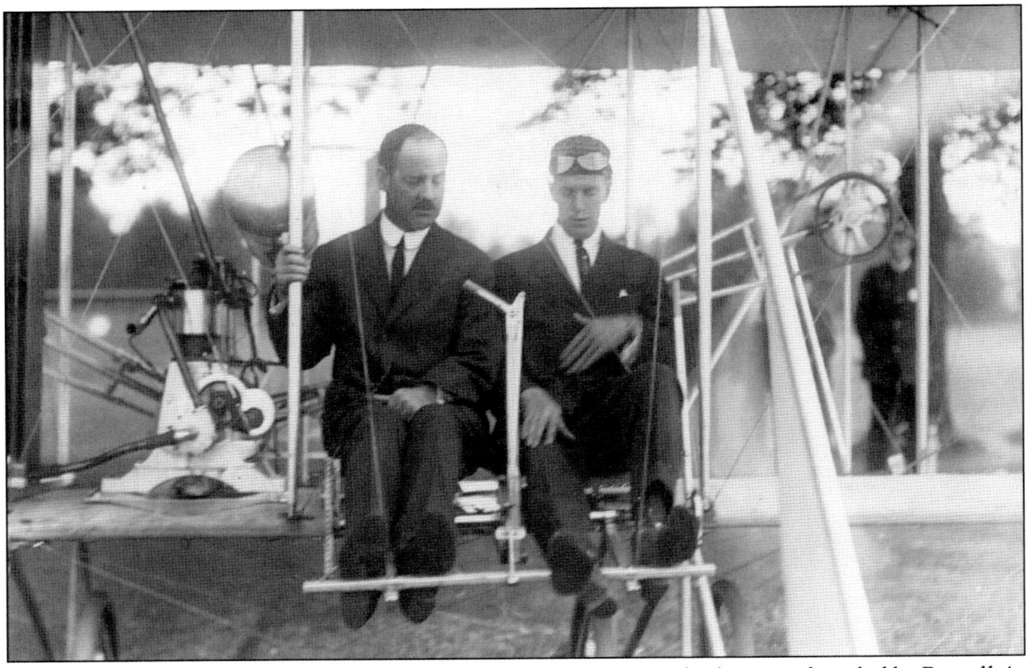

Alvin McCauley was president of Packard Motor Car Company, which was cofounded by Russell A. Alger Jr. McCauley later became an investor in Henry Ford's Stout Metal Airplane Company, which made the Stout ST-1, the first all-metal airplane designed for the navy. Other investors were Roy Chapin, Walter Chrysler, Fred Fisher, Charles Kettering, Ransom Olds, and Barney Everitt.

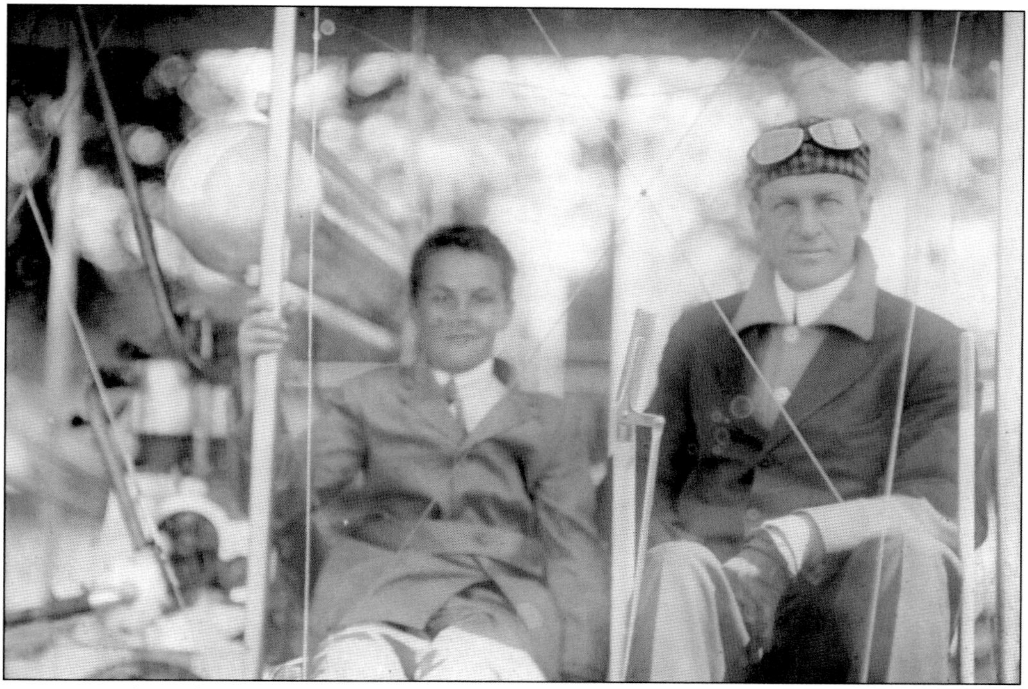

Horace Wadsworth, son of Frederick E. Wadsworth, is seen here with Frank Coffyn.

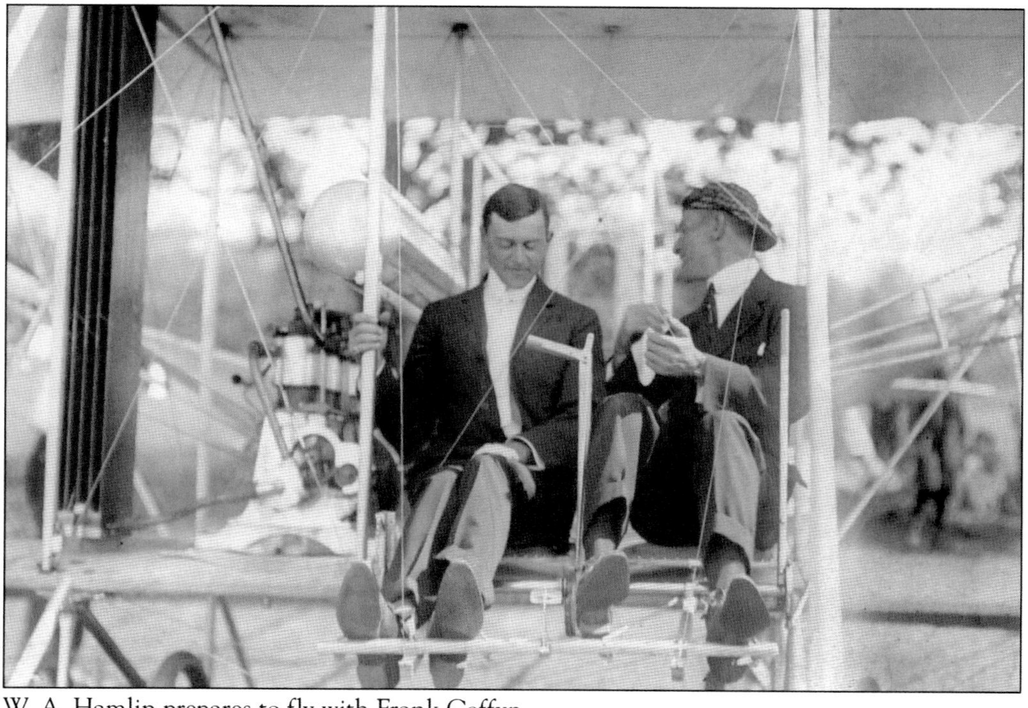

W. A. Hamlin prepares to fly with Frank Coffyn.

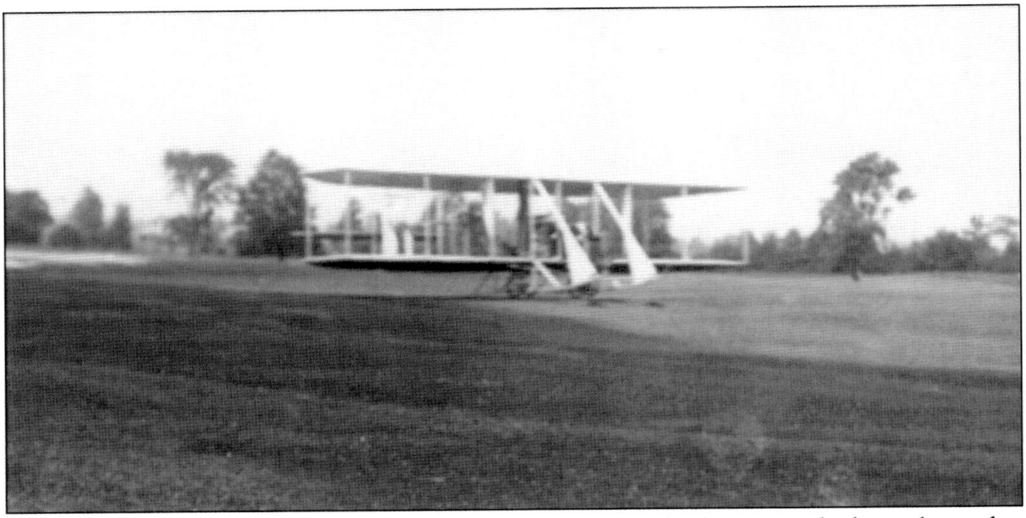

The flights took place at the polo grounds of the Country Club of Detroit, which was located at the time on what is now the athletic field of Grosse Pointe South High School on Fisher Road.

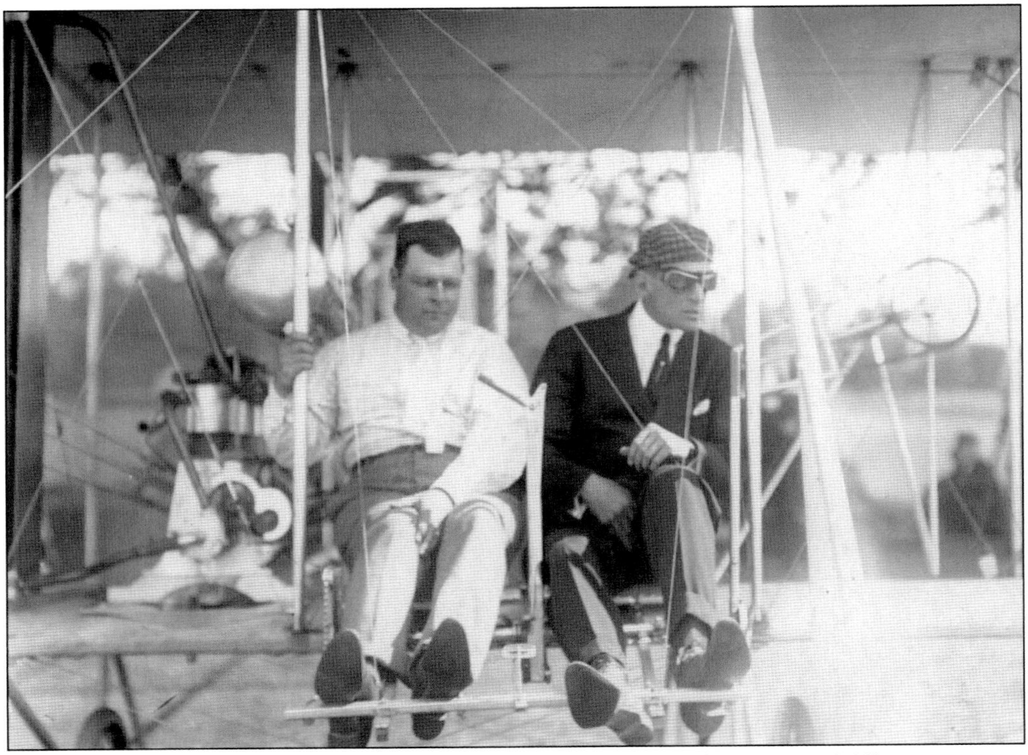

Here with Coffyn is Maurice McMillan, the son of Hugh and Helen Dyar McMillan.

Phillip McMillan was one of the original investors in the Packard Motor Company.

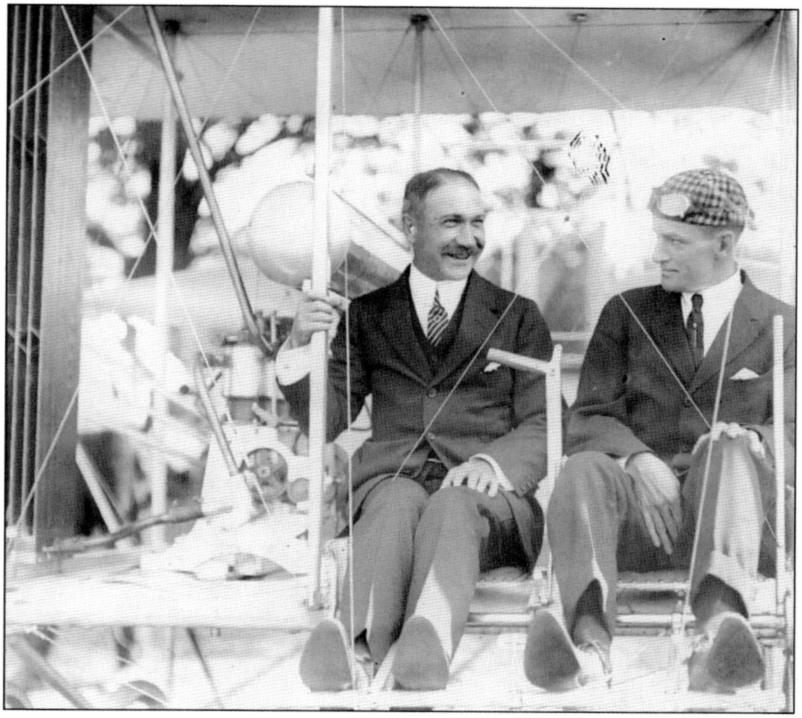

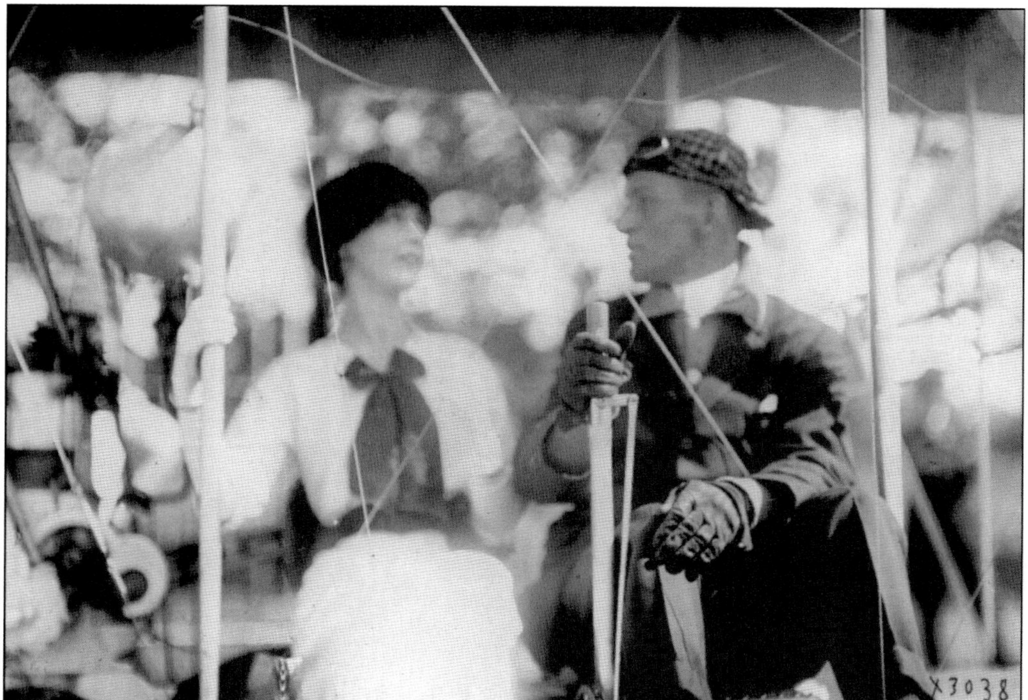

Mrs. Reid Flushing goes for a spin.

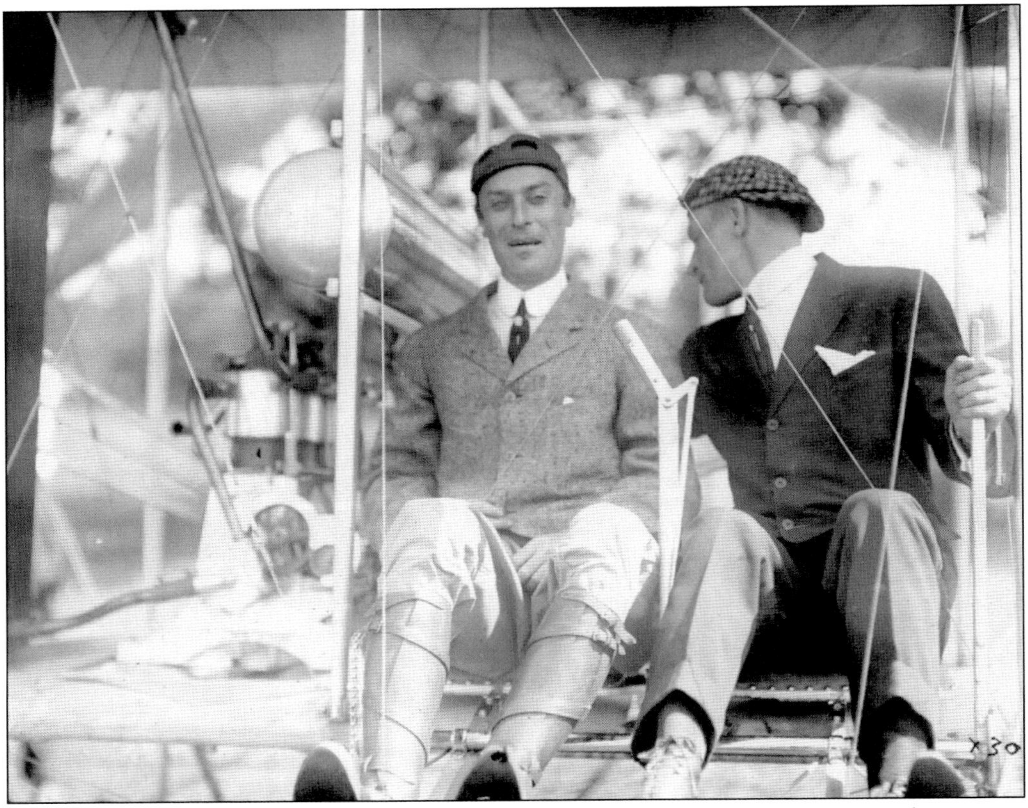

L. H. Taylor, seen here at left, was engineer with the EMF Motor Company, a short-lived car company that was founded by custom auto-body builder Barney Everitt, Cadillac's William Metzger, and Henry Ford's former production manager Walter Flanders.

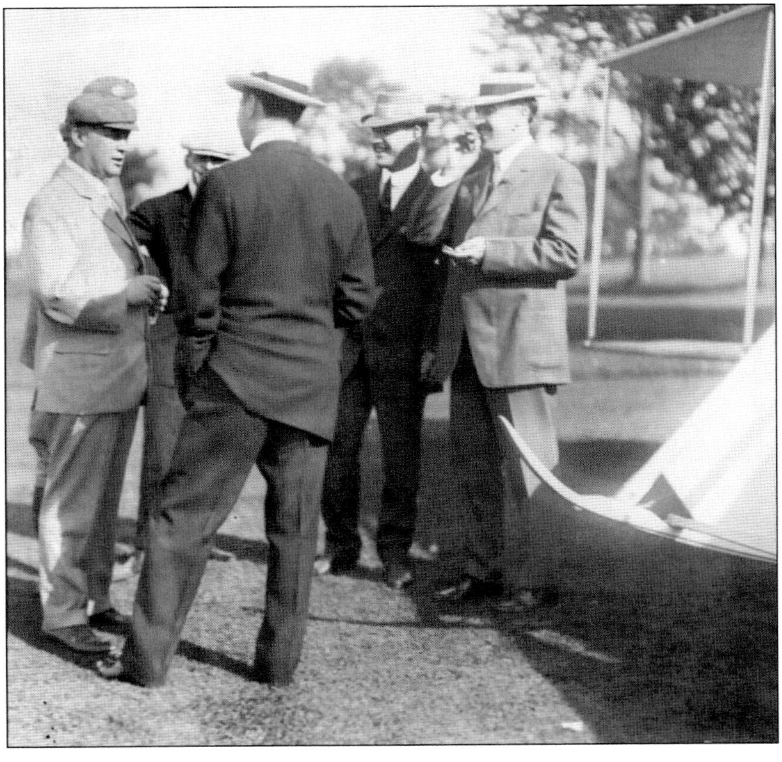

EMF Motor Company's B.F. Barney Everitt (far left) and William Metzger (far right) are pictured here.

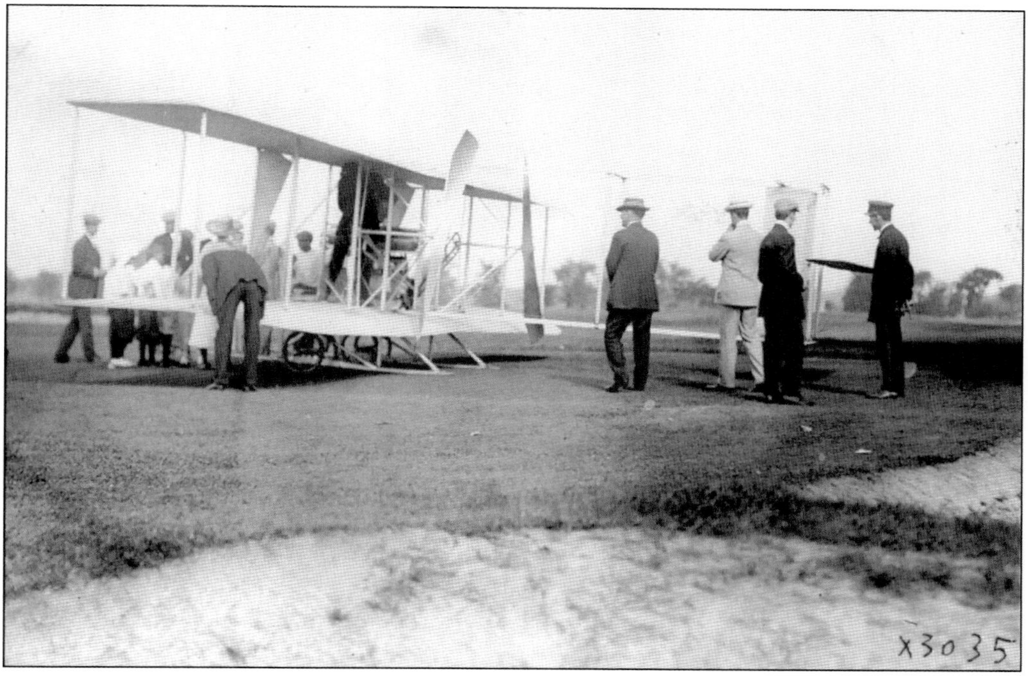

This event not only had the Grosse Pointe community excited, it also attracted the attention of the local media. Stories and photographs of the event made the front page of the Detroit newspapers for days.

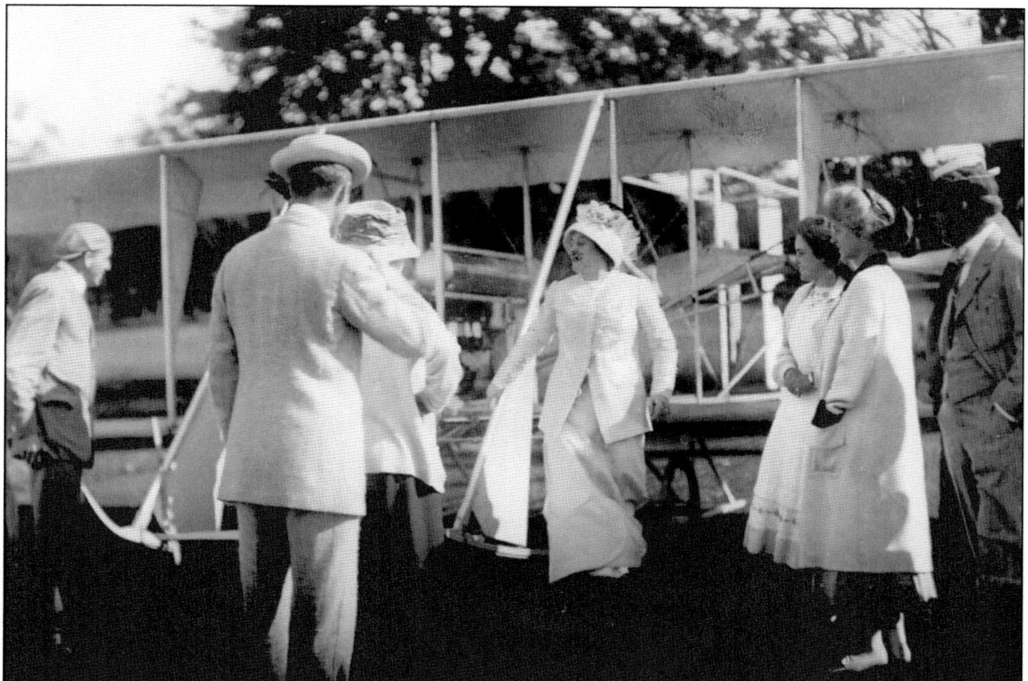
Mary Wadsworth is seen here after the flight. Her husband was one of the founders of the Detroit Aero Club with William Metzger. He built a hydro-airplane named the *Flying Fish* that was designed to skim over the surface of the water.

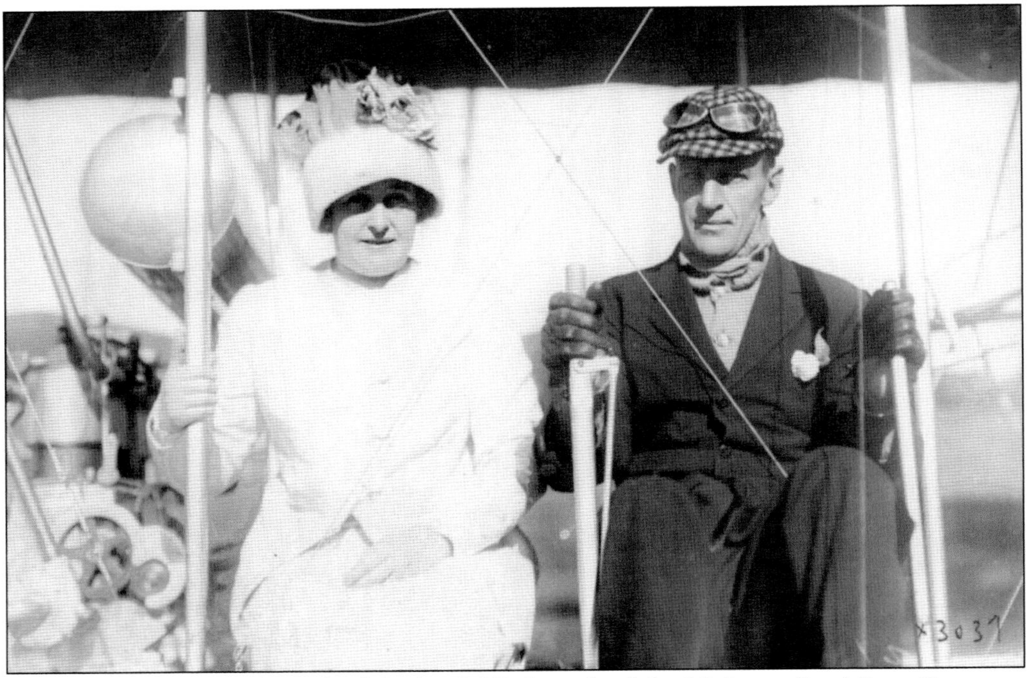

Mary Wadsworth was the wife of Frederick Wadsworth of the Michigan Steel Boat Company. She was formerly Mary Mannering, a prominent actress.

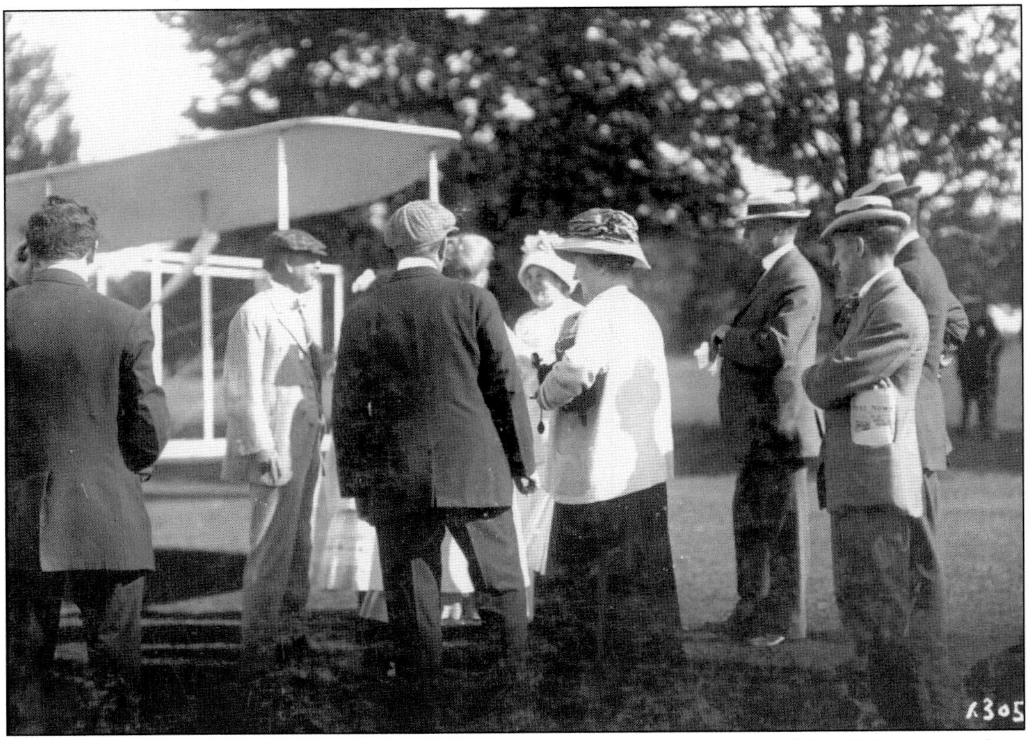

Several onlookers wait to talk to Mary Wadsworth to get her impressions of the flight. According to an article in the *Detroit Free Press*, when Wadsworth flew with Coffyn, he engaged in a race with a passing motorist, much to her delight.

Six

A Lasting Tribute

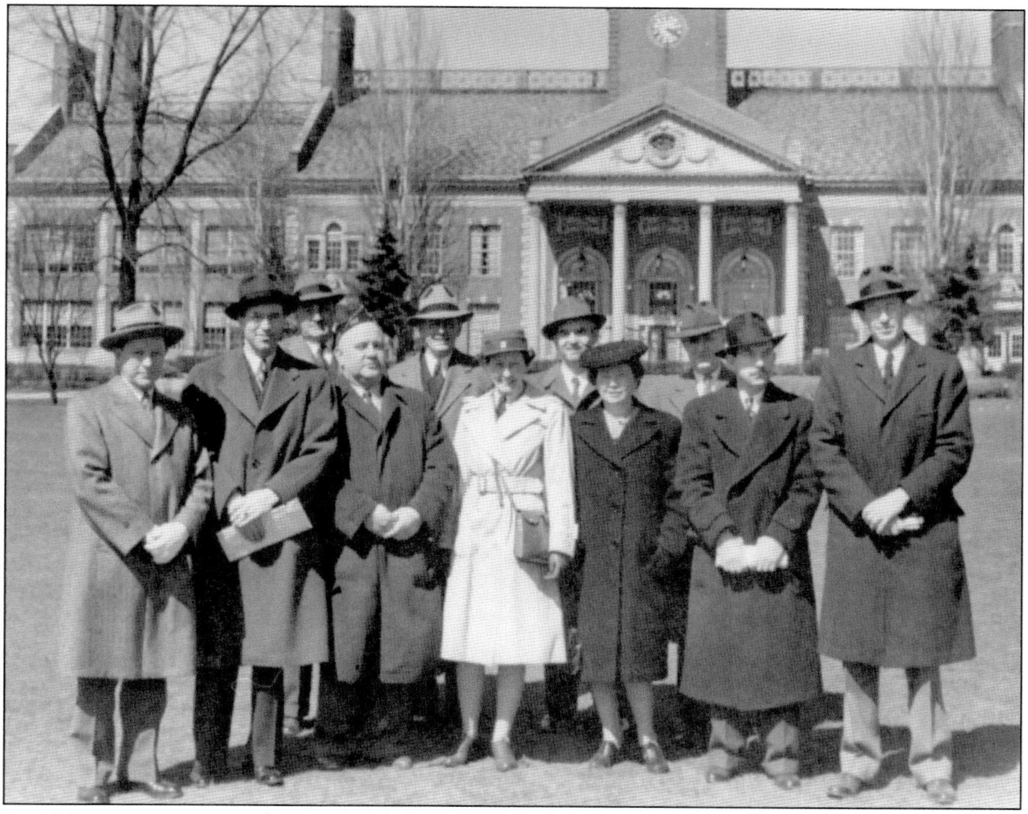

In 1943, a committee of civic-minded Grosse Pointers wanted to honor the men and women of their community who had served in World War II. Most of the group, known as the Grosse Pointe Honor Roll Association, is pictured here, including Alger Shelden on the far right. Other members were Pres. William J. Watkins, Norbert Neff, Judge Kenneth Thomas, Paul Moreland, Florence Severs, Arnold Diesing, Sgt. Julius Stork, George L. Schlaepfer, John J. O'Brien, Clarence Blessed, Frances D. Shelden, and George Elworthy.

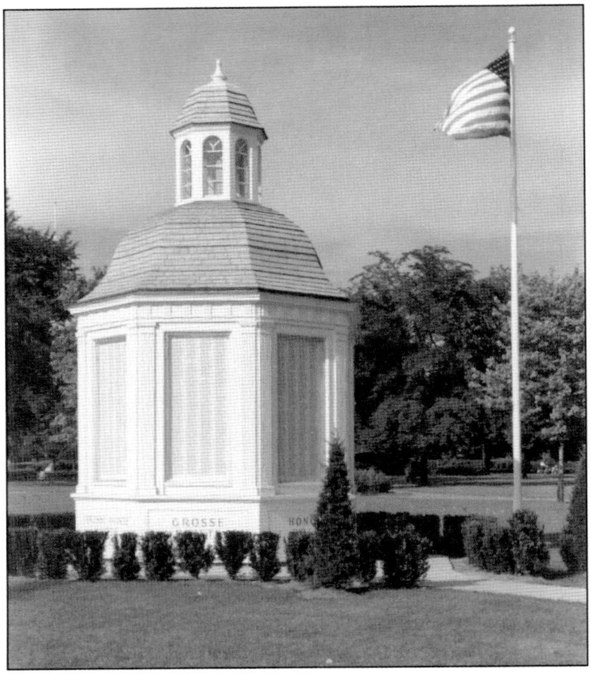

The names of all Grosse Pointers who served in World War II were engraved on this kiosk, the 32 names of those who died in gold lettering. The kiosk, which originally stood on the front lawn of Grosse Pointe High School, was later moved to the lakeside lawn of the War Memorial. It has been replaced by the bronze plaques on the wall of the entrance hall of the house.

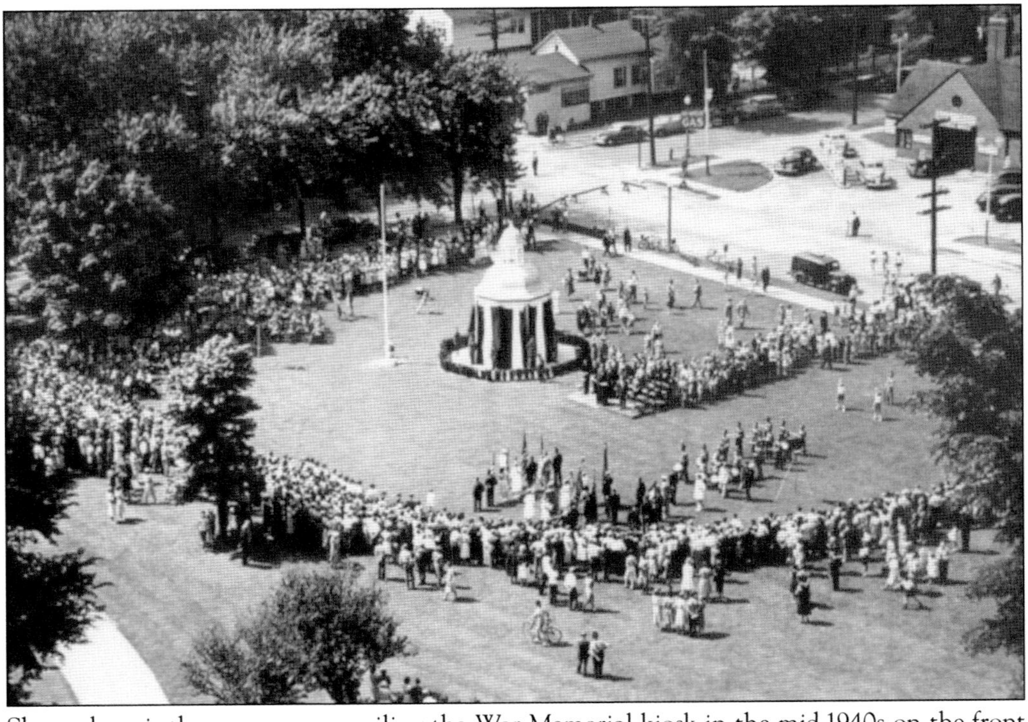

Shown here is the ceremony unveiling the War Memorial kiosk in the mid-1940s on the front lawn of Grosse Pointe High School at the corner of Fisher Road and Grosse Pointe Boulevard. The Honor Roll Association originally had 1,900 names. After putting notices in the *Grosse Pointe News* and *Grosse Pointe Review*, and with the help of air raid wardens who went door-to-door, they ended up with 3,114 names. The project was funded entirely by donations. Michigan governor Wilber Brucker presided over the dedication on Memorial Day 1944.

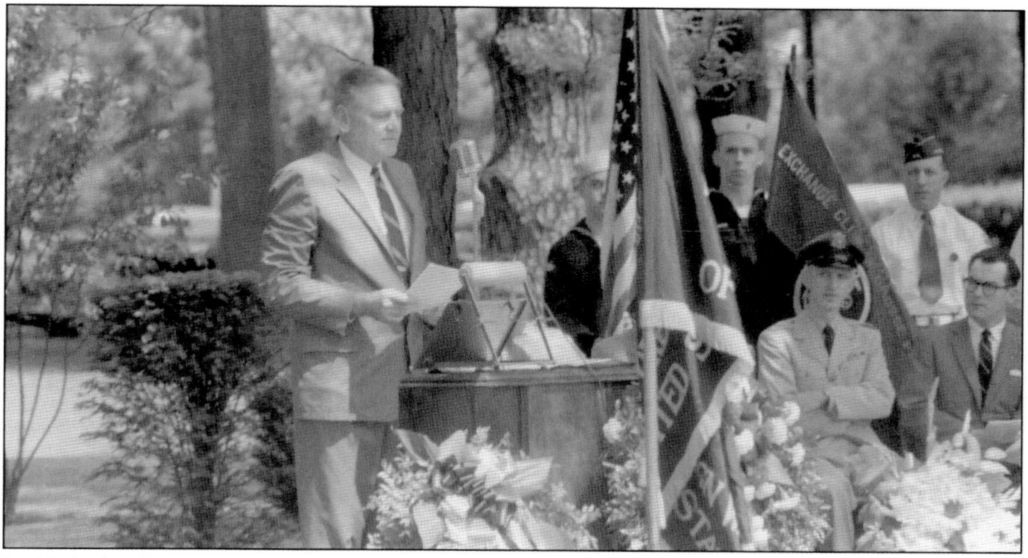

In 1949, the Grosse Pointe War Memorial Association was officially formed to establish a lasting tribute to the men and women who served in World War II, as well as to create a center for the "educational and charitable purposes which will enrich the community life and serve to promote the well being of the public." Pictured here is a Memorial Day service held in the formal gardens, dating from the late 1950s.

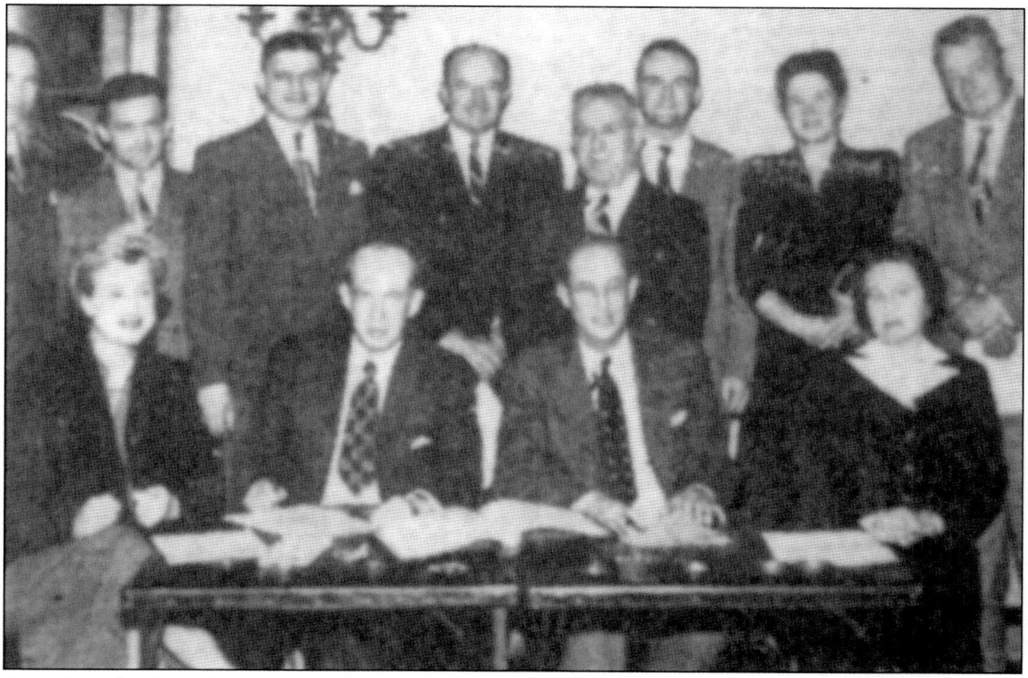

On May 26, 1949, this picture of the very first War Memorial board of directors appeared in the *Grosse Pointe Review*. Pictured, in no particular order, are Mrs. D. Dwight Douglas (seated, left), assistant secretary Remington Purdy, president Alger Shelden, Mrs. Charles T. Ellis, treasurer Paul Moreland (standing, left), assistant treasurer Richard Huegli, Ralph Netting, Ernst Kanzler, Vincent DePetris, Earl Heenan Jr., Mrs. Charles A. Dean, and Norbert Neff. Not pictured were vice president John Kenower, secretary Mrs. H. Goebel, Mrs. Charles B. Lord, and Leo Fitzpatrick.

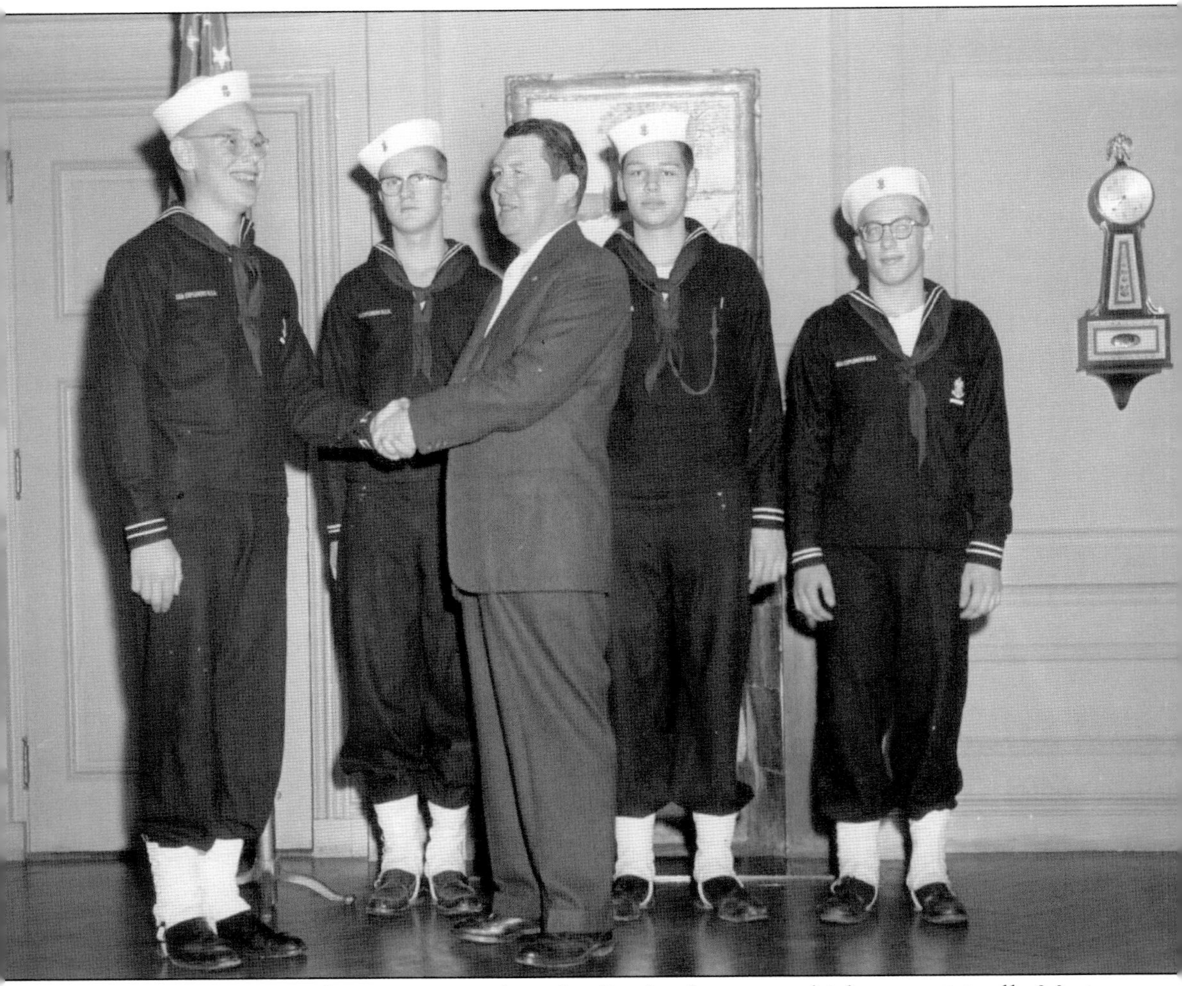

Young navy sea cadets are pictured in the Stackpole room, which was originally Marion Alger's bedroom.

The War Memorial provided many services to the community, enlisted men and women, and veterans. Red Cross blood drives like these were held annually. In recent years, the center has organized supply drives and letter writing campaigns to those stationed overseas. Today the center has numerous projects and exhibits to recognize Grosse Pointe veterans.

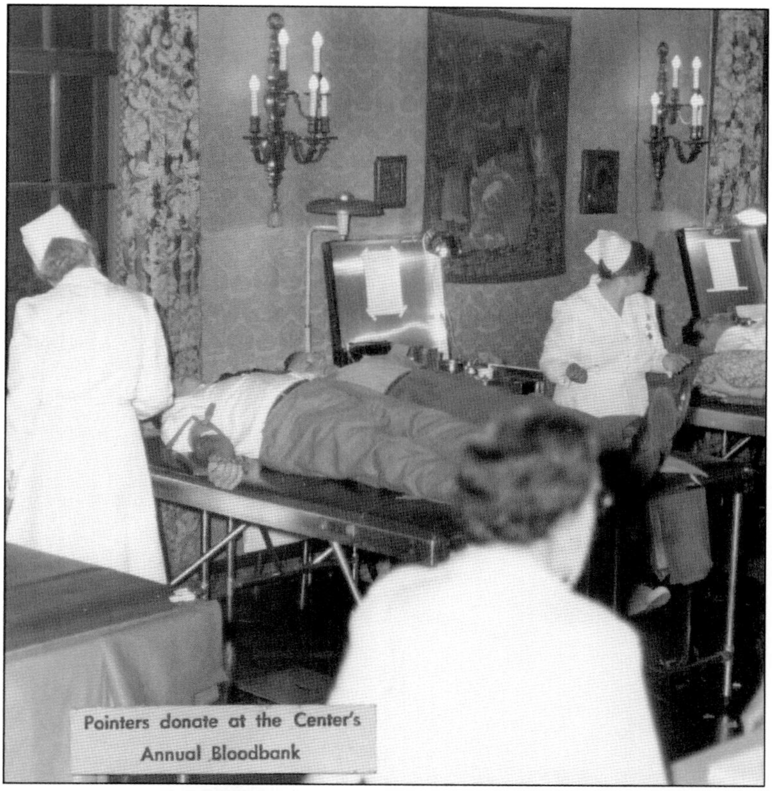

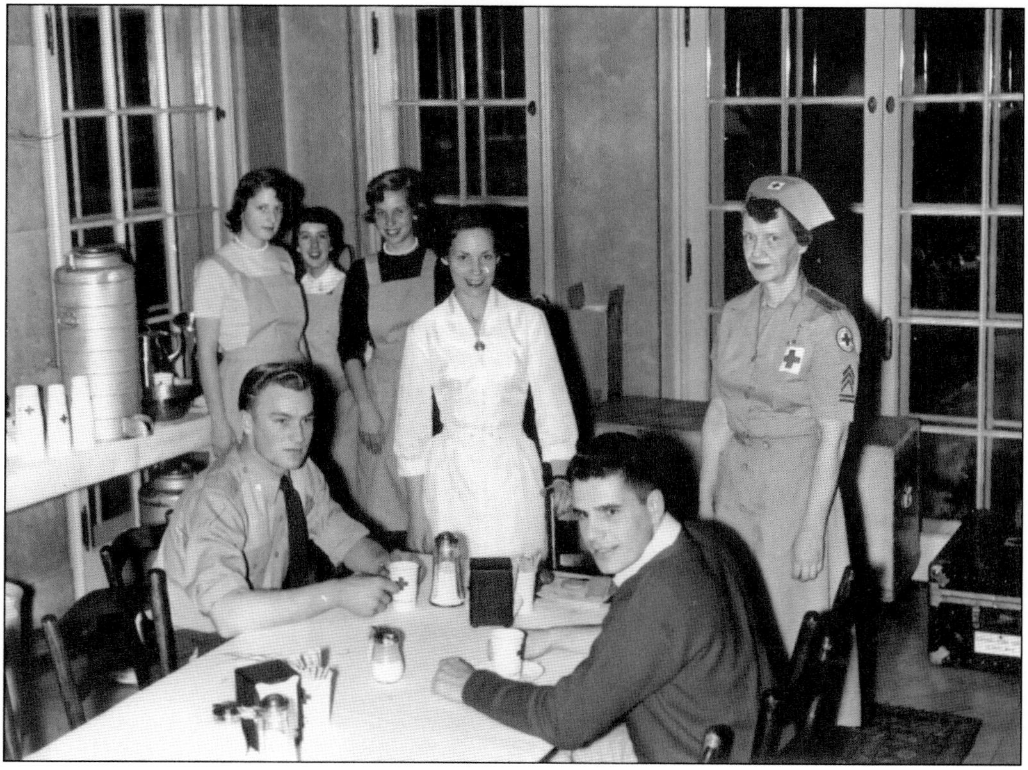

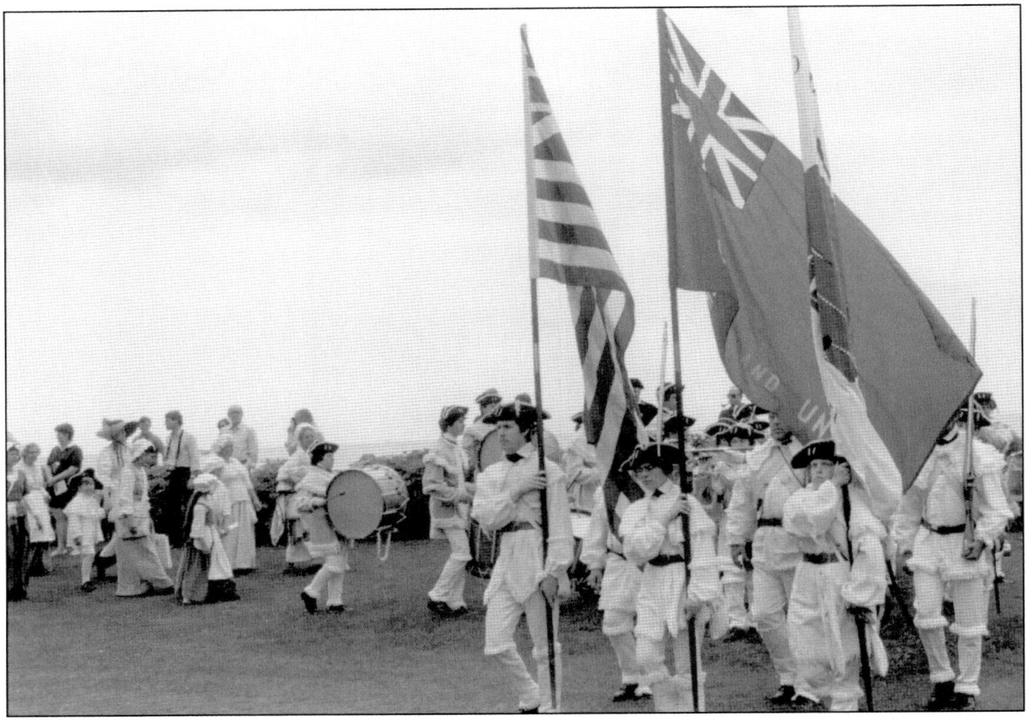

Historic reenactments, like this one of the British troops that likely marched on this very spot in the 1700s, still take place periodically on the grounds of the War Memorial.

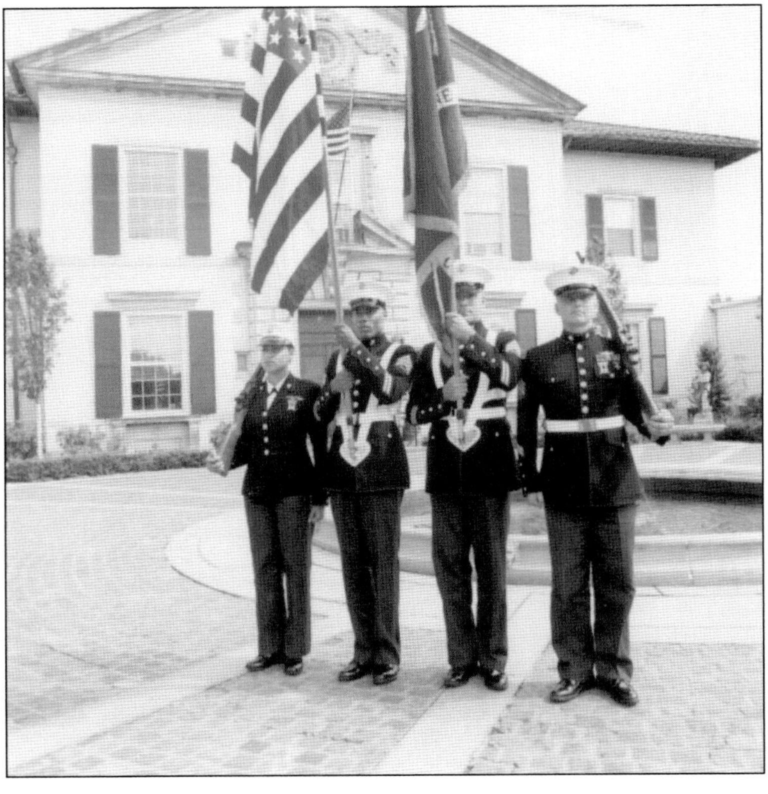

The decades-old mission of the Grosse Pointe War Memorial continues today: "Honoring those who served our country in the Armed Forces, the War Memorial provides educational, cultural, civic and patriotic programs, services and facilities to enrich the lives of the community."

Seven

Honoring, Enlightening, and Entertaining

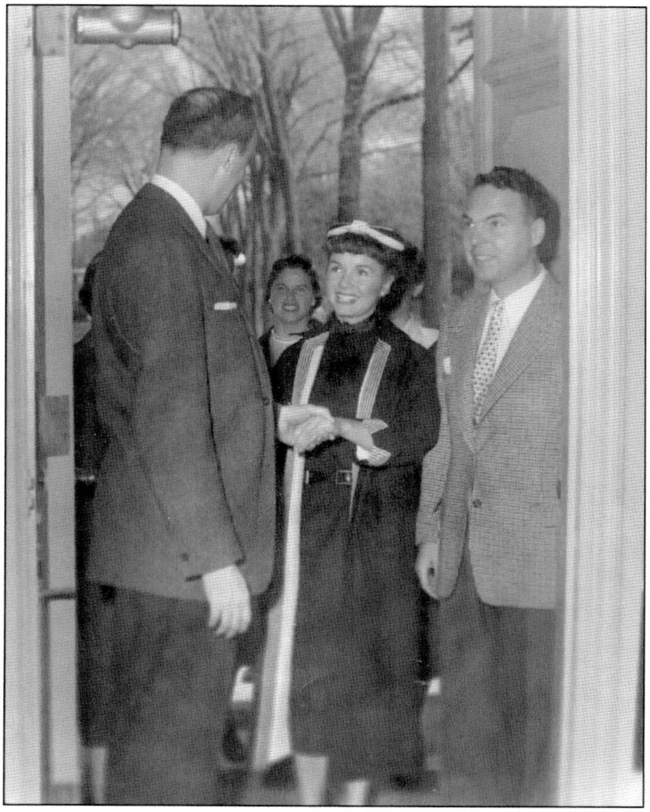

Film star Debbie Reynolds is welcomed to the Grosse Pointe War Memorial. Reynolds was the guest of Grosse Pointe travel agent and teacher Chet Sampson (right), who organized legendary trips to Hollywood for local high school students in the 1950s and 1960s.

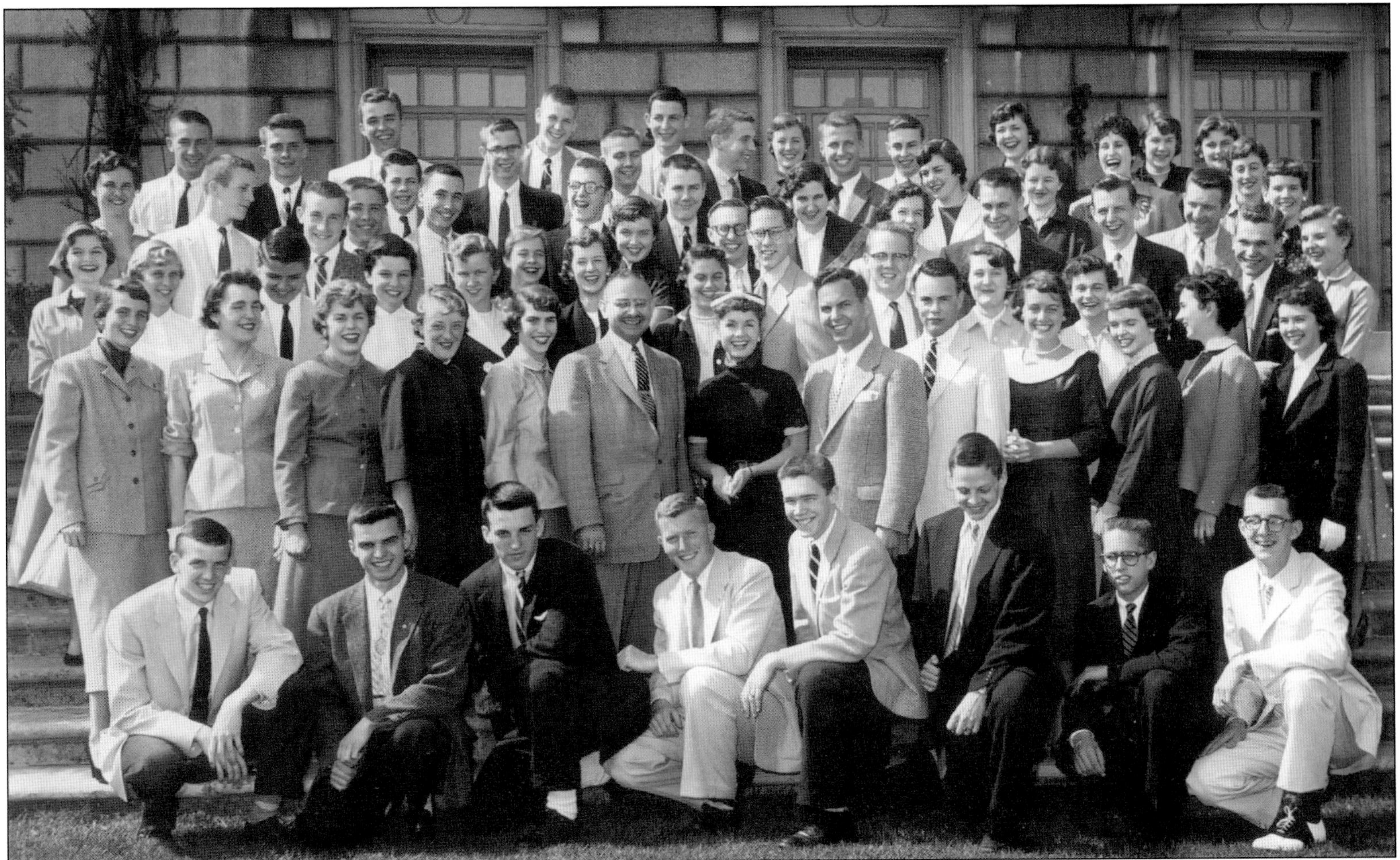

Debbie Reynolds is surrounded by adoring admirers on the terrace steps of the War Memorial. She was in town with her then-husband, Eddie Fisher, to attend the dedication of the new gymnasium/auditorium at Grosse Pointe High School in 1954.

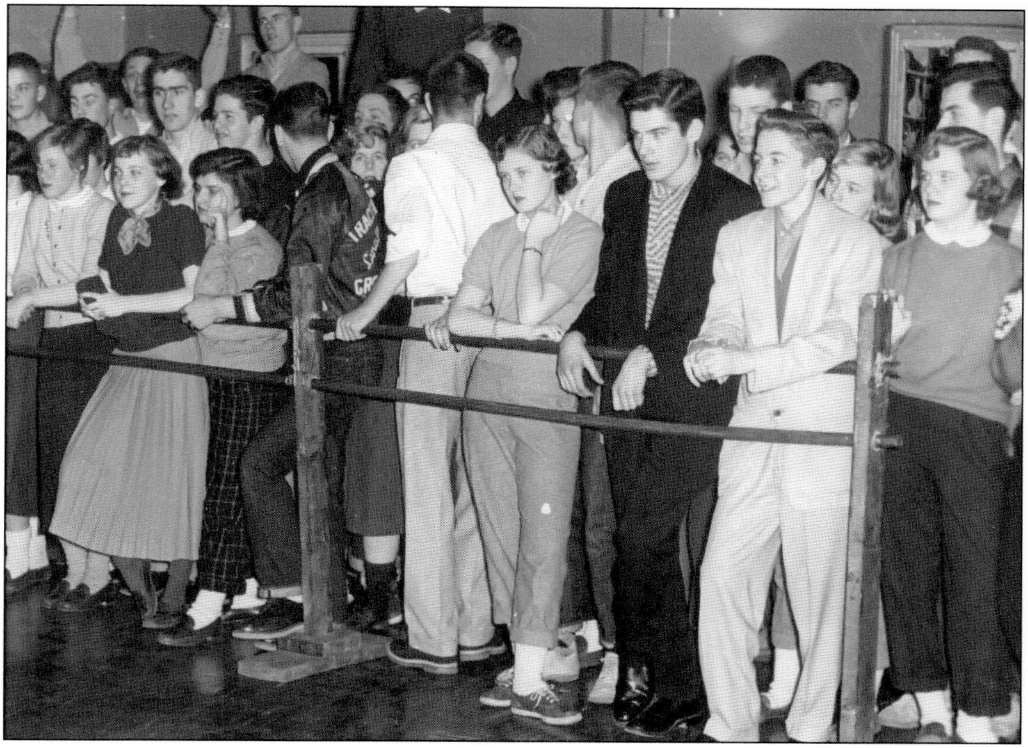

Fans wait in line to see movie star Debbie Reynolds.

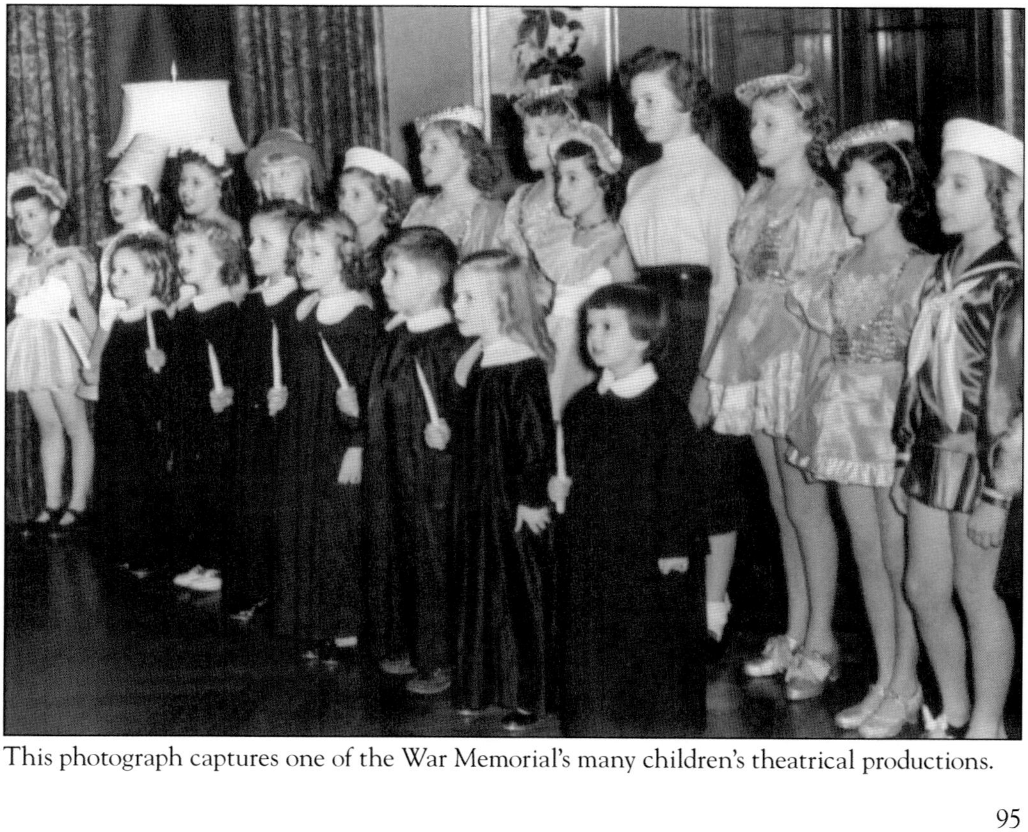

This photograph captures one of the War Memorial's many children's theatrical productions.

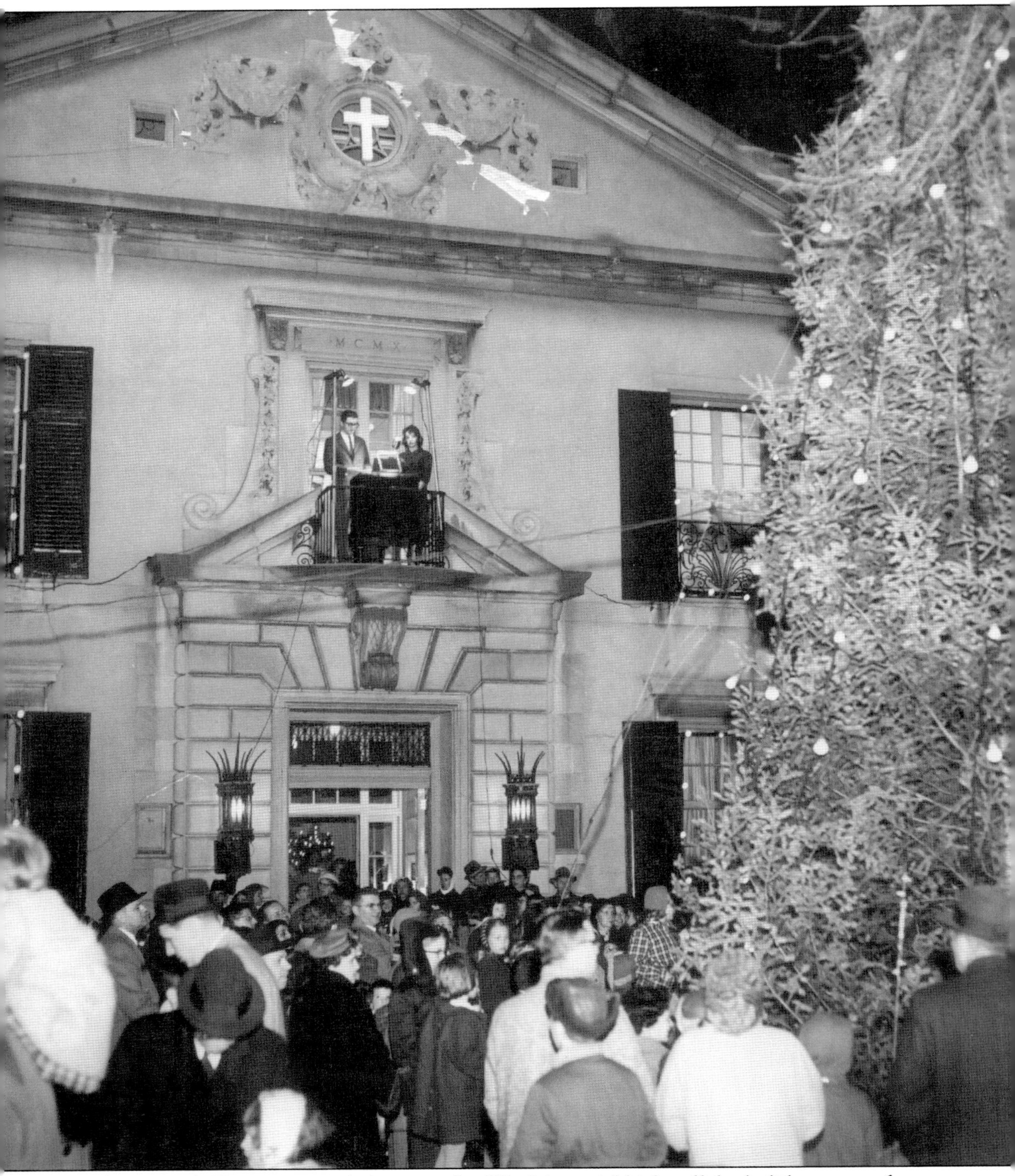

The annual Christmas tree lighting at the War Memorial kicks off the holiday season for many residents. It is a tradition that continues today.

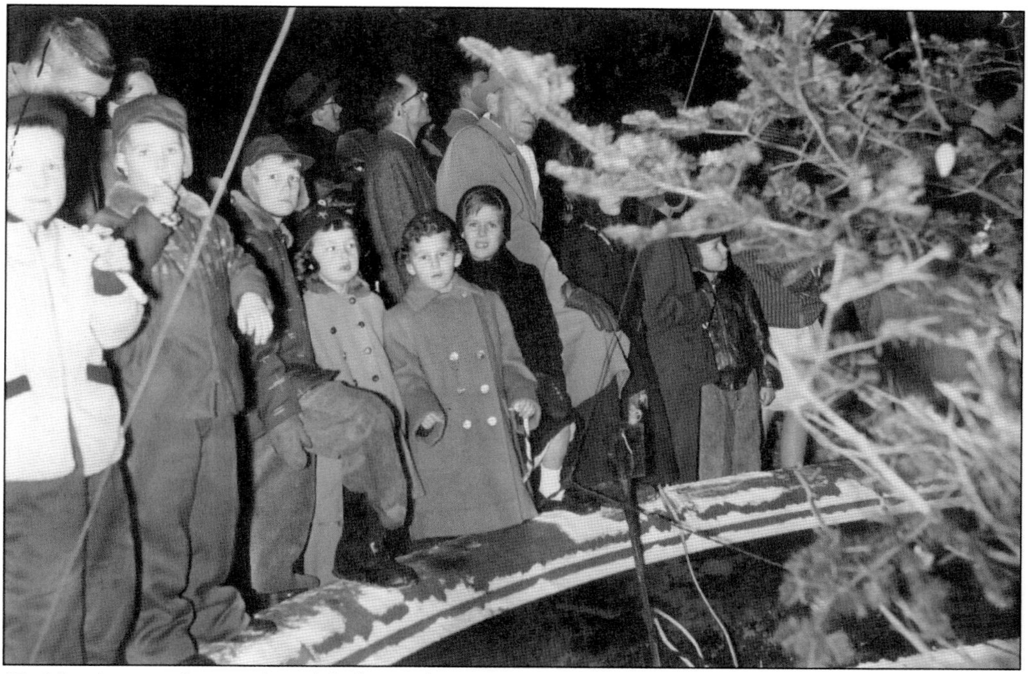

Children's eyes glow as they delight in the radiant Christmas tree.

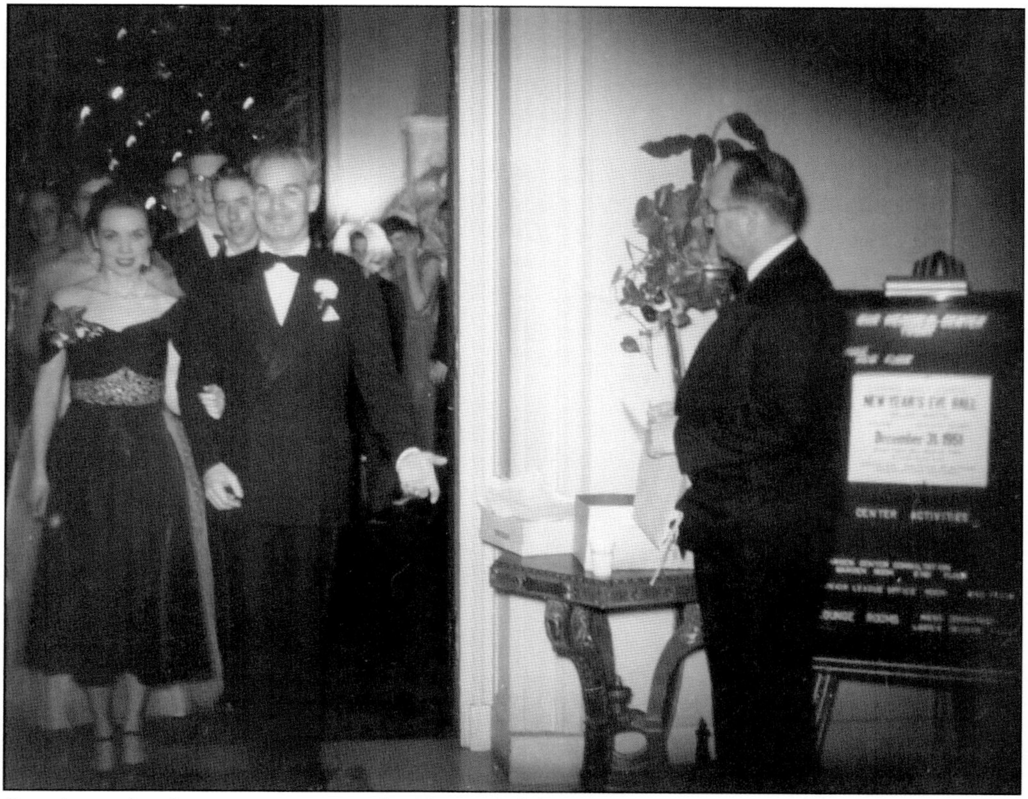

Couples make their appearance at the Young Adult New Year's Eve Ball, 1951.

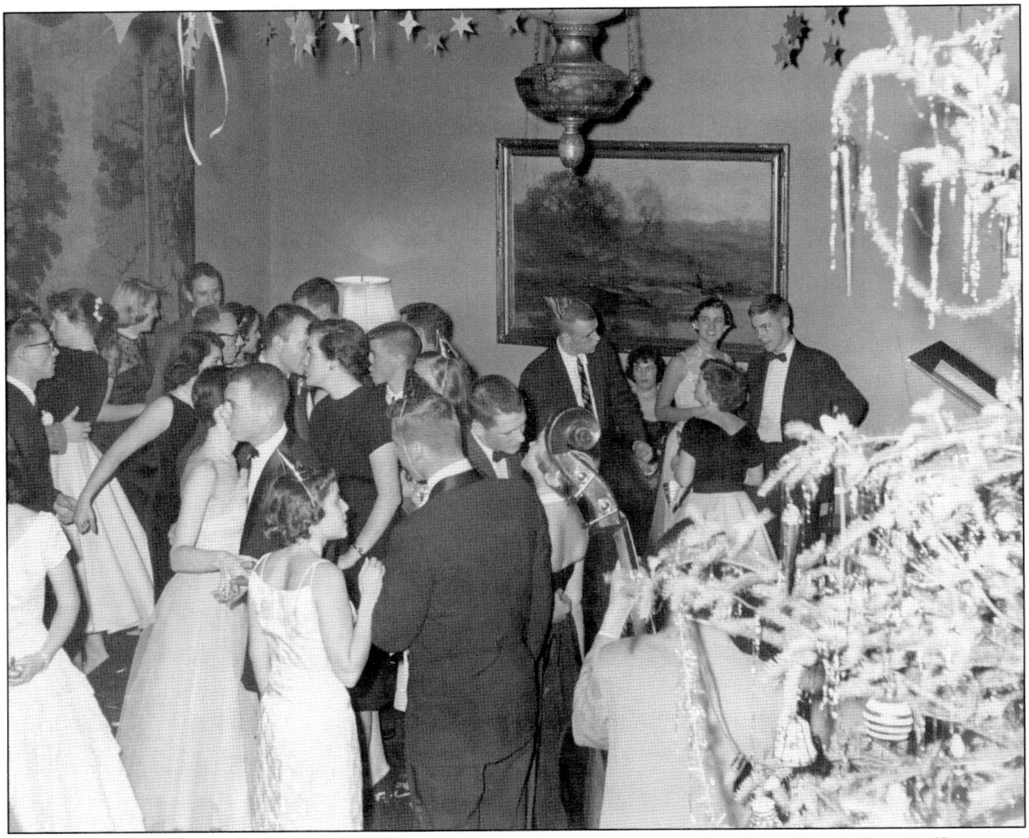

Party hats and a decorated tree add to the festive atmosphere at the New Year's Eve Ball.

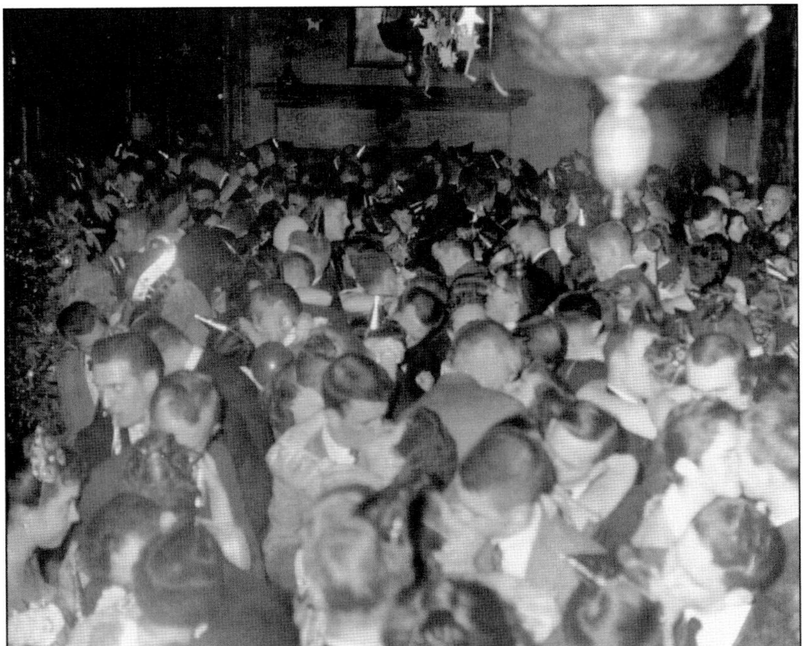

Happy New Year! Dancers celebrate at midnight with a kiss.

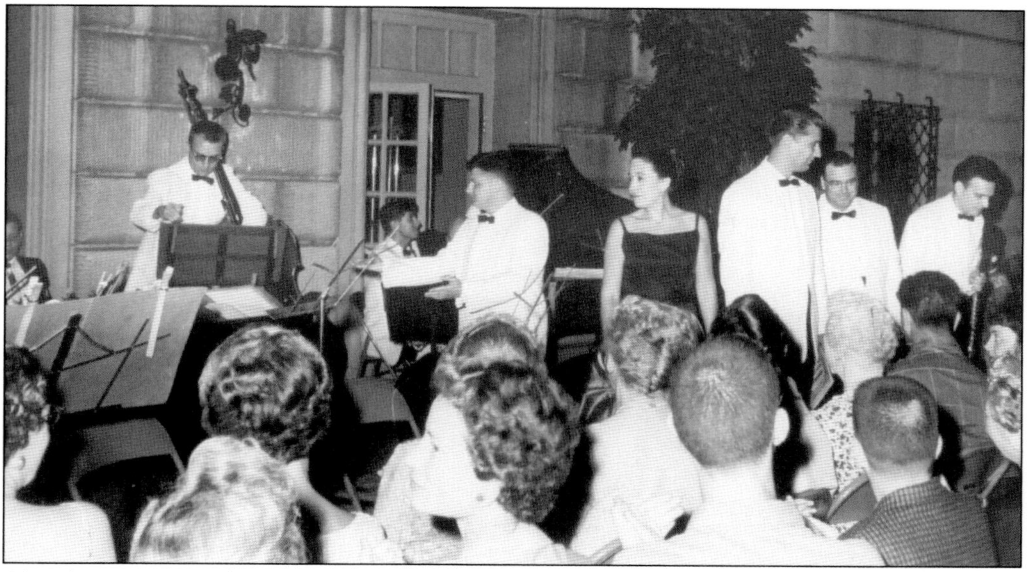

Chamber musicians from the Detroit Symphony Orchestra perform at the second season of the Grosse Pointe Summer Music Festival in 1959. The concert took place on the terrace at the War Memorial.

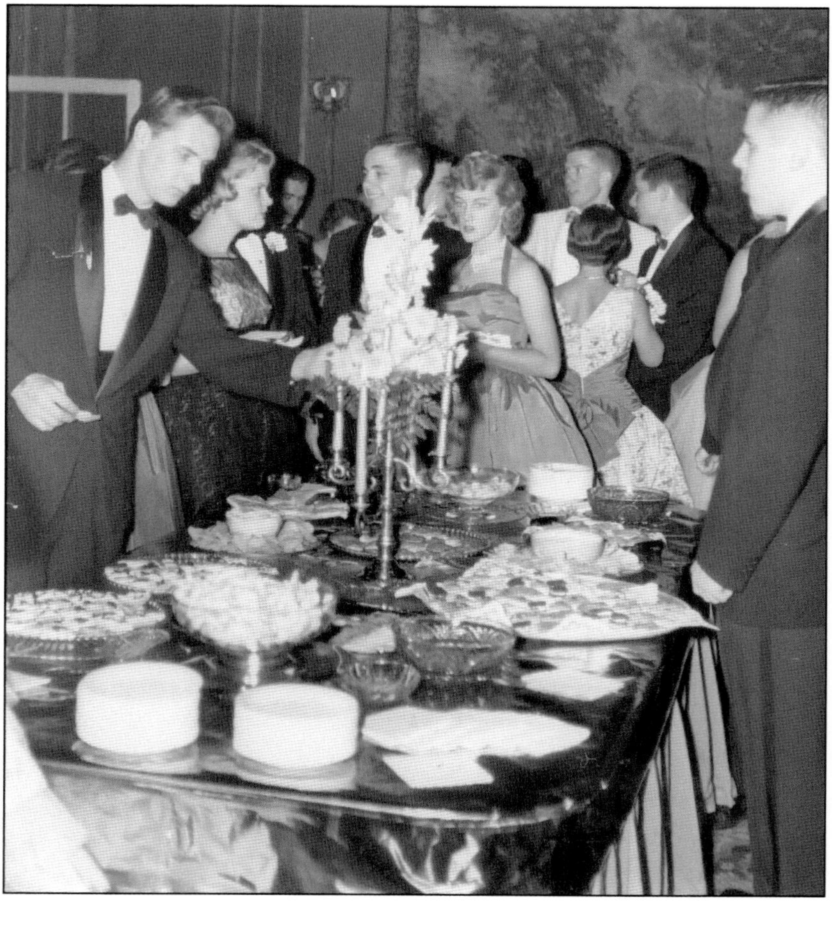

Guests sample the sumptuous spread at a formal affair.

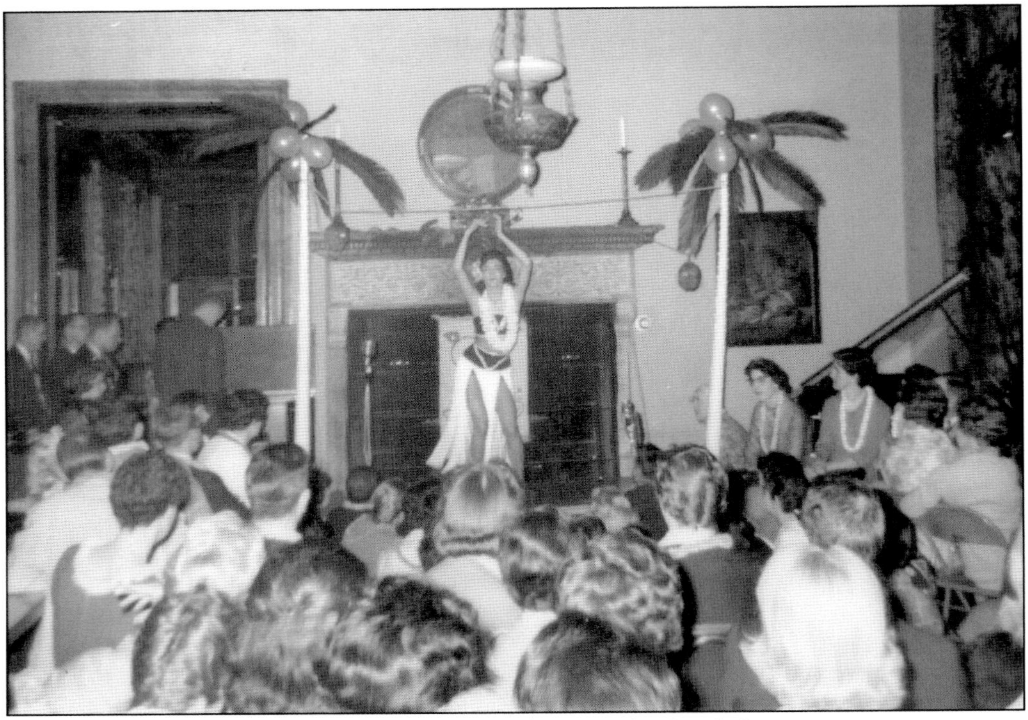

A dancer illustrates the proper way to do the Hula at a 1950s South Seas party.

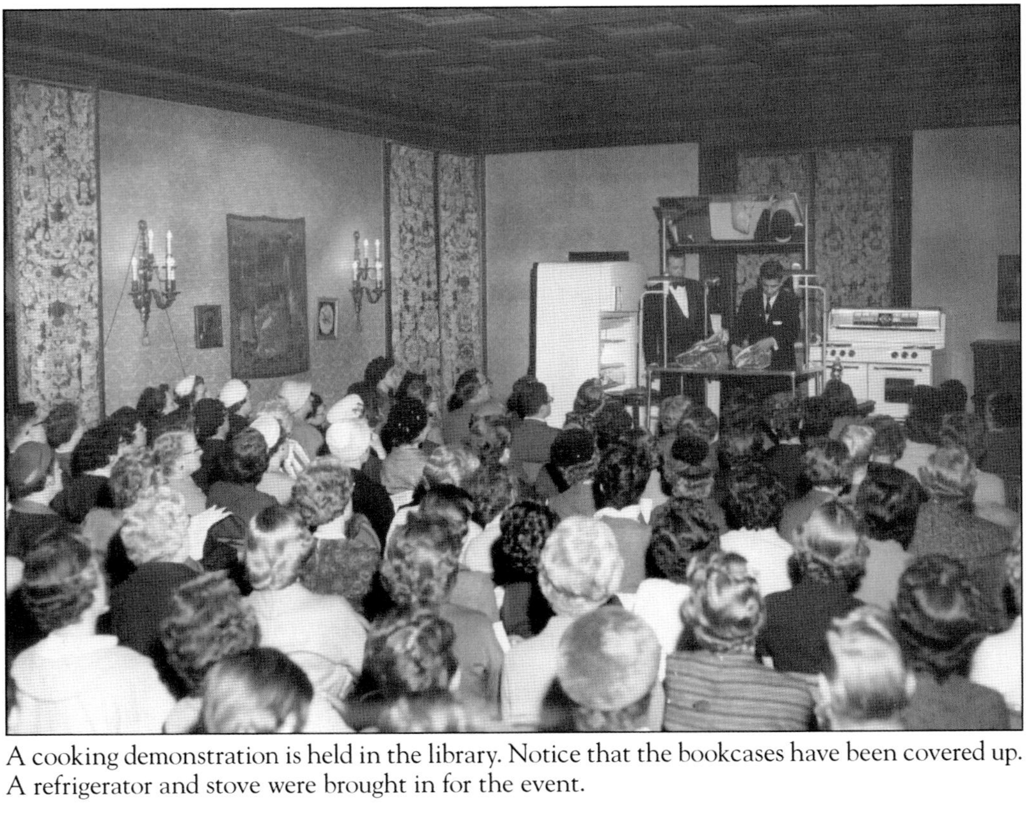

A cooking demonstration is held in the library. Notice that the bookcases have been covered up. A refrigerator and stove were brought in for the event.

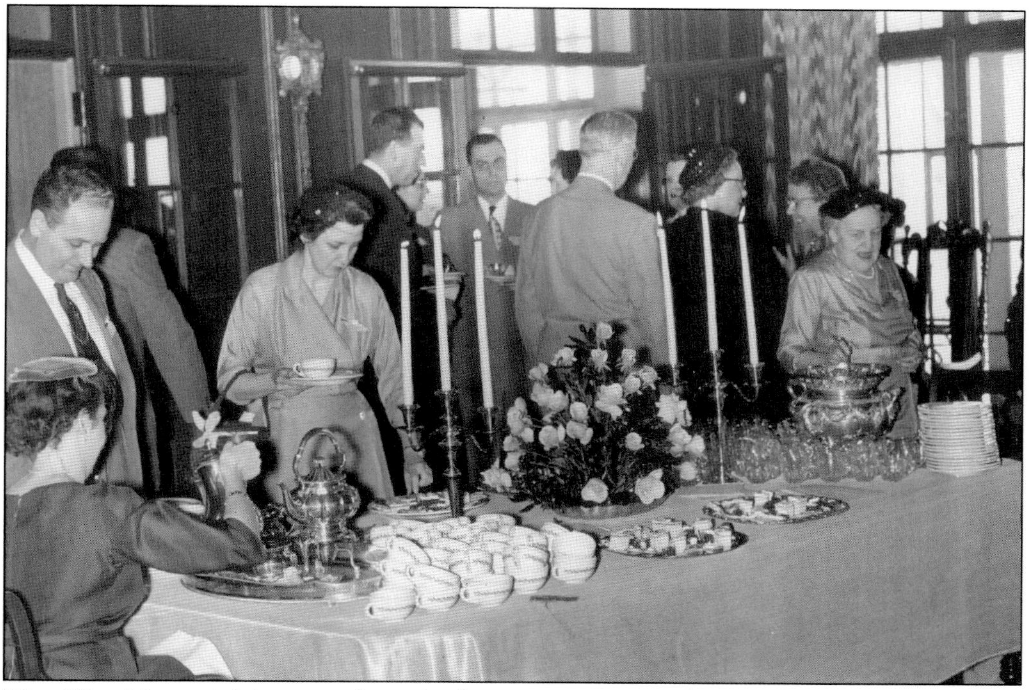

The War Memorial hosts a formal afternoon tea complete with finger sandwiches and petit fours.

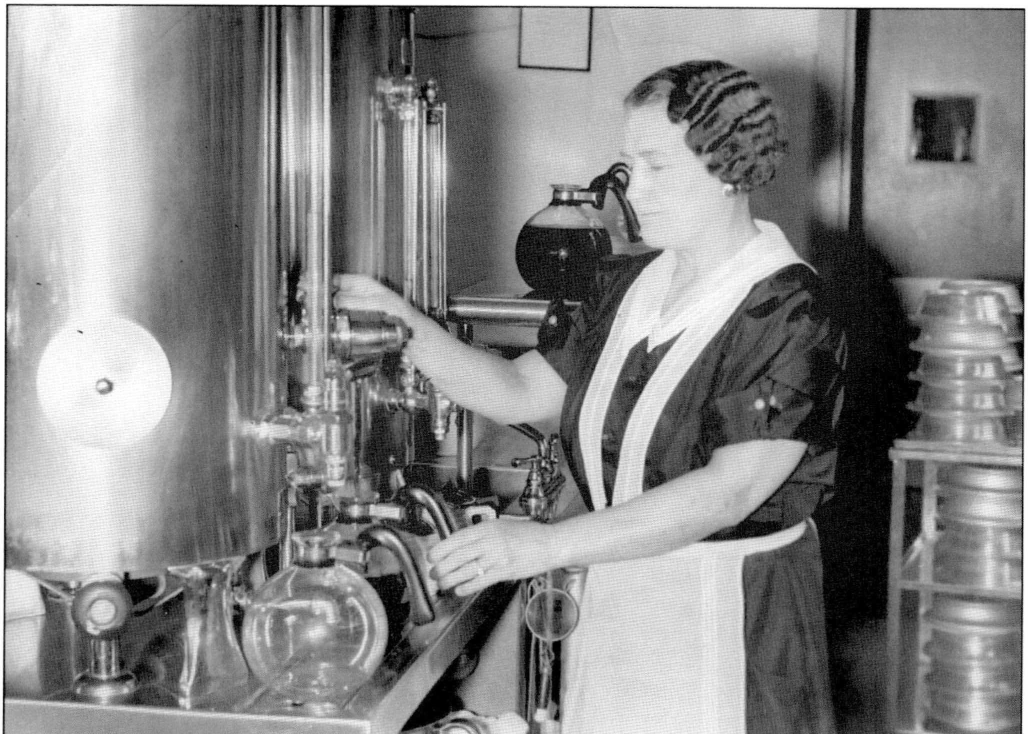

Faithful kitchen staff members have been a staple at the War Memorial. Mildred Marx took care of the center's guests for decades.

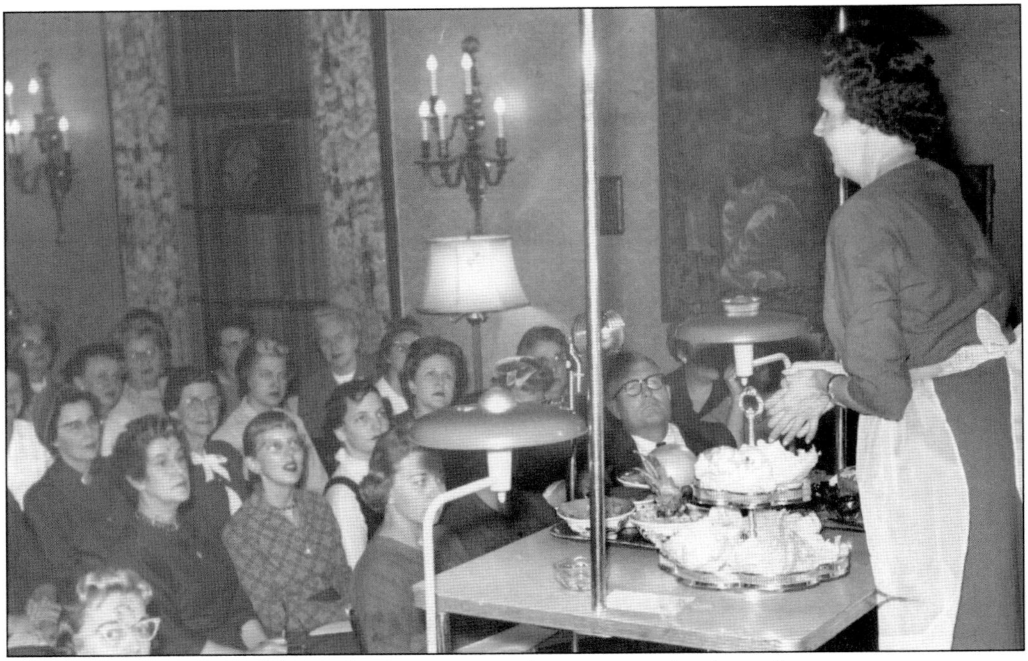

Women (and a few men) learn the finer points of creating perfect hors d'oeuvres.

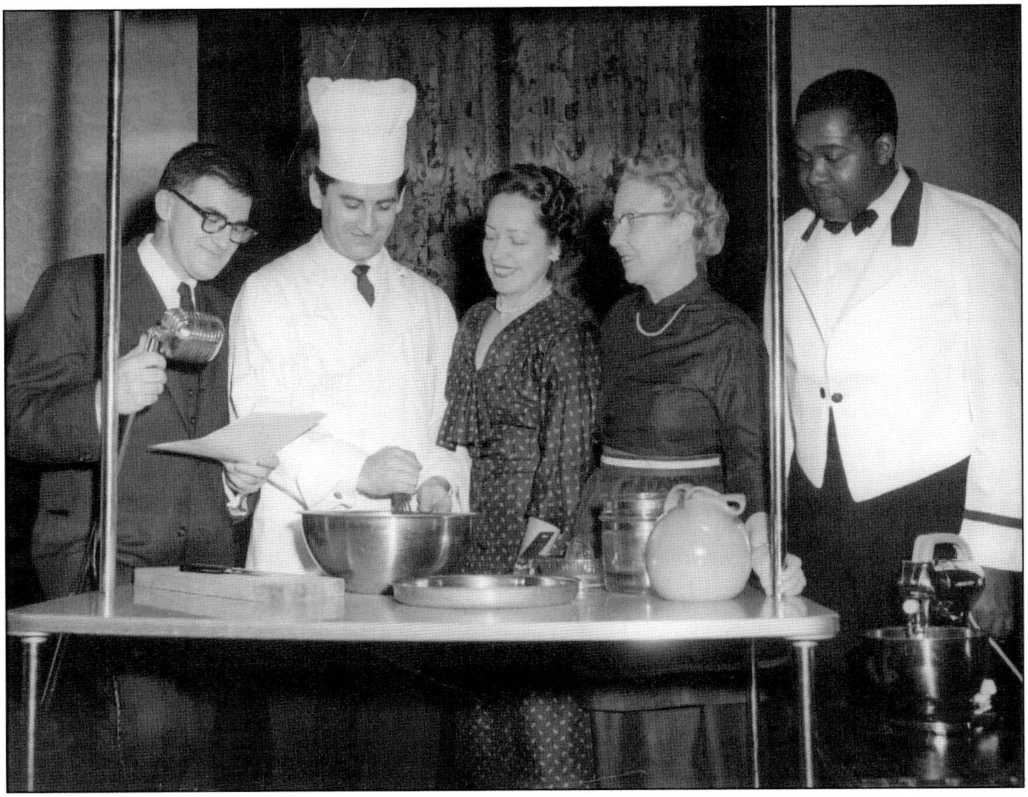

The staff at the War Memorial, from chefs to organizers to servers, provide excellent service to the community.

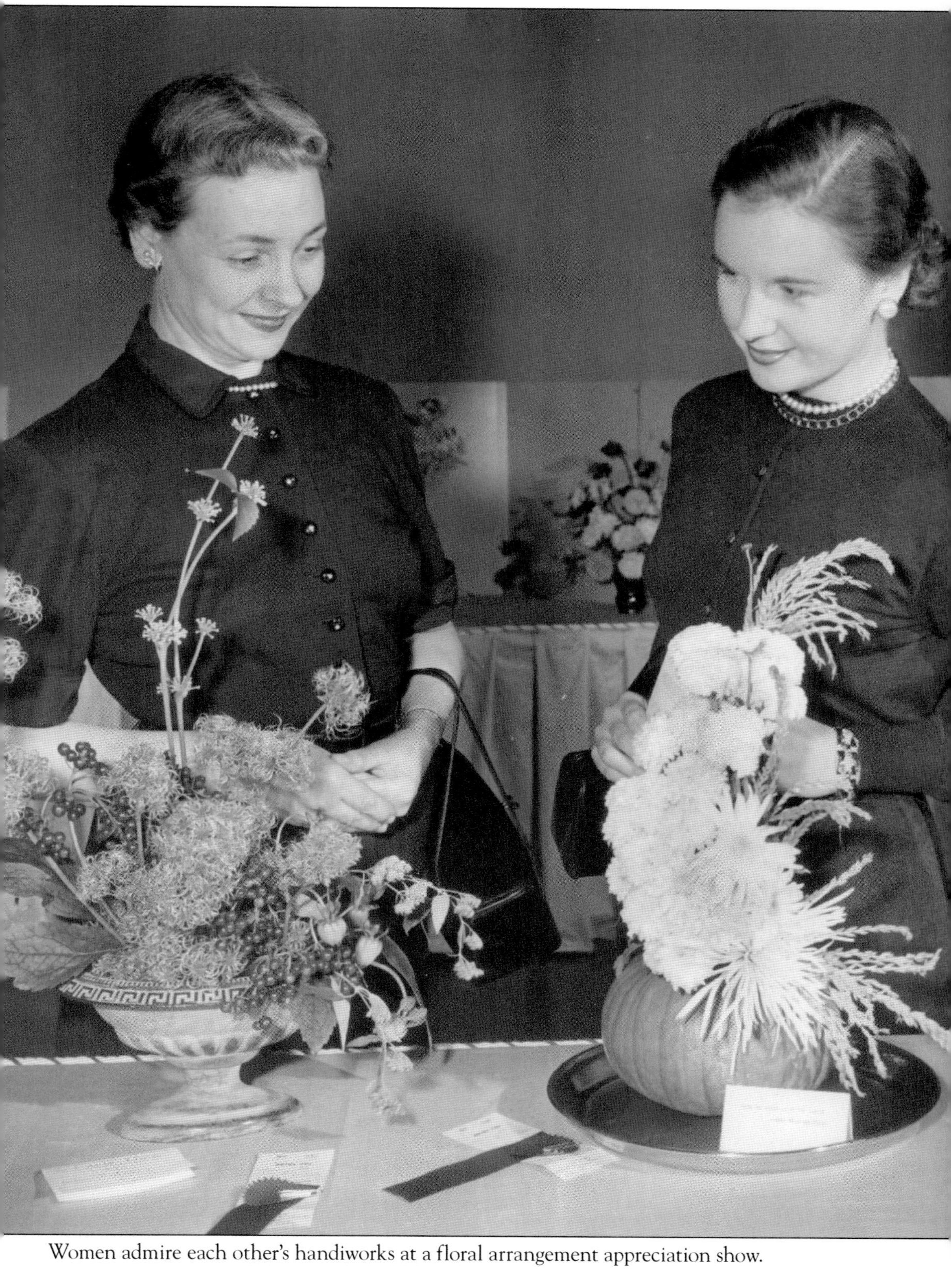

Women admire each other's handiworks at a floral arrangement appreciation show.

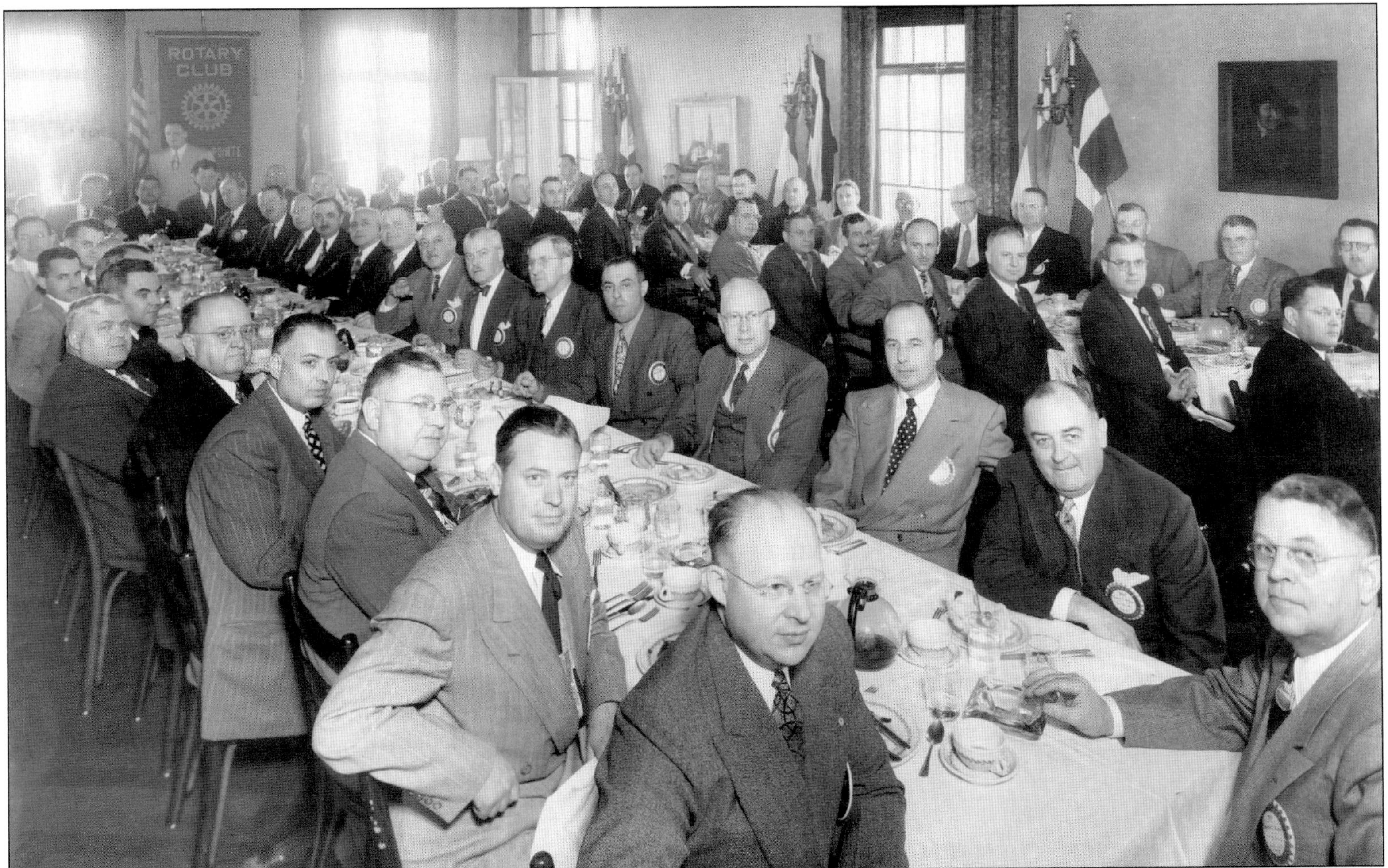

The Rotary Club of Grosse Pointe has been meeting at the War Memorial since the early 1950s.

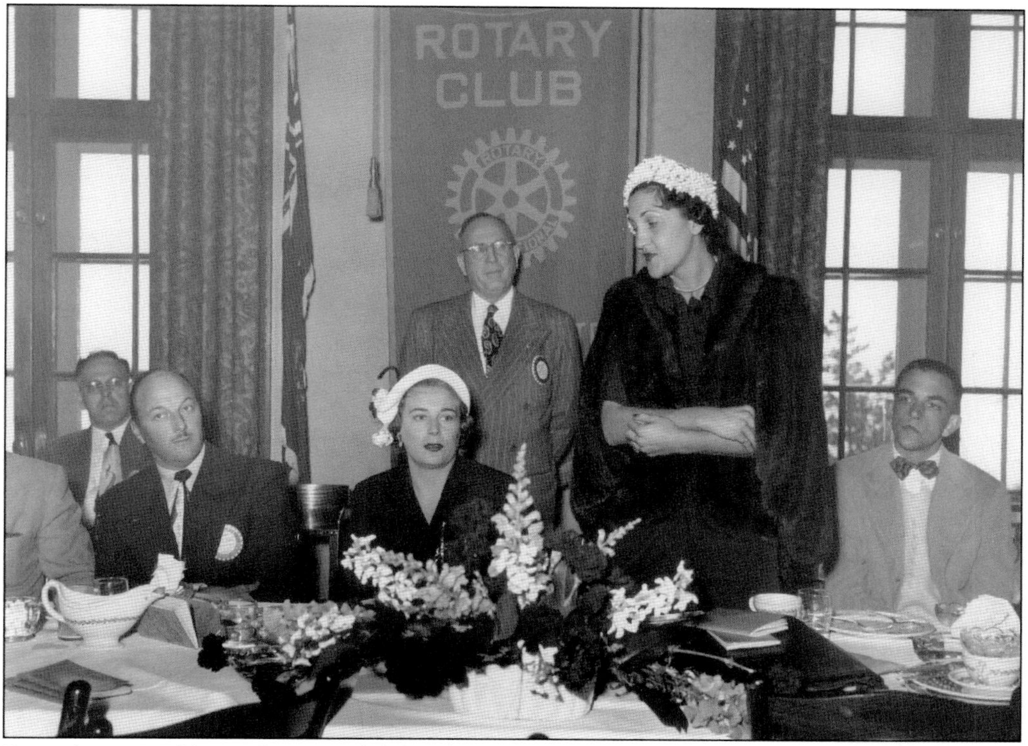

Special guests address a Rotary Club luncheon.

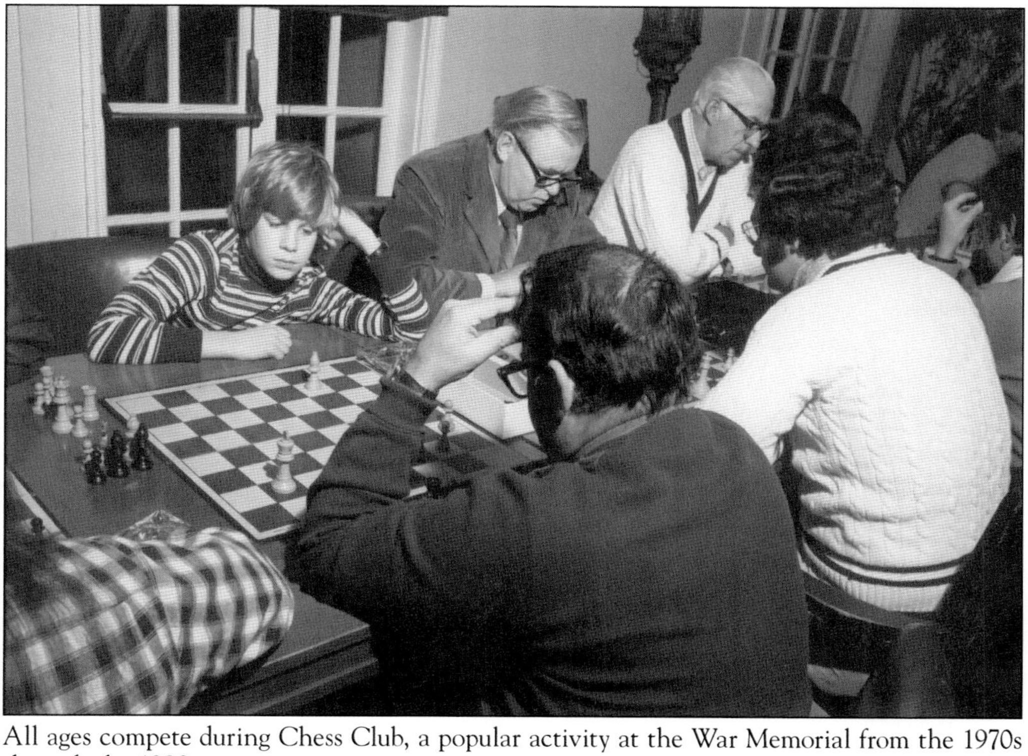

All ages compete during Chess Club, a popular activity at the War Memorial from the 1970s through the 1990s.

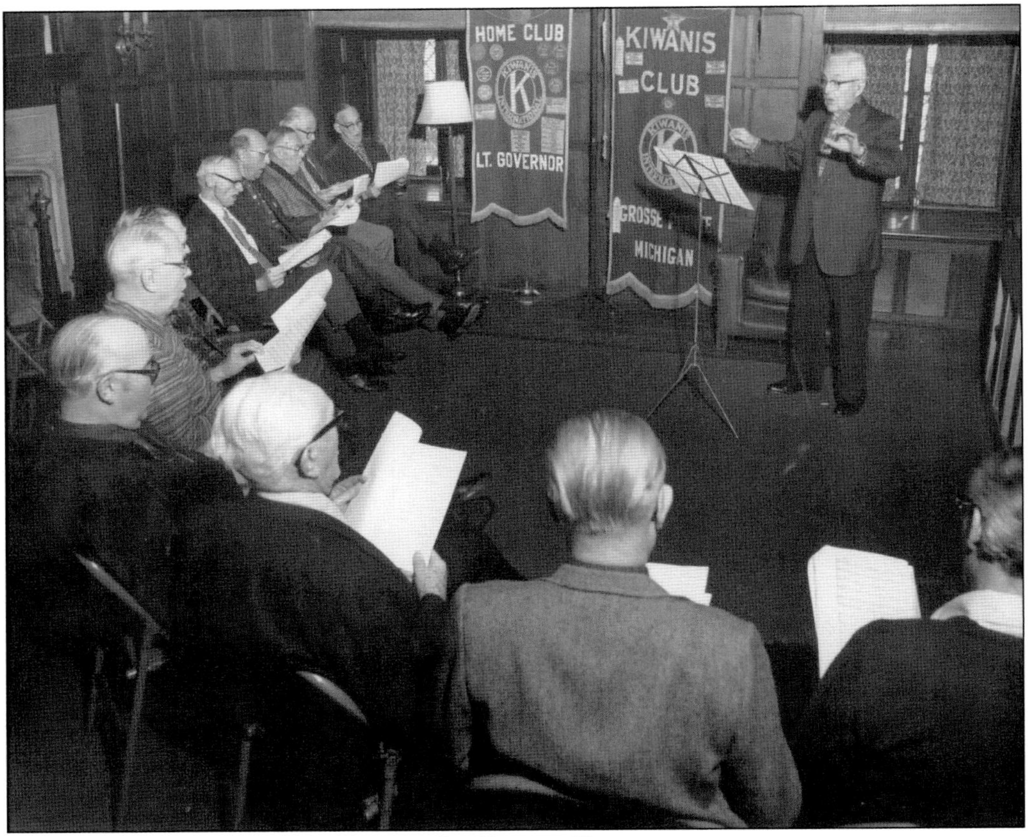

Kiwanis Club members croon a tune in the Veterans Room.

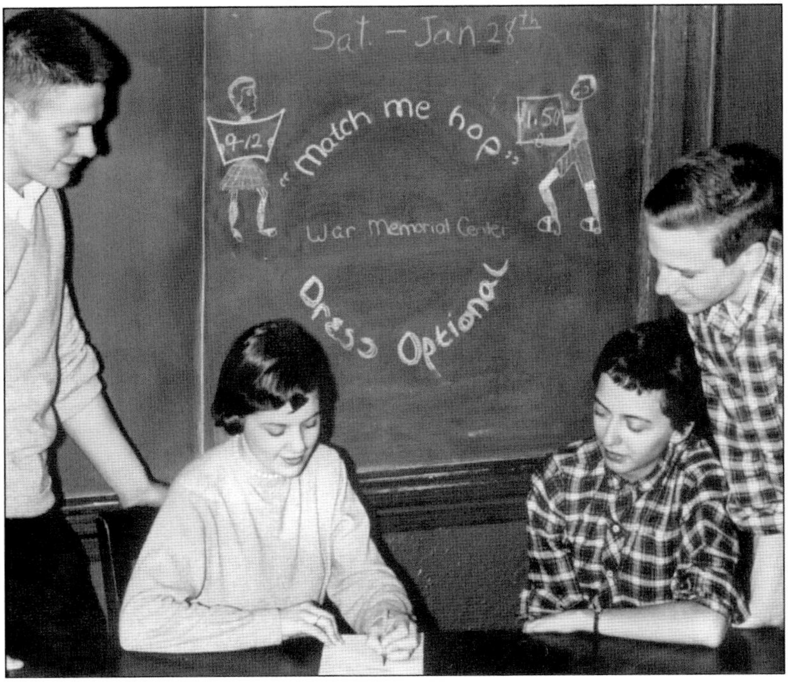

Junior high schoolers organize a "dress optional Match Me Hop" in the 1950s. Tickets were $1.50.

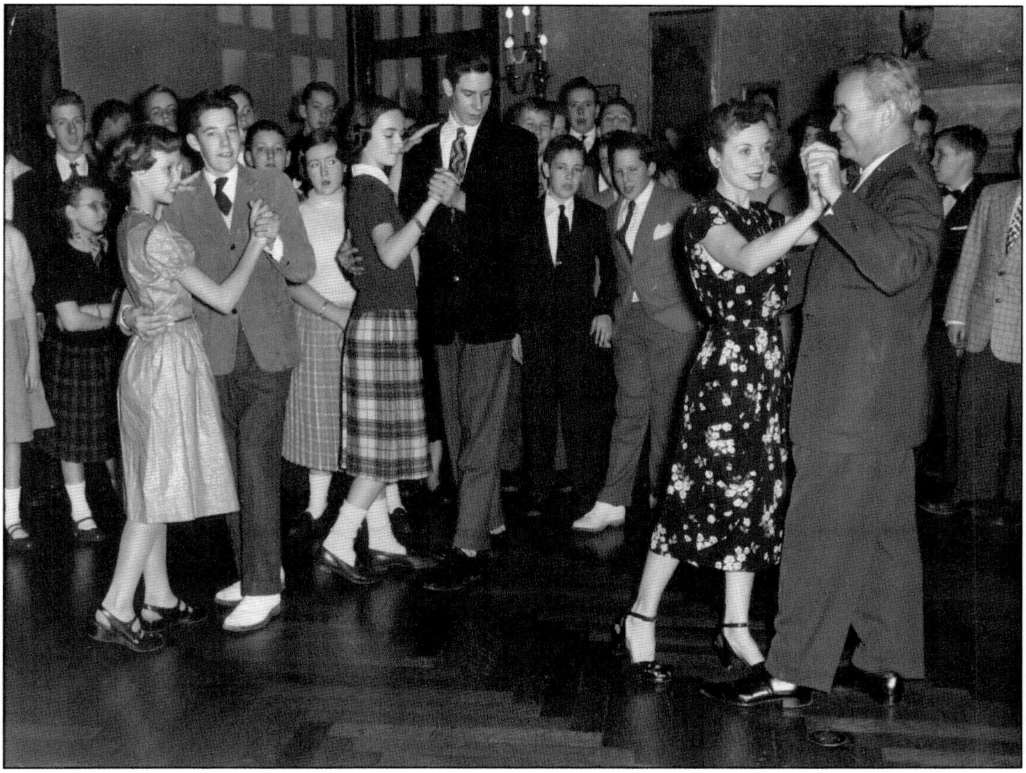

Lillian Forrest (above, right) instructs the younger set in the magic of ballroom dancing. Lillian has been teaching at the War Memorial since 1963.

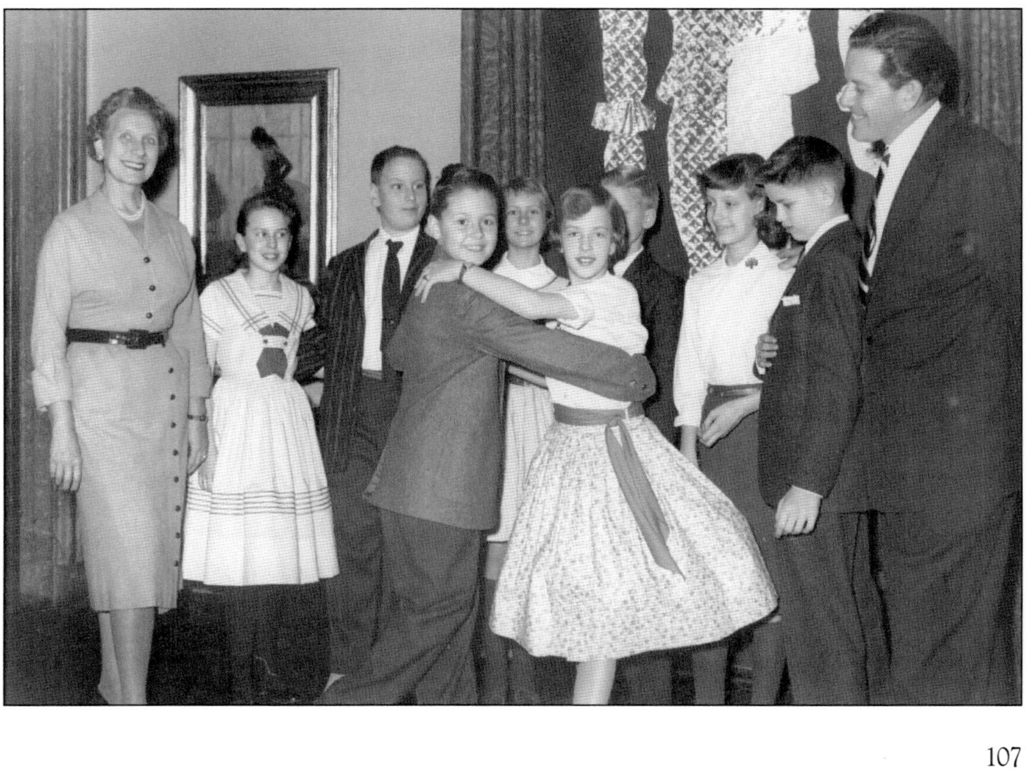

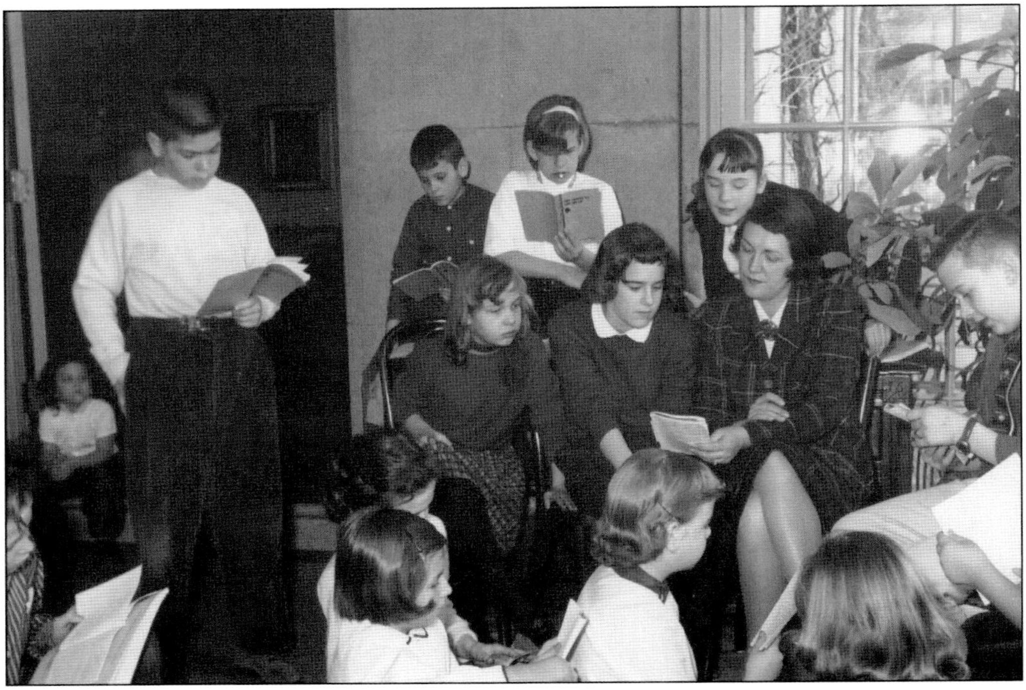

Above, renowned local director Sally Reynolds works with a group from the children's theater program. She taught for nearly 50 years. Below, local children star in an enchanting children's theater production.

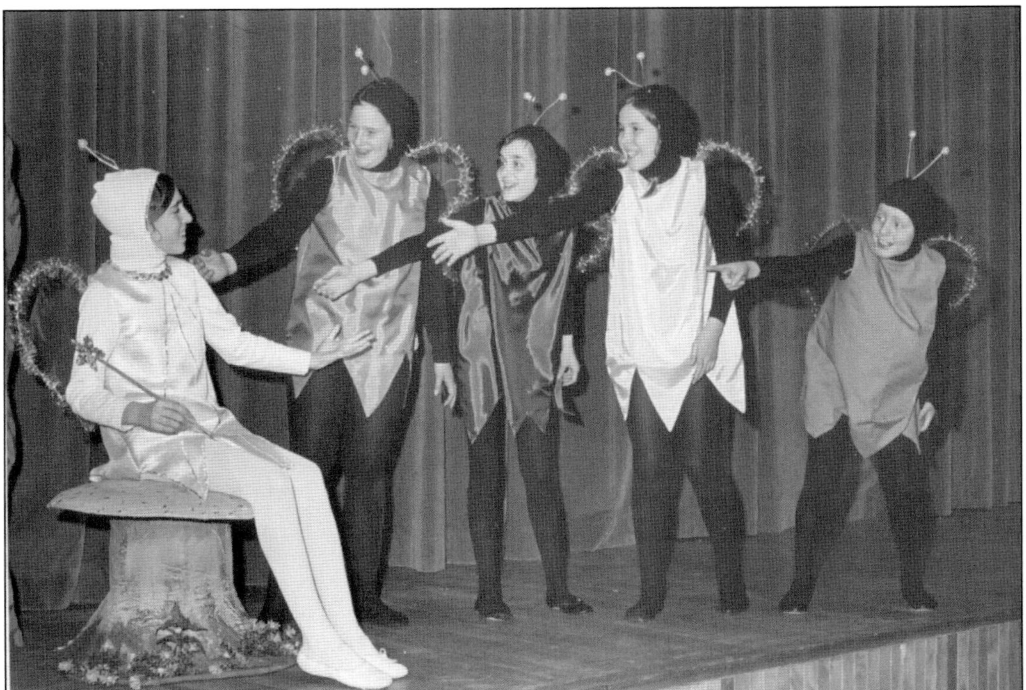

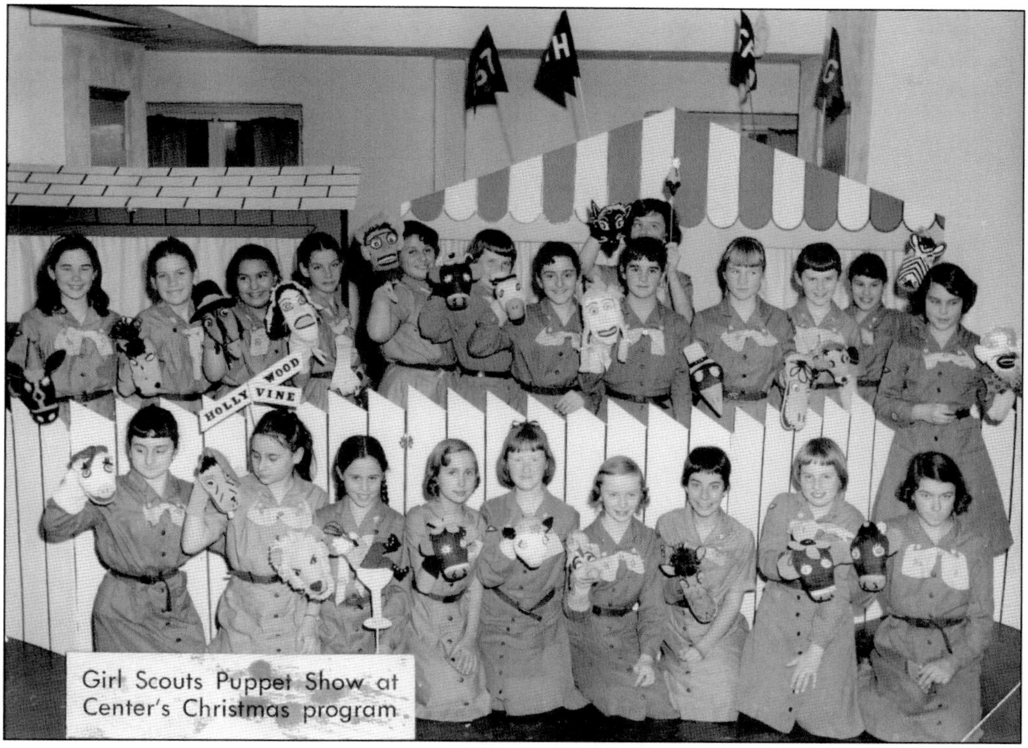

Girl Scouts perform a puppet show at the War Memorial's Christmas program.

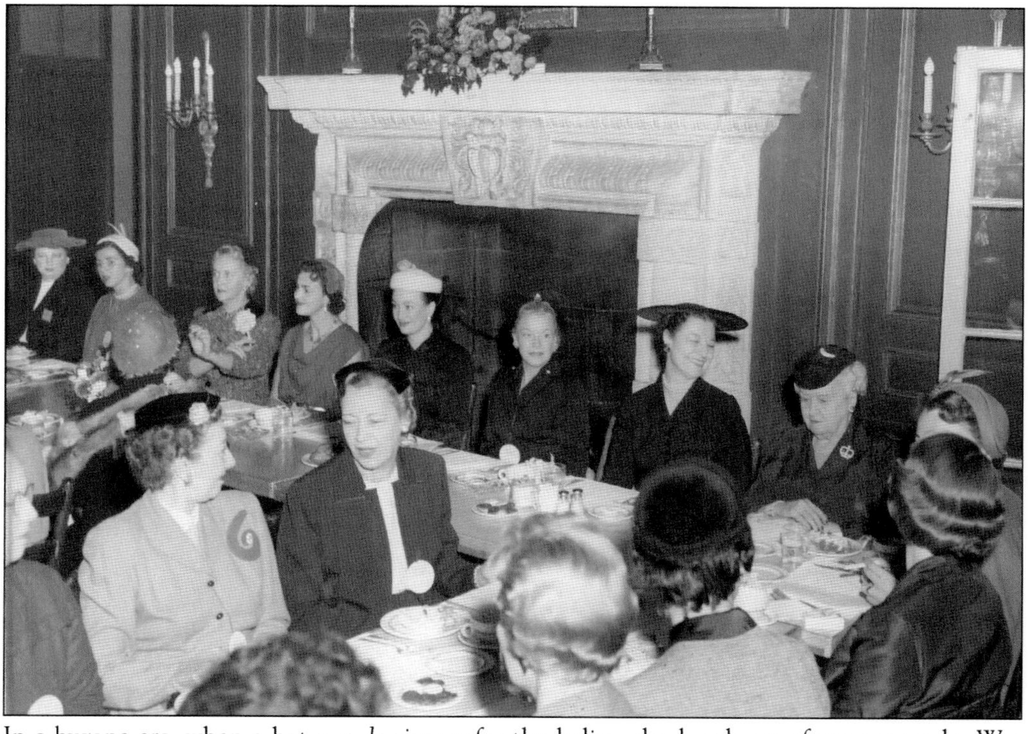

In a bygone era, when a hat was *de rigueur* for the ladies who lunch, an afternoon at the War Memorial was a special treat.

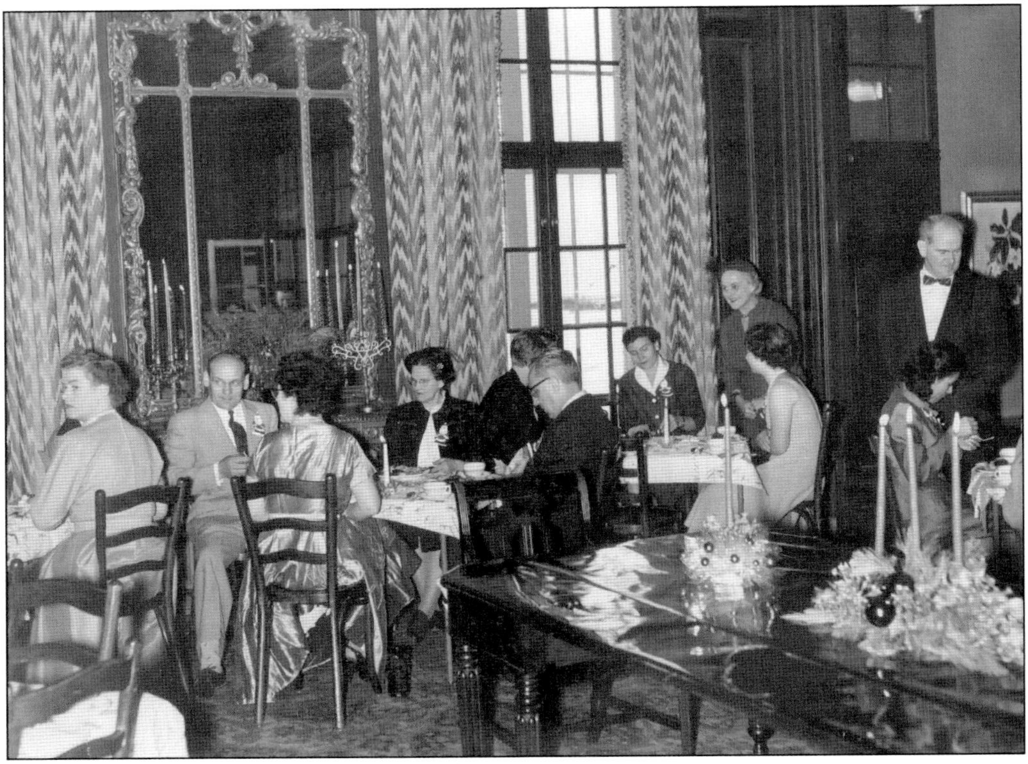

Celebrants enjoy a holiday dinner in the dining room.

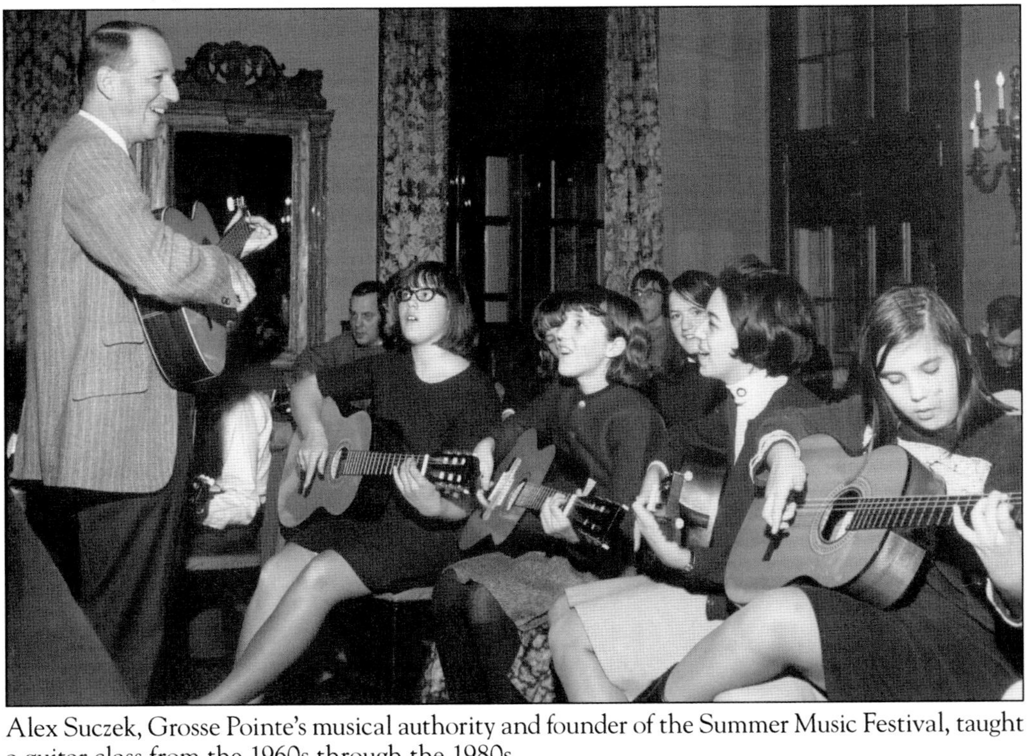

Alex Suczek, Grosse Pointe's musical authority and founder of the Summer Music Festival, taught a guitar class from the 1960s through the 1980s.

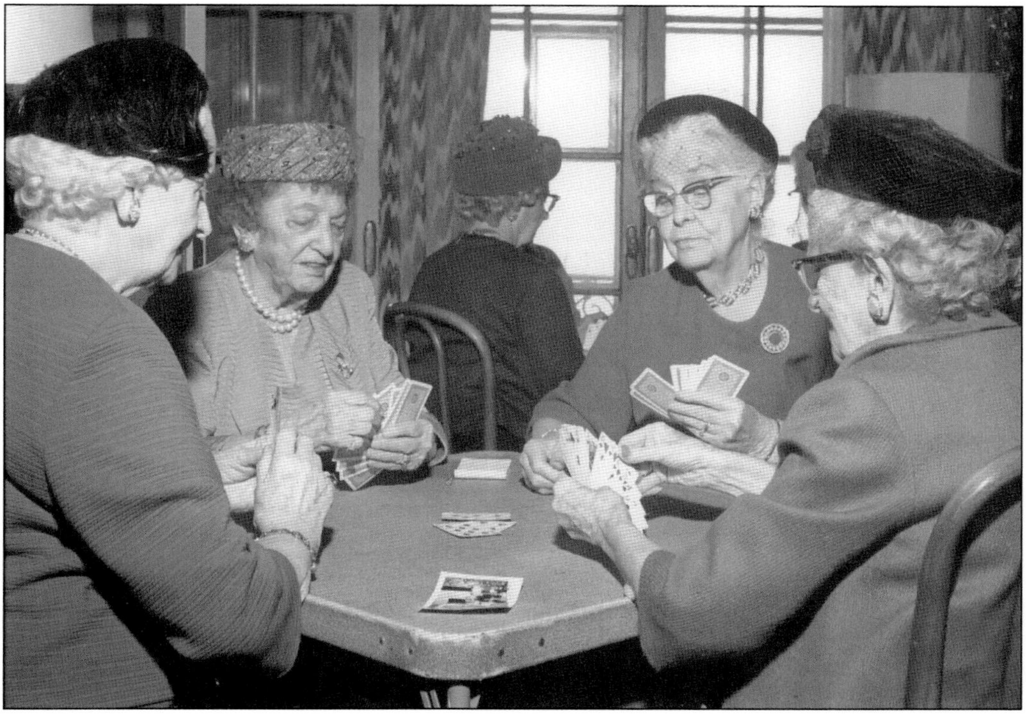

Bridge Club is a long-standing tradition at the War Memorial. The card players still meet every Monday, but now they allow men to participate.

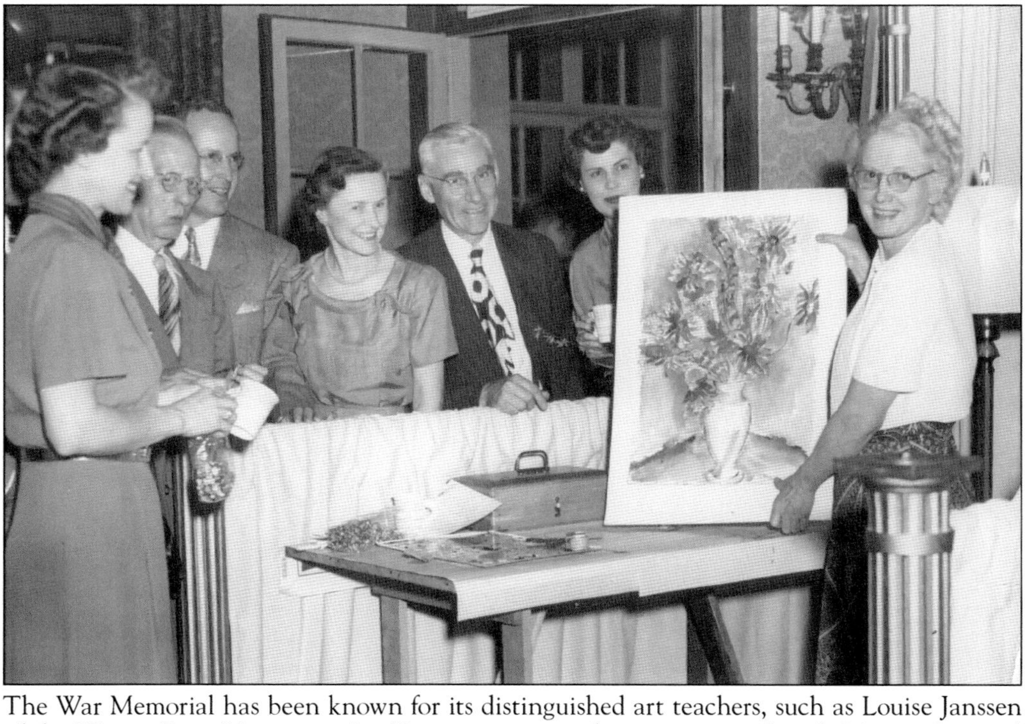

The War Memorial has been known for its distinguished art teachers, such as Louise Janssen of the Wayne State University Art Department; noted portrait artist Joseph Maniscalco; and William Bostick, former Detroit Institute of Arts administrator.

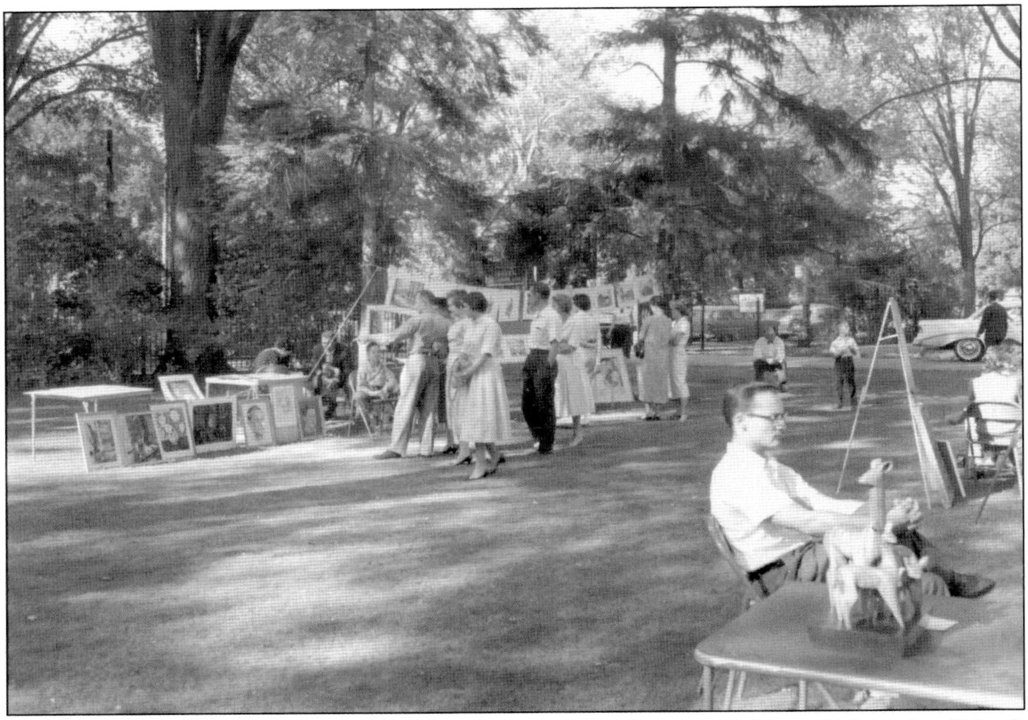

The War Memorial grounds provide a lovely setting for the annual Grosse Pointe Art Fair. A parking lot is now located on this site.

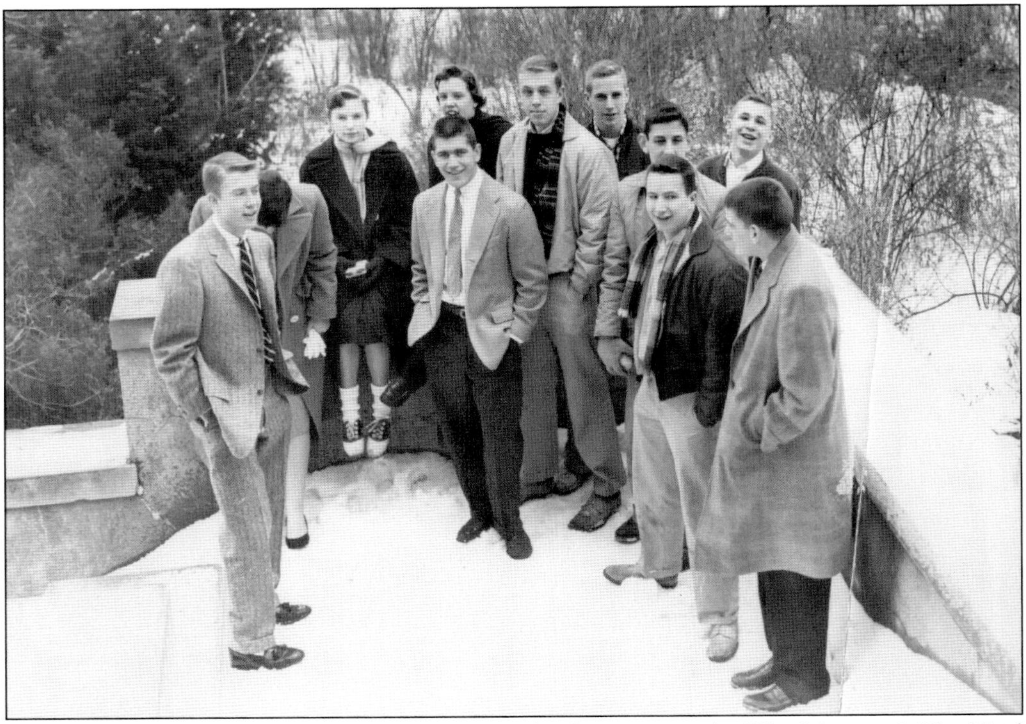

Grosse Pointe High School student government leaders meet at the War Memorial. The Trial Gardens are located behind them today.

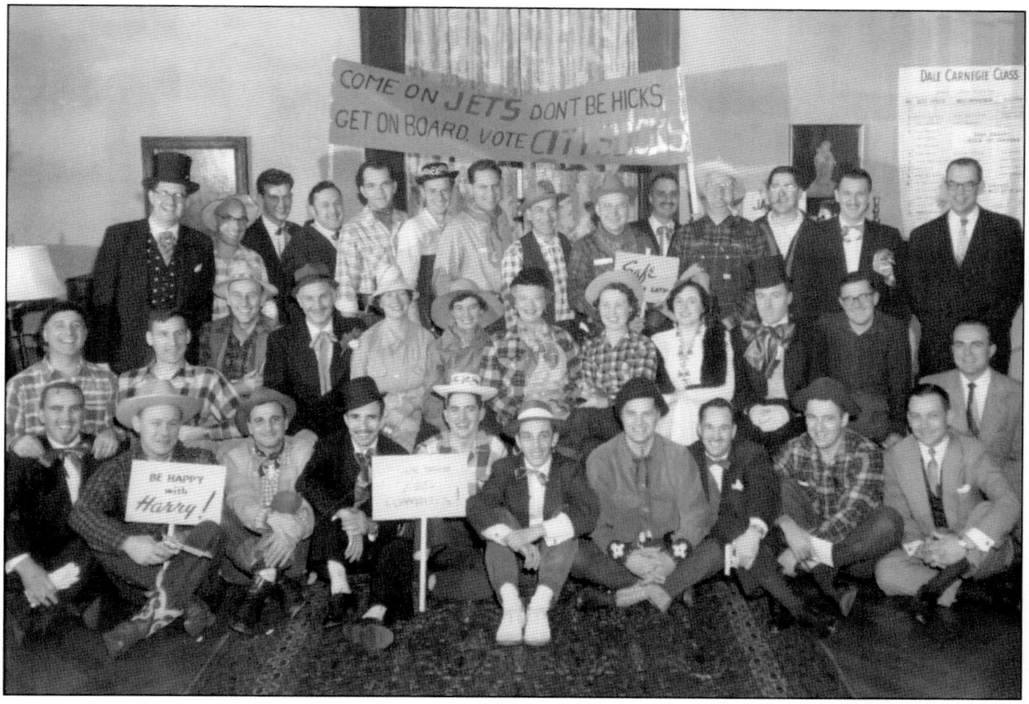

A Dale Carnegie class in public speaking helps Grosse Pointers come out of their shells.

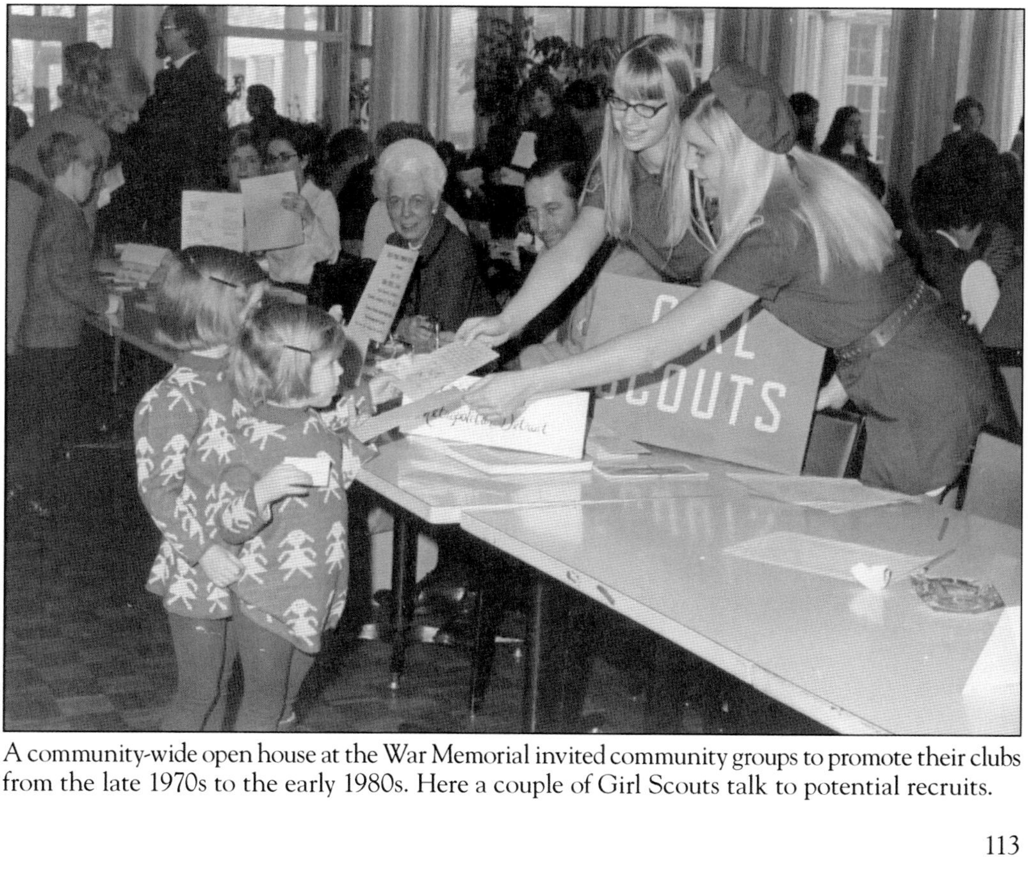
A community-wide open house at the War Memorial invited community groups to promote their clubs from the late 1970s to the early 1980s. Here a couple of Girl Scouts talk to potential recruits.

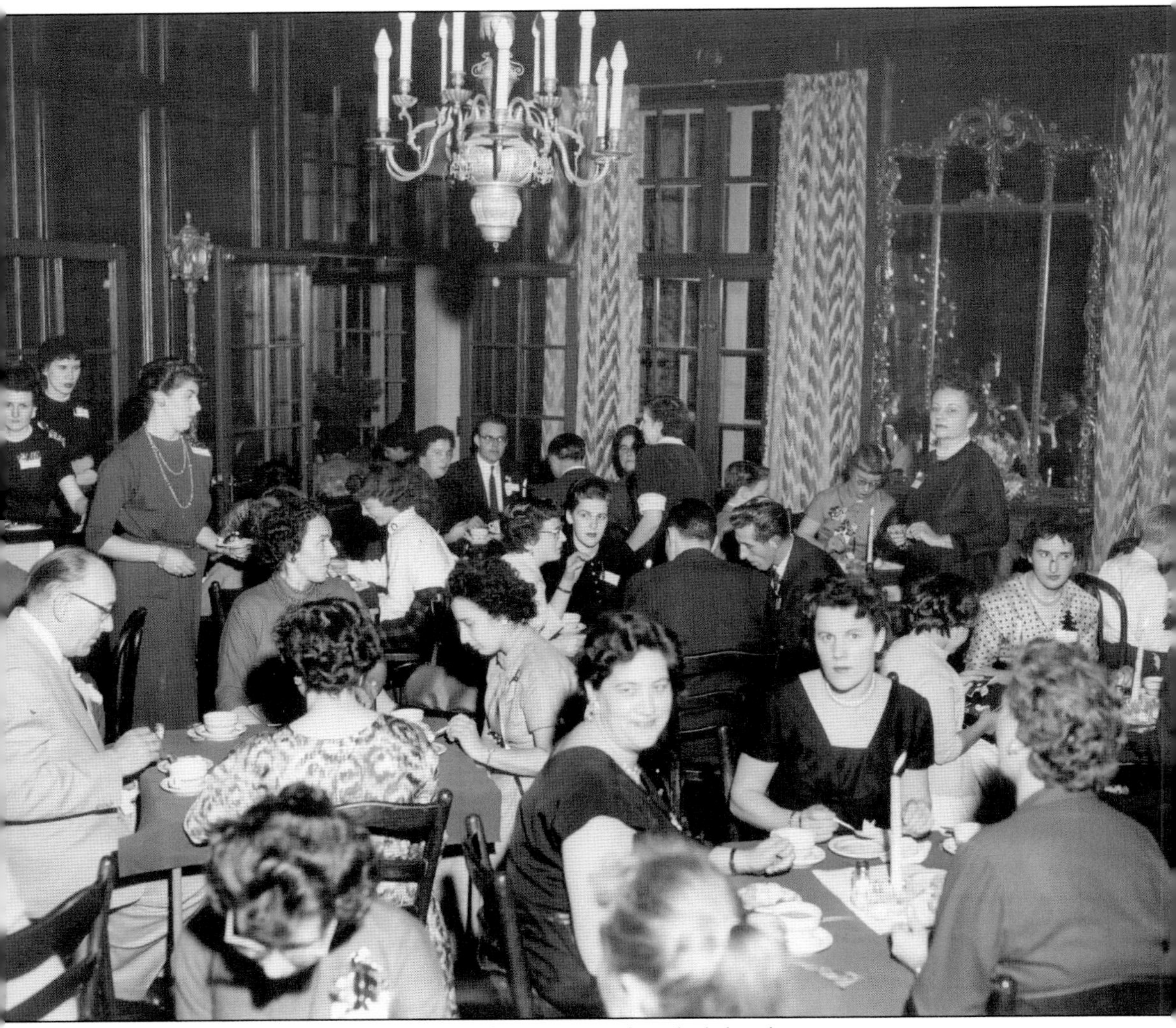

Community members gather in the dining room for a holiday dinner.

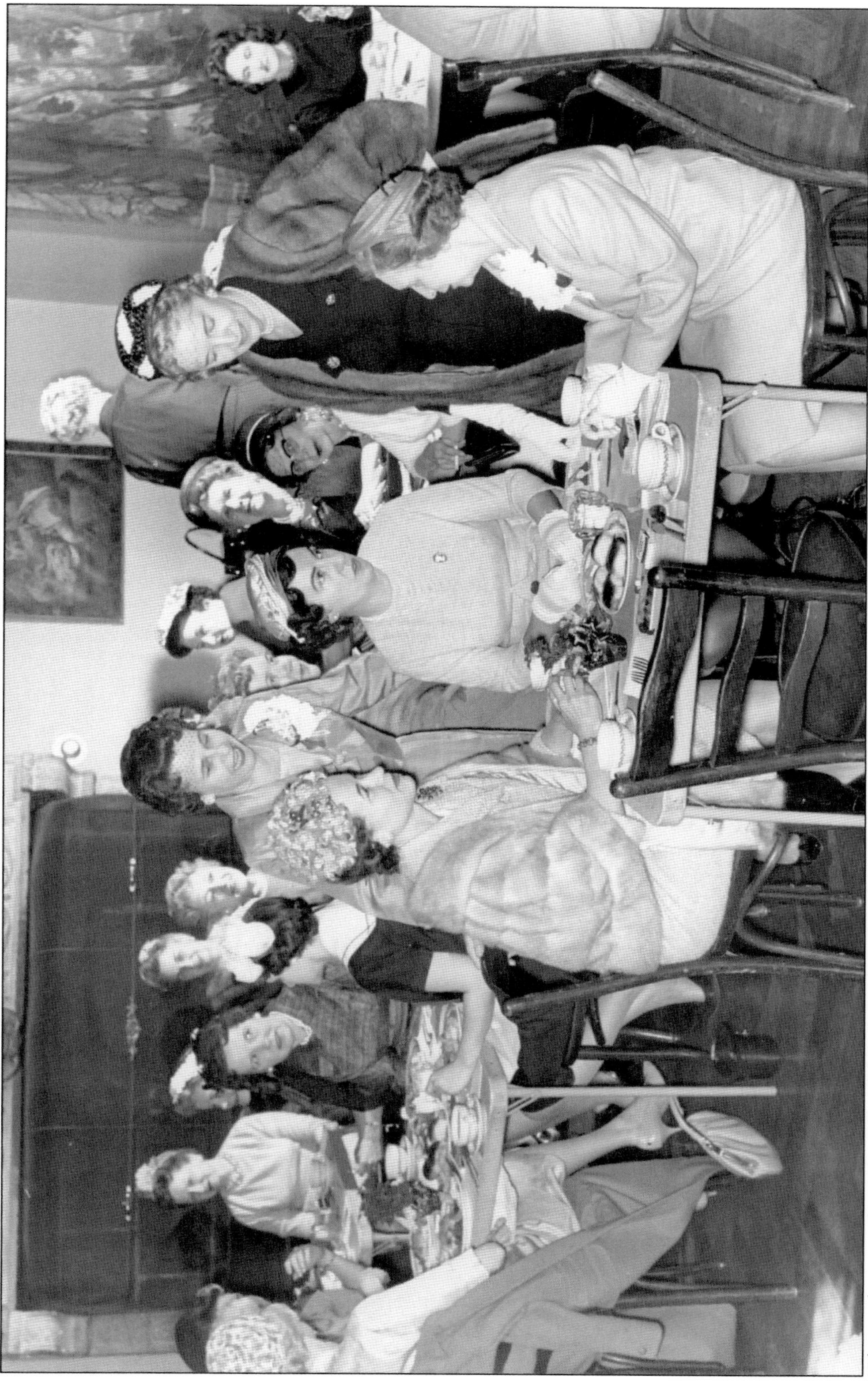

Gloves, hats, and mink stoles defined an era when women whiled away the afternoon at a luncheon at the War Memorial.

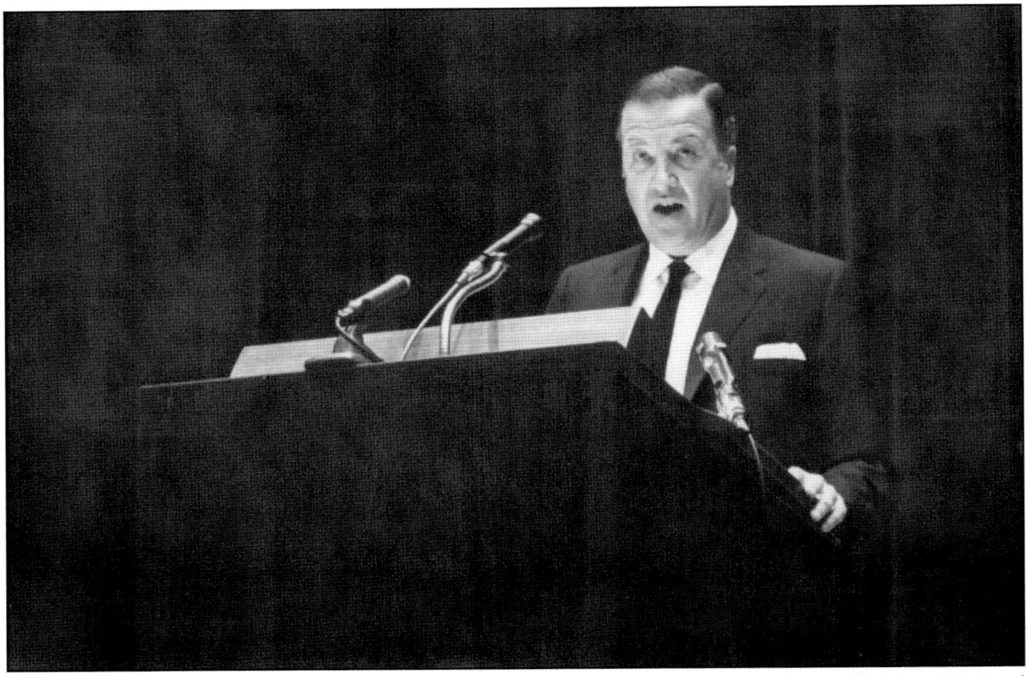

Henry Ford II, or Hank the Deuce as he was called, was a contemporary of Russell Alger III. Ford was largely credited with strengthening the Ford Motor Company in the postwar years.

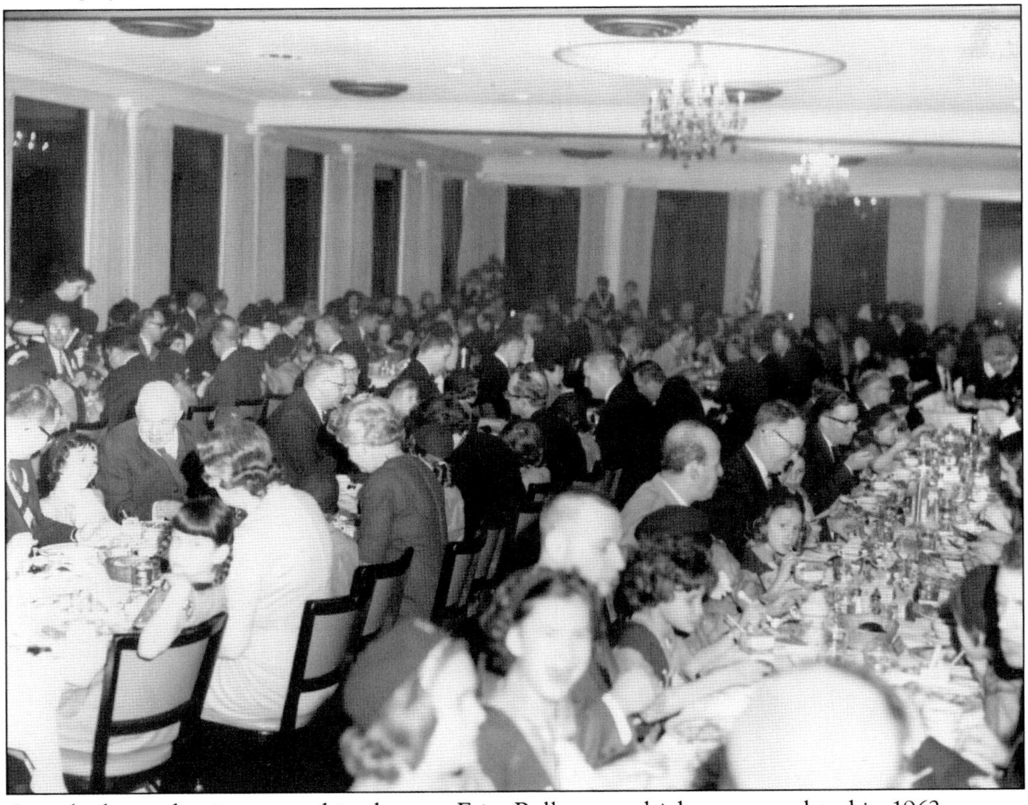

A packed crowd enjoys a meal in the new Fries Ballroom, which was completed in 1962.

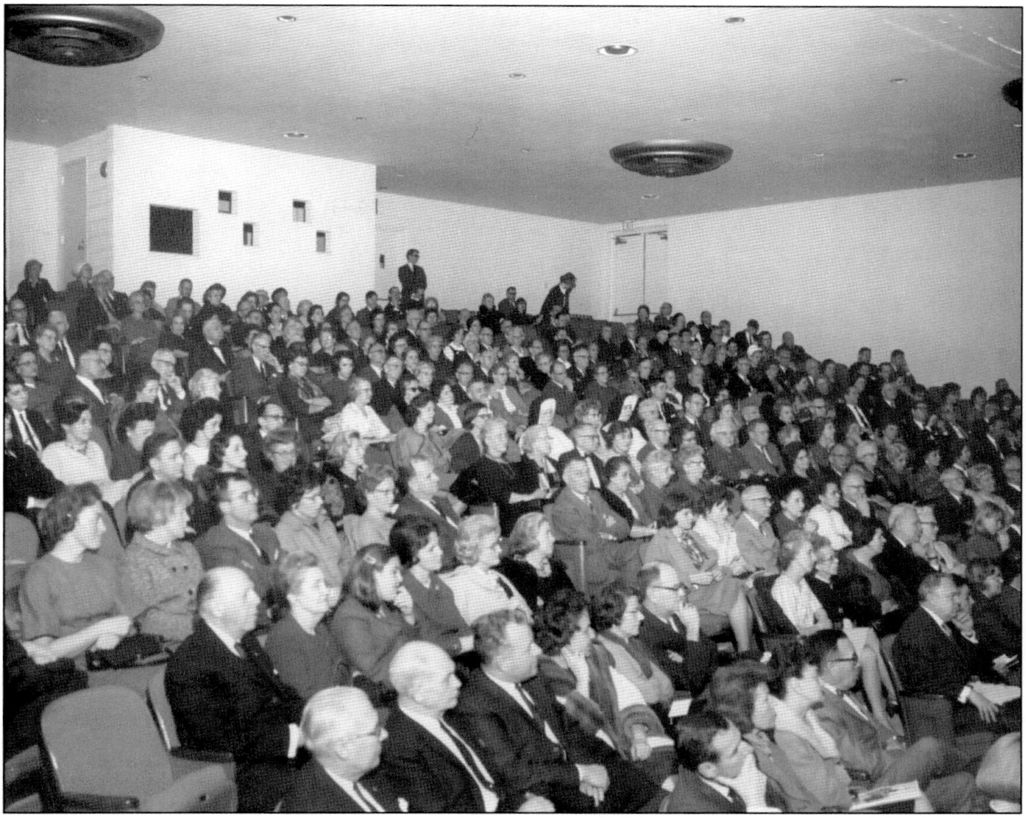

The Fries Auditorium enjoys a full house. The auditorium was built below the ballroom and provided much needed space for music, dance, and theater performances, as well as films.

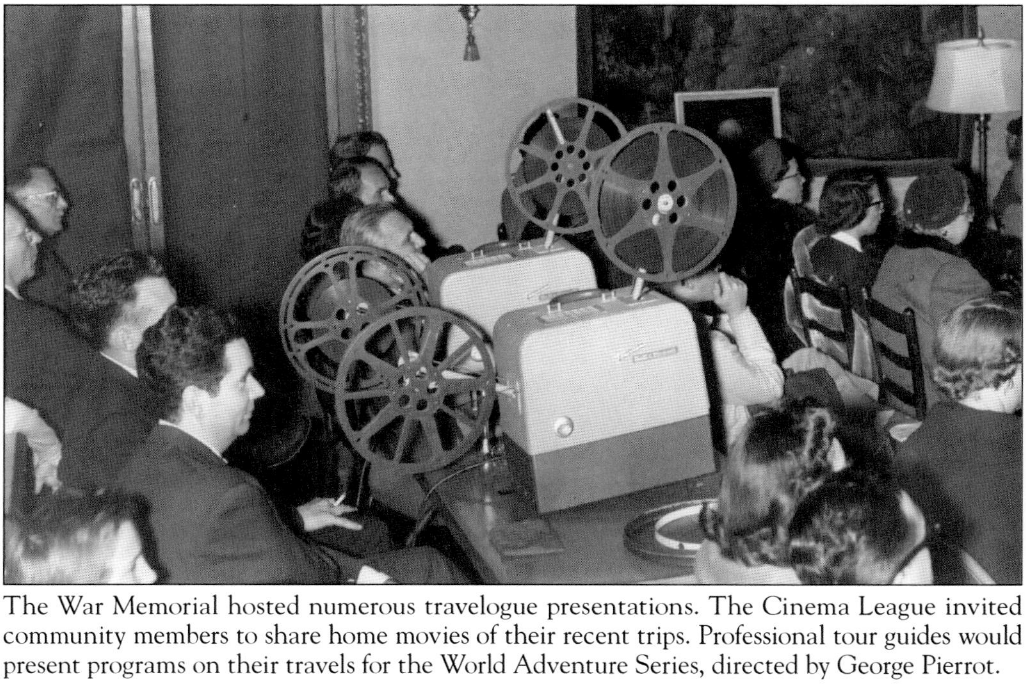

The War Memorial hosted numerous travelogue presentations. The Cinema League invited community members to share home movies of their recent trips. Professional tour guides would present programs on their travels for the World Adventure Series, directed by George Pierrot.

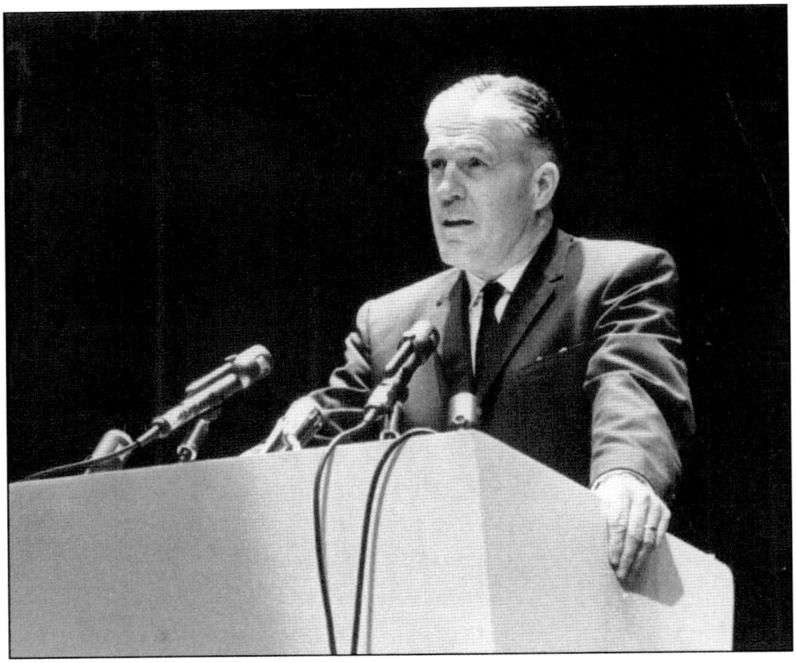

Former Michigan governor George Romney was one of the many prominent officials to speak at the War Memorial.

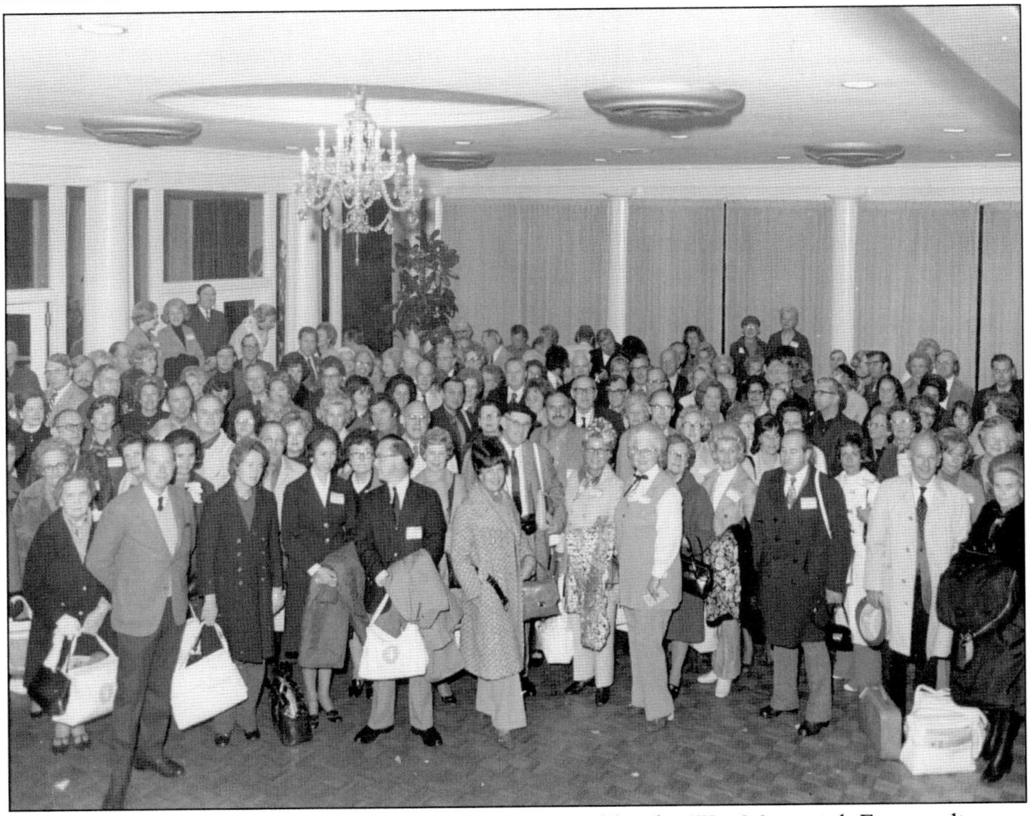

Anxious travelers prepare to depart on a trip sponsored by the War Memorial. Former director John Lake would charter airplanes and take as many as 100 vacationers on trips across the country and around the world in the 1960s and 1970s.

Martial Arts classes teach self-defense for all ages.

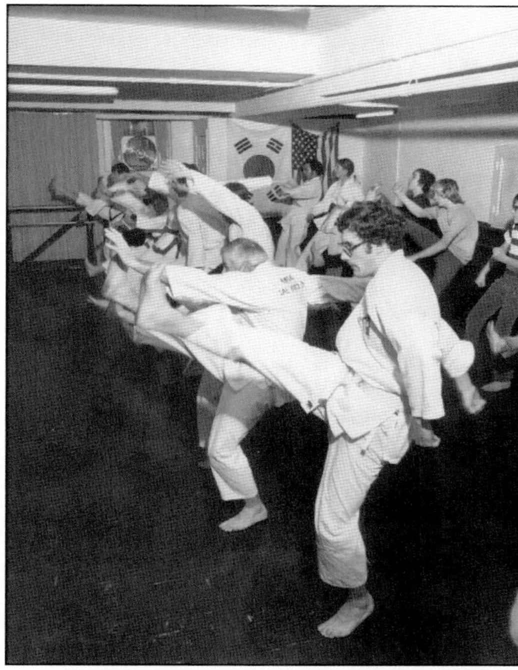

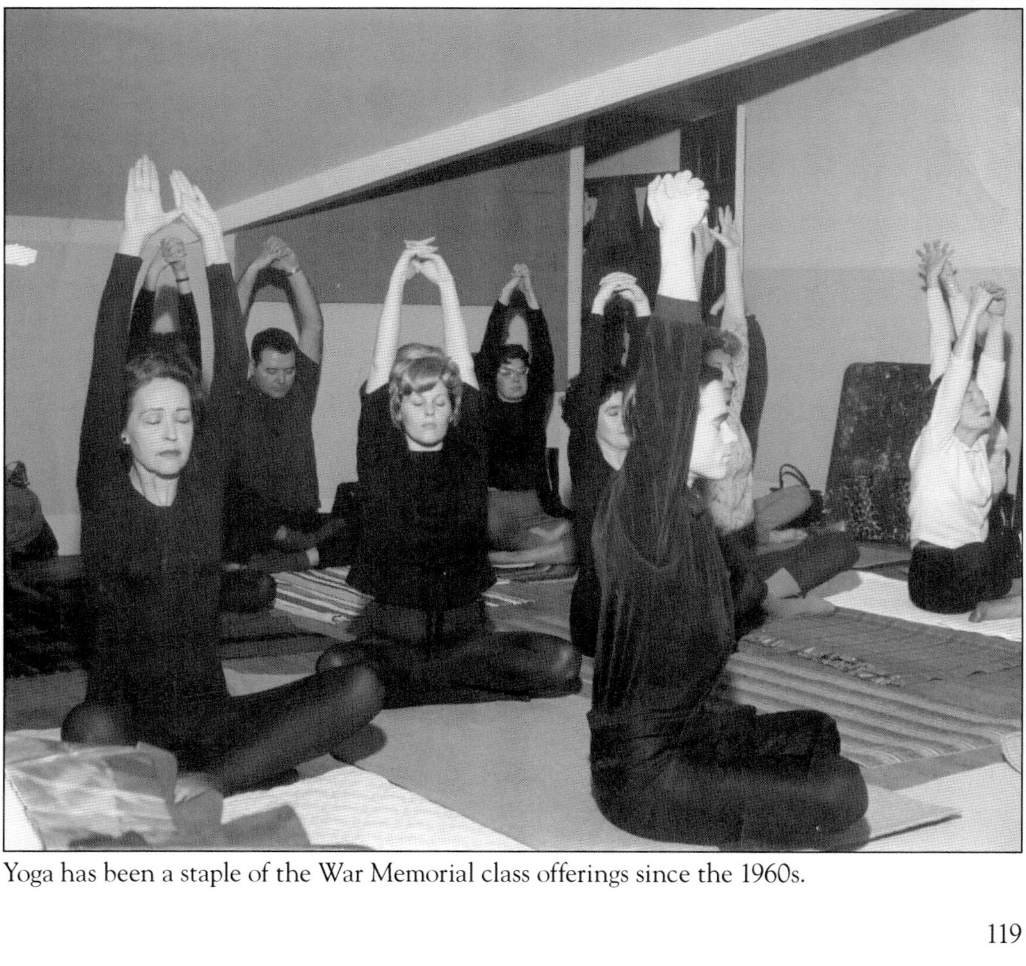

Yoga has been a staple of the War Memorial class offerings since the 1960s.

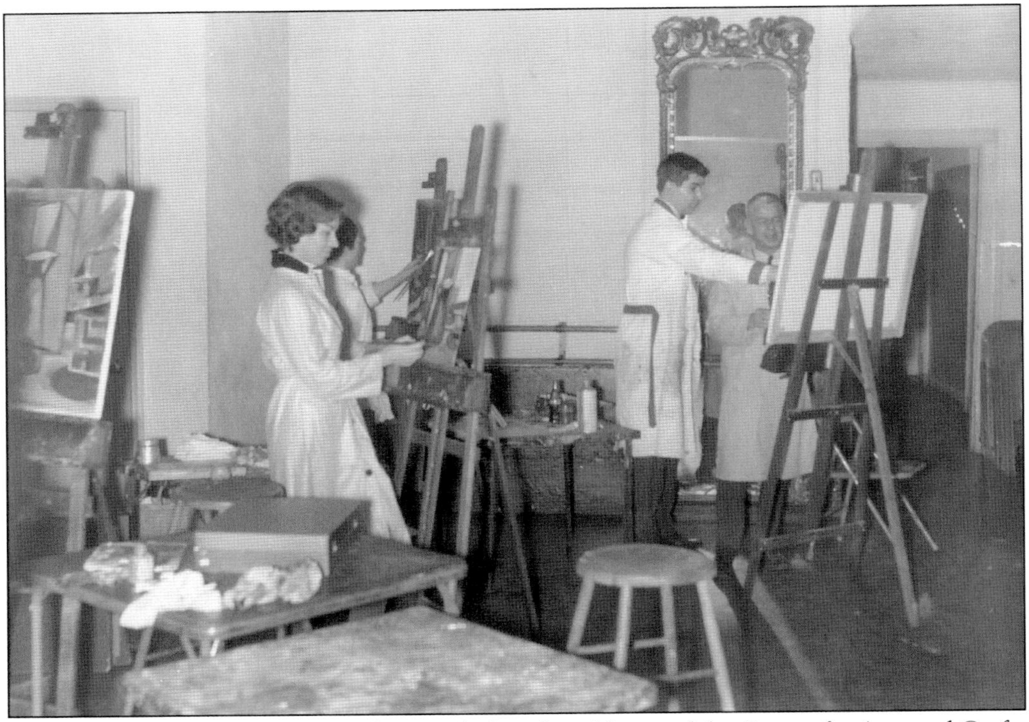

Oil painting classes were held in the attic before the addition of the Center for Arts and Crafts in 1977. At a cost of $150,000, the new wing provided two large classrooms, storage and clean-up facilities, and an office.

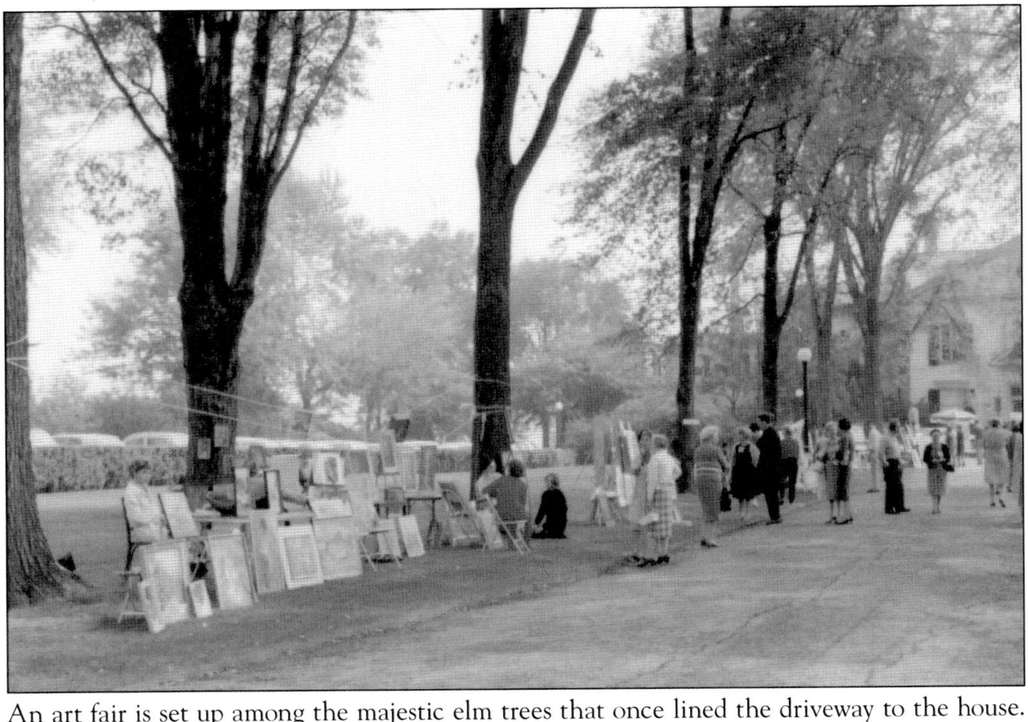

An art fair is set up among the majestic elm trees that once lined the driveway to the house. Sadly, all the trees were lost to Dutch elm disease in the 1960s and 1970s.

Grosse Pointe teens buy tickets to a Battle of the Bands concert. The event featured three bands in the ballroom and three in the auditorium, with attendees going up and down the stairs to listen to all the groups and cast their vote. Bob Seger was one of the most famous contestants.

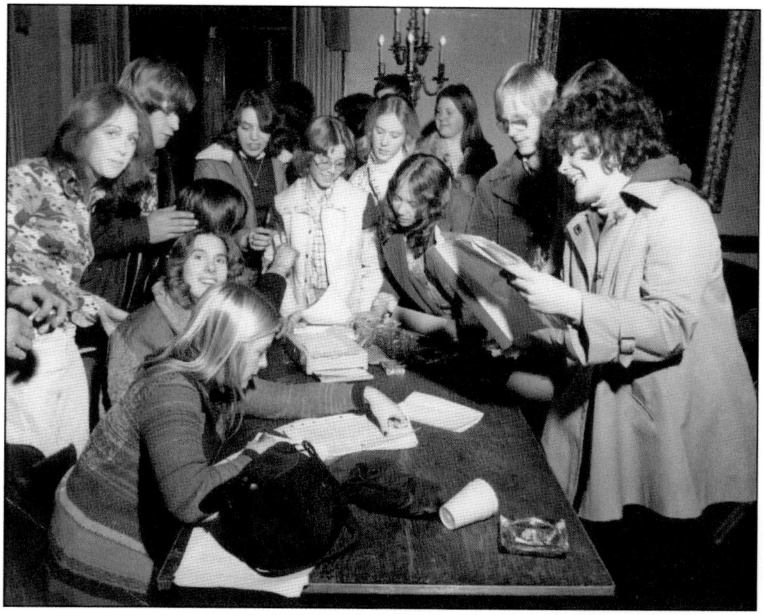

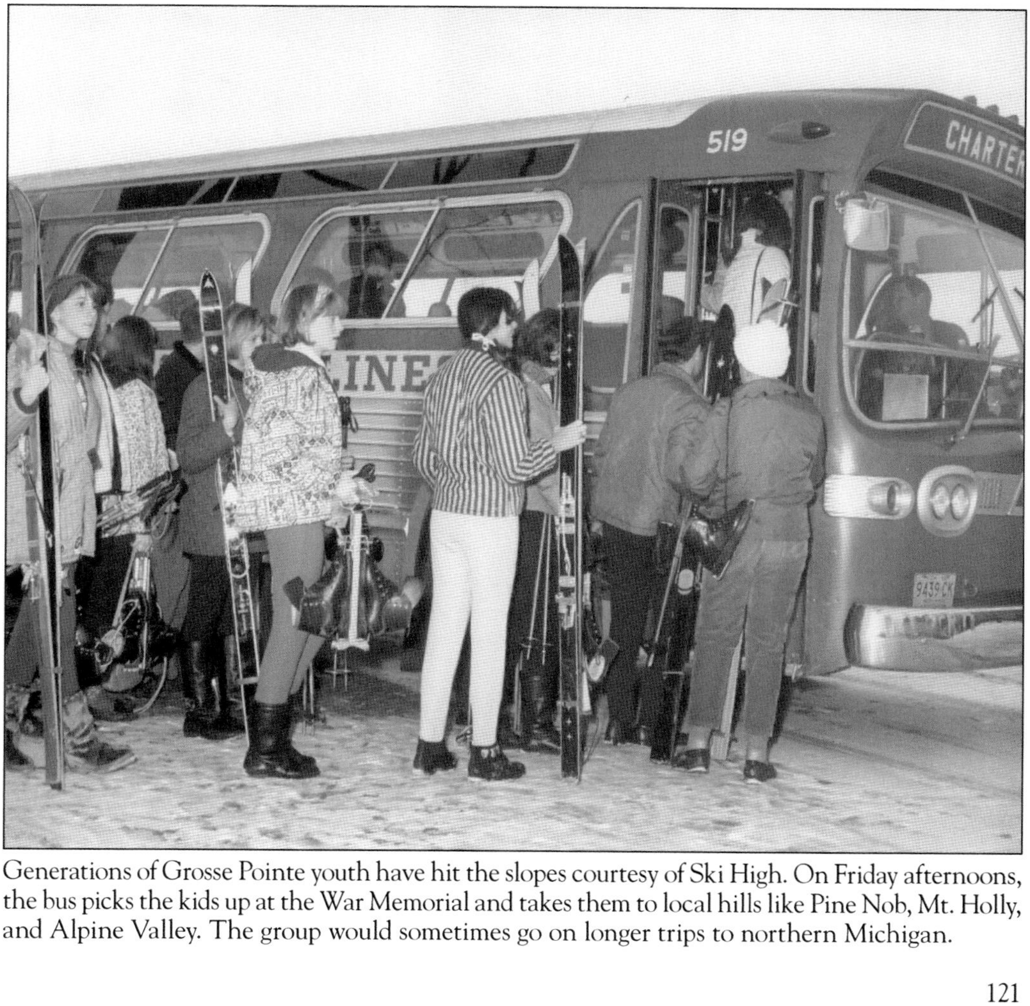

Generations of Grosse Pointe youth have hit the slopes courtesy of Ski High. On Friday afternoons, the bus picks the kids up at the War Memorial and takes them to local hills like Pine Nob, Mt. Holly, and Alpine Valley. The group would sometimes go on longer trips to northern Michigan.

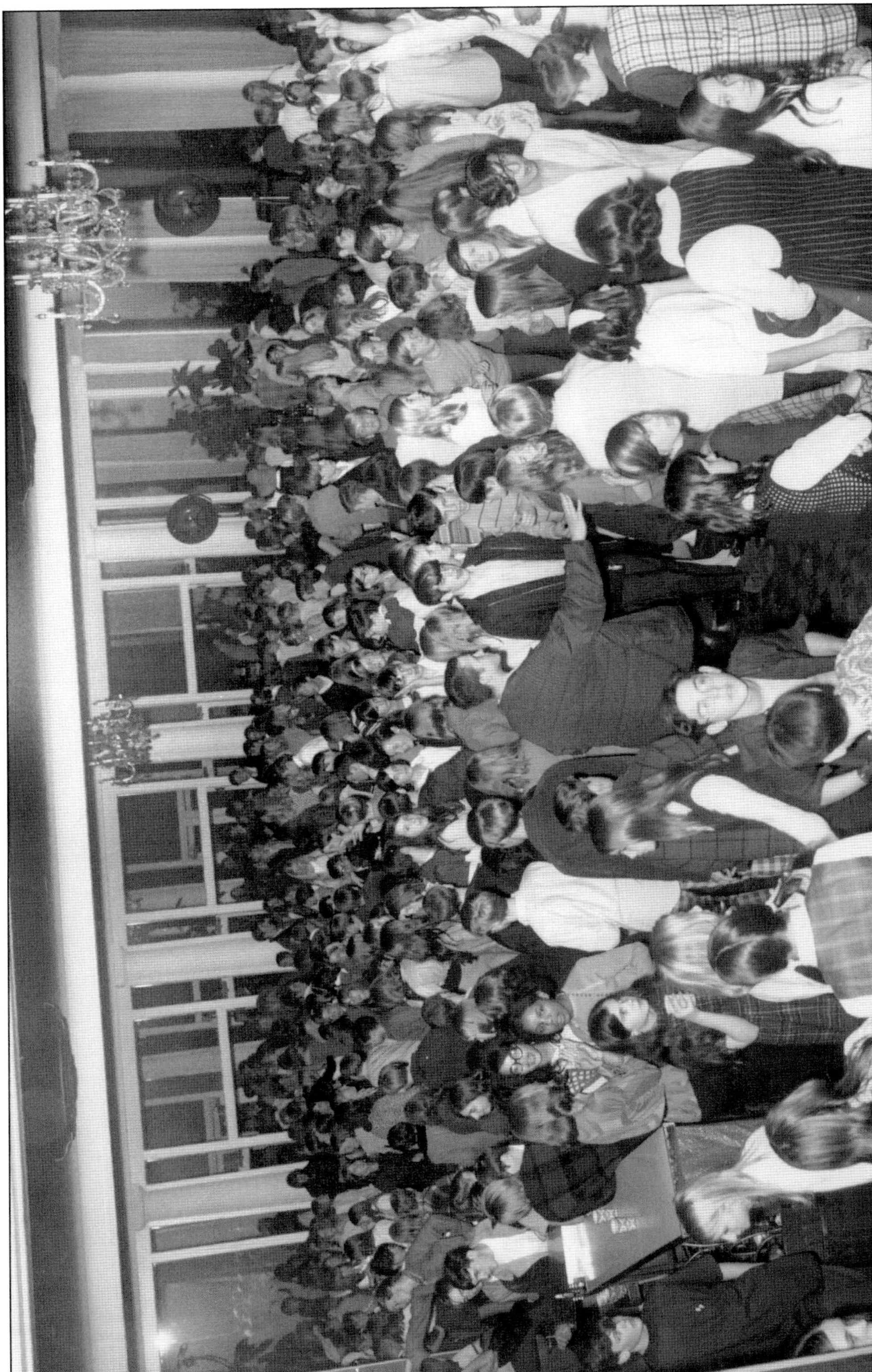

As many as 500 junior high students would squeeze into the ballroom for the youth dances.

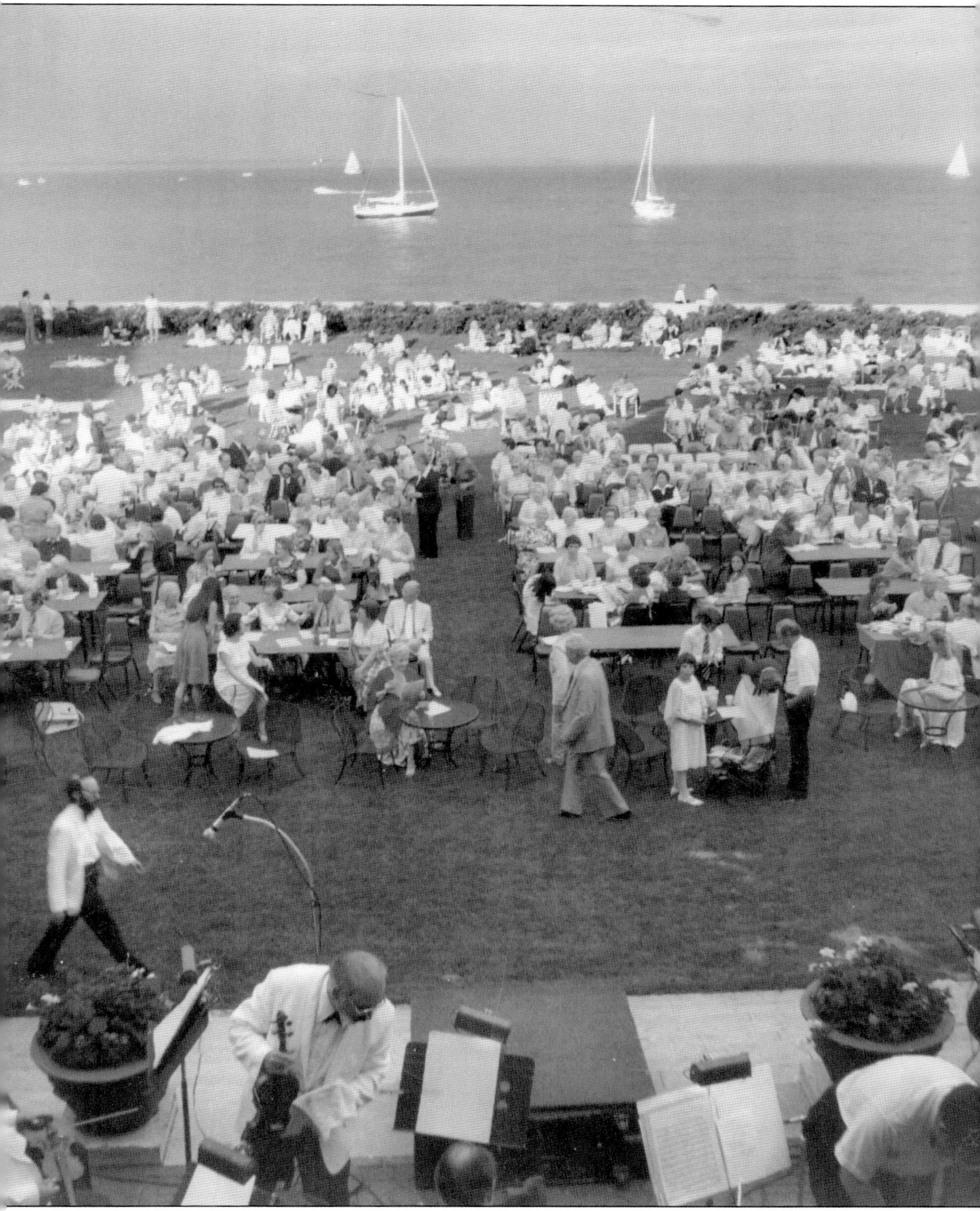

The melodic strains of the Grosse Pointe Symphony waft over guests on the lawn and out across the waves of Lake St. Clair during a summer evening concert.

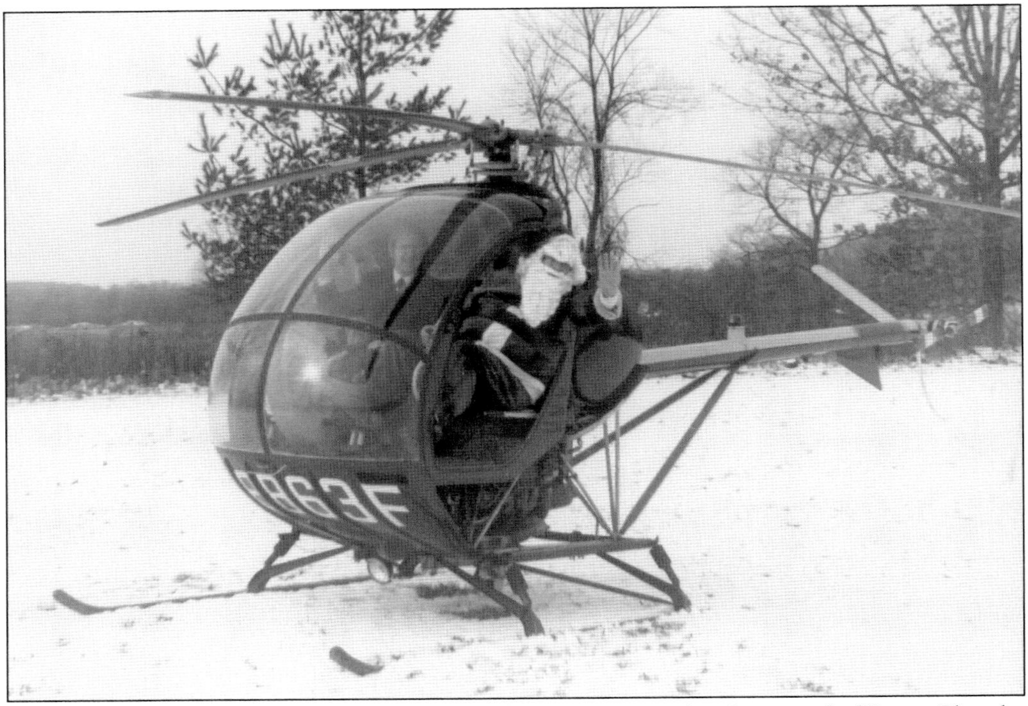

One of the most anticipated holiday events at the War Memorial is the arrival of Santa Claus by helicopter on the back lawn, which children still enjoy today.

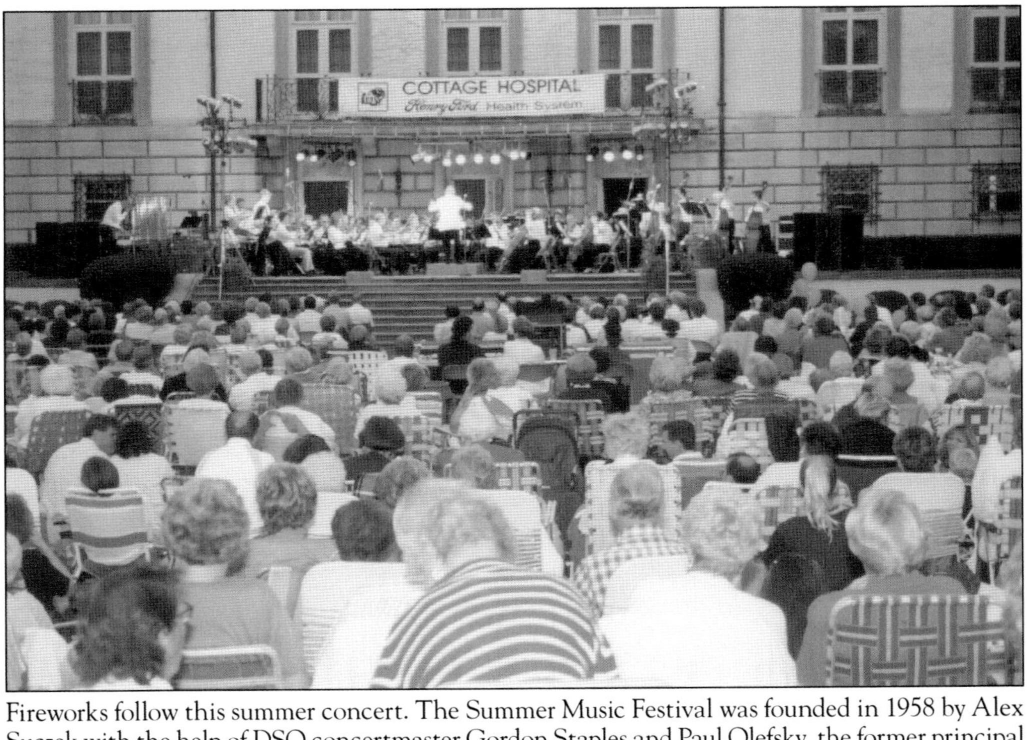

Fireworks follow this summer concert. The Summer Music Festival was founded in 1958 by Alex Suczek with the help of DSO concertmaster Gordon Staples and Paul Olefsky, the former principal cellist. Olefsky was the festival's first music director.

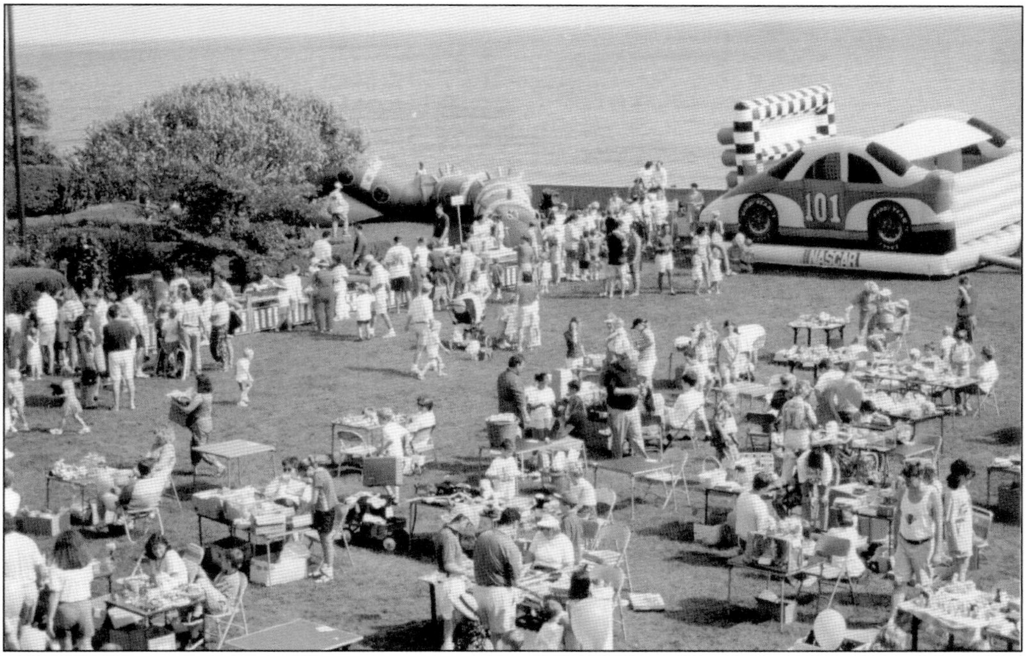

Family Fun Days, held in the 1980s and 1990s, included unique inflatable bounce houses.

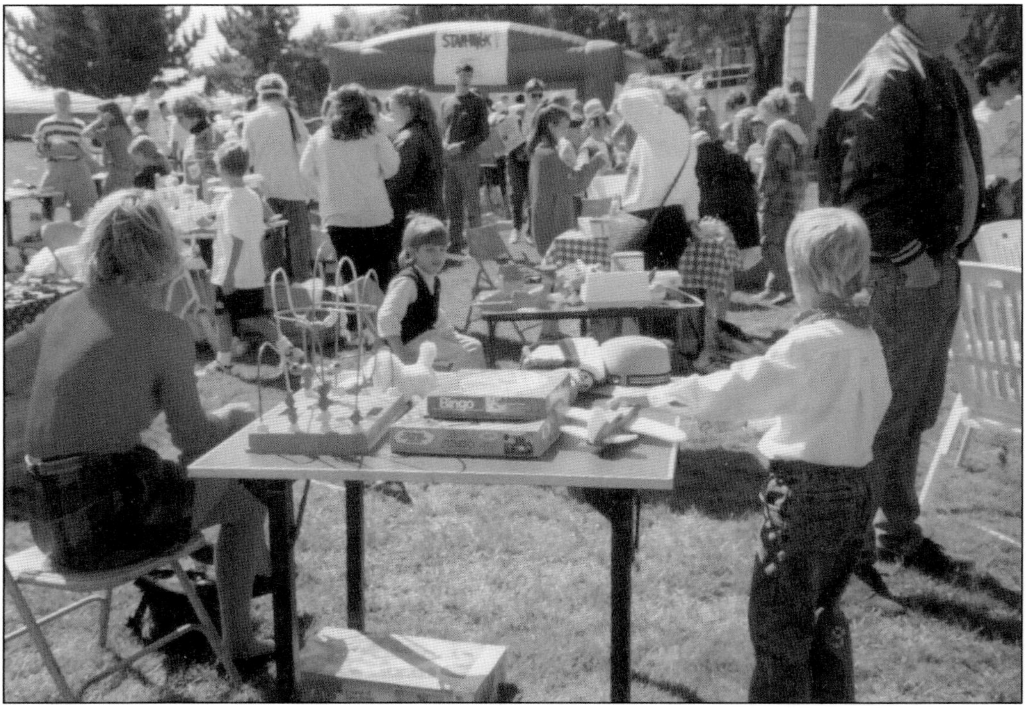

At the Swap Shop, children could bring their old toys and swap them with other kids.

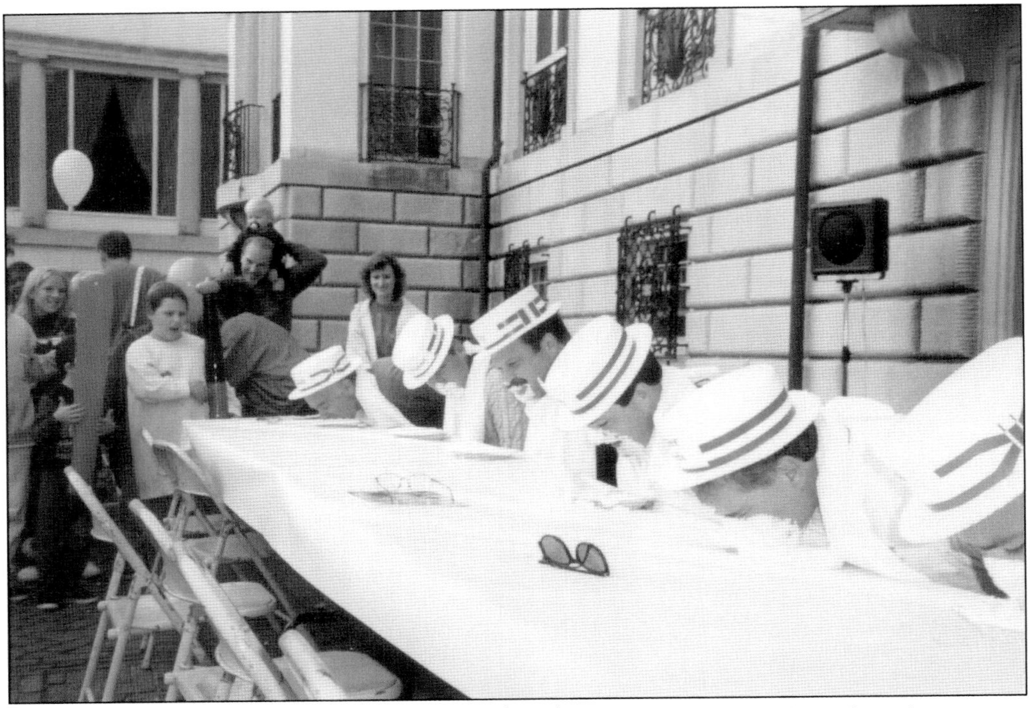

A representative of each of Grosse Pointe's police departments compete in a pie-eating contest as part of Fun Day.

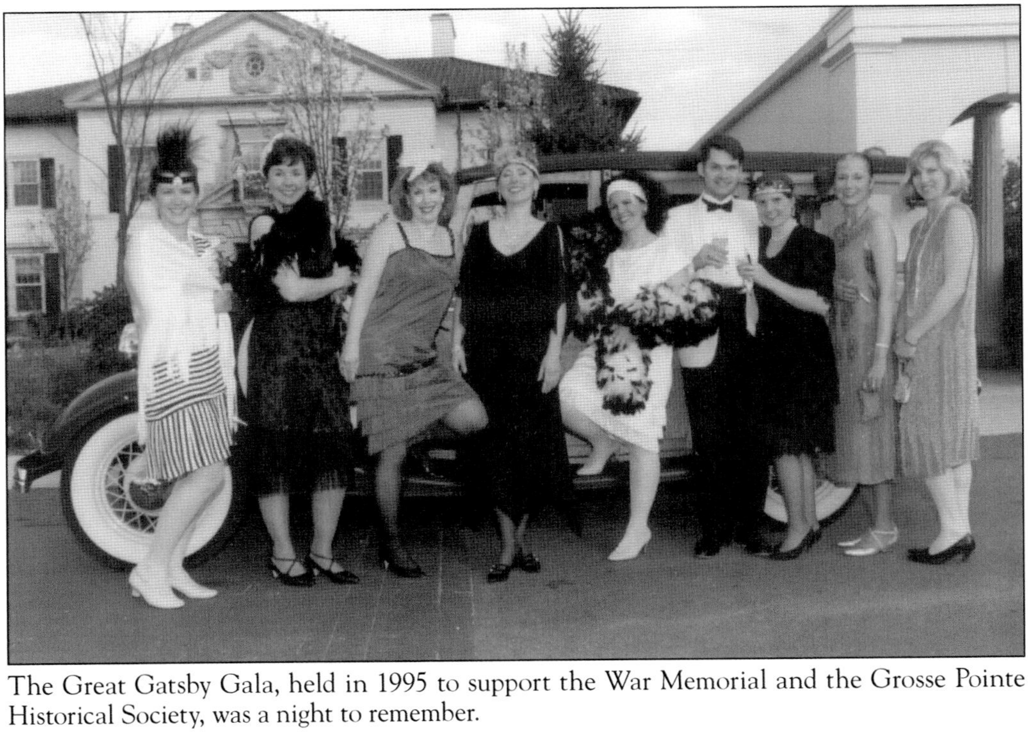

The Great Gatsby Gala, held in 1995 to support the War Memorial and the Grosse Pointe Historical Society, was a night to remember.

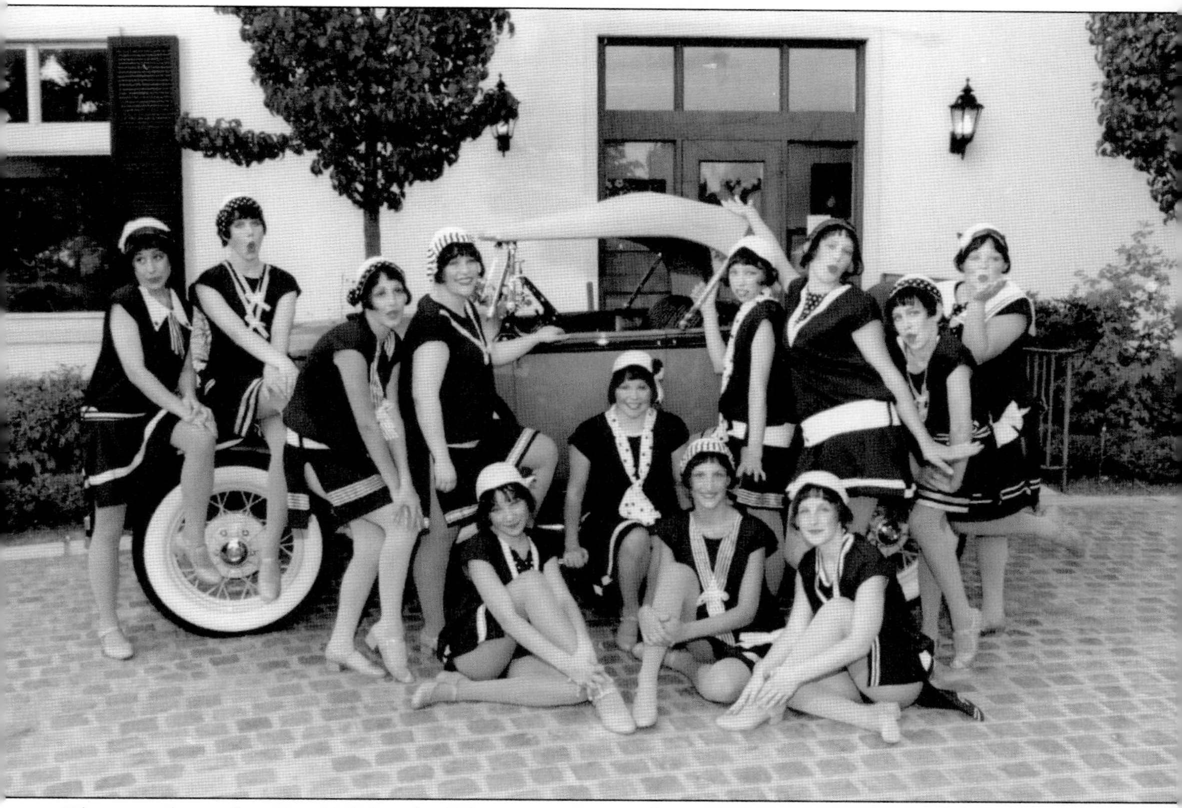

Flappers from the Casali School of Dance studio performed the Charleston and other 1920s dances for the guests of the Great Gatsby Gala.

Russell Alger built a home for his family that would last for generations. The laughter of their children and the beautiful dinner parties have evolved into a wide range of educational, cultural, and community-based events. What began as one man's dream has become a community jewel enjoyed by thousands of patrons every year. Undoubtedly, the Algers would not have wanted it any other way. In 2010, their home celebrates 100 years, and the community will forever be indebted to the Alger family for their gracious gift.

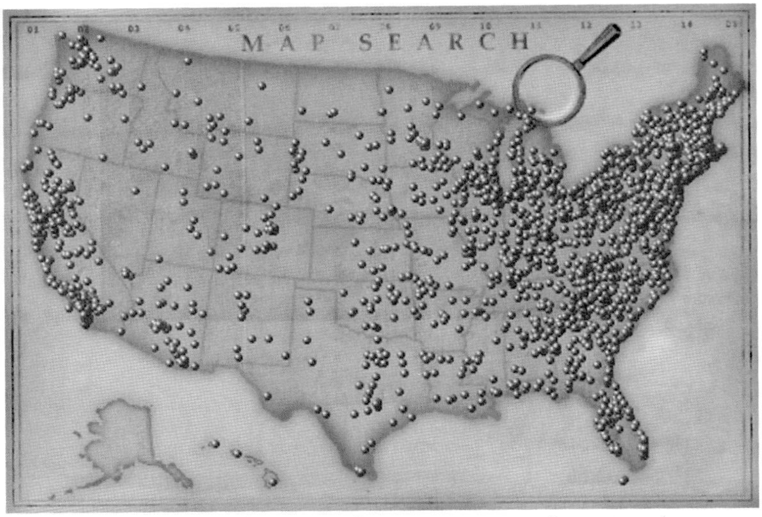
MAP SEARCH